THE BEGINNINGS OF STRATEGIC AIR POWER

G000070877

By the same author

The Origins of Strategic Bombing (1973)

Air Chief Marshal Sir Edgar Ludlow-Hewitt, Air Officer Commanding-in-Chief, Bomber Command from September 1937 to April 1940

THE BEGINNINGS OF
STRATEGIC
AIR POWER

A History of the
British Bomber Force
1923 – 1939

NEVILLE JONES

FRANK CASS

First published in 1987 in Great Britain by
FRANK CASS PUBLISHERS
Crown House, 47 Chase Side, Southgate
London N14 5BP

and in the United States of America by
FRANK CASS PUBLISHERS
c/o ISBS, 5824 N.E. Hassalo Street
Portland, Oregon, 97213-3644

Website: www.frankcass.com

Copyright © 1987 Neville Jones
Paperback edition 2002

British Library Cataloguing in Publication Data

Jones, Neville
    The beginnings of strategic air power: a
    history of the British bomber force 1923–39
    1. Great Britain. *Royal Air Force–*
    History   2. Bombers – History
    I. Title
    358.4′2′0941   UG635.G7

            ISBN 0-7146-3307-0 (cloth)
            ISBN 0-7146-8322-1 (paper)

    Library of Congress Cataloging-in-Publication Data

Jones, Neville.
    The beginnings of strategic air power.
    Bibliography: p.
    Includes index.
    1. Great Britain. Royal Air Force – History.
2. Strategic forces – Great Britain – History.
3. Bombers – Great Britain – History.   4. Bombing, Aerial –
Great Britain – History.   I. Title.
UG635.G7J55 1987   358.4′00941   86-32644

*All rights reserved. No part of this publication may be reproduced, stored in or introduced
into a retrieval system or transmitted in any form or by any means, electronic, mechanical,
photocopying, recording or otherwise, without the prior written permission of
the publisher of this book.*

Printed in Great Britain by Antony Rowe Ltd

To the Memory of
Group Captain H. A. Williamson CMG AFC
a former officer of the Royal Naval Air Service
who found himself 'the odd man out'
in the Air Ministry of the 1920s

CONTENTS

List of Illustrations   viii

Acknowledgements   ix

Introduction   xi

1. British Air Strategic Thought and Practice up to 1918   1

2. The New Strategic Policy 1919–33   22

3. The Expansion of the Bomber Force 1923–33   47

4. The Early Expansion Programmes 1934–5   71

5. Re-arming the Bomber Force 1936–7   100

6. Preparations for War 1938–9   126

7. Bombing Policy and Plans October 1938 to
   September 1939   150

8. Conclusions   168

   Notes   174

   Bibliography   185

   Index   187

LIST OF ILLUSTRATIONS

Air Chief Marshal Sir Edgar Ludlow-Hewitt   *frontispiece*

facing page

1. Viscount Tiverton, 1918   50
2. The Vimy crew which made the first flight to Australia in 1919   51
3. A Handley Page 0/400 of Handley Page Transport, 1920   54
4. A DH 9 of KLM, 1920   54
5. Vickers Virginia   55
6. Hawker Hart   55
7. E. V. Appleton, Wheatstone Professor of Physics, University of London   64
8. Handley Page HP 42 *Hannibal* of Imperial Airways, 1931   65
9. Douglas DC-2 *Uiver* (Stork) of KLM, 1934   65
10. Erhard Milch   130
11. General Walther Wever   130
12. Junkers Ju 52, 1932   131
13. Focke-Wulf FW 200 (Condor), 1938   131
14. A Formation of Hawker Hurricanes   136
15. The prototype Vickers Wellington   137
16. Handley Page Hampden   146
17. Armstrong Whitworth Whitley   146
18. Neville Chamberlain on his return to Heston on 30 September 1938   147

Credits

Frontispiece and No. 11 are reproduced by courtesy of the Imperial War Museum; No. 1 by courtesy of the Earl of Halsbury; Nos. 2, 5 by courtesy of Vickers Ltd.; Nos. 3, 8, 18 by courtesy of British Airways; Nos. 4, 9 by courtesy of KLM Royal Dutch Airlines; Nos. 6, 14, 15 by courtesy of British Aerospace; No. 7 by courtesy of King's College, London; Nos. 10, 12, 13 by courtesy of Lufthansa; No. 16 by courtesy of Handley Page Association; No. 17 by courtesy of Armstrong Whitworth Ltd.

ACKNOWLEDGEMENTS

The author wishes to thank the Controller of Her Majesty's Stationery Office for permission to quote from Crown Copyright material held in the Public Record Office.

He also wishes to thank the following for granting permission to quote from printed copyright material: Oxford University Press for extracts from *The War in the Air* by Sir Walter Raleigh and H.A. Jones; Collins Publishers for extracts from *Empire of the Air* by Viscount Templewood, *Bomber Offensive* by Sir Arthur Harris and *Architect of Air Power* by W.J. Reader; Harrap Ltd. for extracts from *From Many Angles* by Major-General Sir Frederick Sykes; Oliver & Boyd for an extract from *Studies of War* by P.M.S. Blackett; Cassell PLC for an extract from *The Royal Air Force and Two World Wars* by Sir Maurice Dean; The Macmillan Press Ltd for an extract from *Wings of Destiny* by the Marquess of Londonderry; Her Majesty's Stationery Office for extracts from *Miscellaneous Pamphlet No. 9 1939* (Cmd. 6106) and *The Strategic Air Offensive against Germany 1939–1945* by Sir Charles Webster and Noble Frankland; Royal United Services Institute for Defence Studies for extracts from the Journal of the Royal United Service Institution; Times Newspapers Ltd. for extracts from *The Times*; Mail Newspapers p.l.c. for an extract from the *Daily Mail*.

He also wishes to thank those who were so helpful in providing the photographs to illustrate this book: The Earl of Halsbury, Norman Barfield and John Godden of British Aerospace, Brian Wexham of Vickers, A.H. Fraser-Mitchell of the Handley Page Association, M.R. Owen of KLM and Christine Howarth of Lufthansa.

Finally, he wishes to express special thanks to Professor Geoffrey Best for his kind encouragement and advice.

INTRODUCTION

Strategic bombing may be described as the type of bombing which is directed against the enemy's war-making capacity as opposed to his armed forces. It was developed by the British air services during the First World War, yet in spite of the existence of a vast amount of source material relating to military aviation both in the war and in the following years, the task of writing an accurate and balanced account of British air strategic thought and practice up to the outbreak of the Second World War has its own special difficulties for the historian. Many of these may be traced to the nature of the basic source of information covering the origins and early development of British air power, the official history of the air war 1914–18; and others to the considerable accretion of myths surrounding the events and personalities associated with aviation, some of which had their origins in wartime propaganda, others in the mass of literature published in the inter-war years. It is therefore considered an essential preliminary to indicate to the reader some of the important areas where this study gives a different account and interpretation of events from those generally accepted, and to offer some explanation for these divergences.

The official air history of the First World War, the six volume *The War in the Air* (Raleigh and Jones, 1922–37) has always been regarded as a full and accurate account of British naval and military aviation from the origins up to the end of the First World War, and because of the high reputation which it acquired as a work of scholarship historians have tended to use it as a basic source of information, even after the official papers covering this period were open for public inspection. In fact, this work gives nothing like the full and unbiased account of the air war that its great detail would suggest; for it concentrates mainly on the activities of the military squadrons on the Western Front, and has almost nothing to offer on the planning and execution of strategic bombing carried out by the Navy. As a result, the origins of air strategic thought and practice, which are firmly rooted in the First World War, are hardly mentioned.[1]

It is not generally known that this history was commissioned by the Air Ministry; or that the Air Force was at that time very much moulded in the image of the military air service, and not, as might be expected, a reflection of the two services from which it was formed. The most senior posts were held by officers formerly of the Flying Corps, and although some officers from the Naval Air Service did continue to serve in the Air Force (others opted to return to the Navy)[2] their influence on air policy was negligible. The new service was almost wholly military in its traditions and policy, and this influence is plainly seen in the approach adopted by the two official historians. They saw the air war primarily as an army co-operation war. They accepted as axiomatic that air power had its raison d'être in army support, and described the development of this work, beginning with pure reconnaissance, and gradually being extended to include artillery spotting and aerial photography, and eventually to fighting and tactical bombing, as being the natural order of things.

The Navy, on the other hand, had a long tradition of striking directly at the territory even of a distant enemy, by bombarding his ports and coastal defences and attacking his shipping in his own waters, and when the aircraft was added to the naval armament it was quickly recognized as a potential weapon for attacking enemy targets which lay beyond the range of naval guns. Very early in the war plans were made to design aircraft which would be capable of operating from land bases in France to attack German industrial targets, at first mainly those producing materials and components used in the construction of submarines, but later being extended to include other important war products. The first significant advance came with the formation in 1916 of a small bomber force (No. 3 Naval Wing) at Luxeuil, equipped with Sopwith 1½ Strutters, to co-operate with the French Air Force in what was to be the first ever planned strategic air campaign.

The Army vehemently opposed the formation of this wing on the grounds, first, that this type of bombing was a waste of resources, and, secondly, that every available aircraft should be assigned to the squadrons supporting the land battles in France. General H.M. Trenchard, commander of the Flying Corps in France, enlisted the support of the Commander-in-Chief, Sir Douglas Haig, and was able to secure the immediate transfer of many of the Sopwiths to the military squadrons, and, soon after that, to bring about the disbandment of the naval wing. The Luxeuil wing operated on what can only be described as a small scale — though, it was later discovered, with conspicuous success — but this does not affect the unique place it holds in British air history; yet its activities are covered in a mere seven pages in the six volumes of the official history.[3]

By the time No. 3 Wing was disbanded in the spring of 1917 the Flying Corps had secured for their squadrons the greater part of Britain's aircraft production. Nevertheless, the Naval Air Service continued to support the concept of long-range strategic bombing. They encouraged manufacturers to design aircraft of longer range and greater lifting power; and, what was equally important, they initiated at staff level investigations into the nature of strategic bombing and the kinds of technical problems likely to be created by this type of operation. The results of this staff work were of outstanding value, and this was in no small measure due to the efforts of one man, Lord Tiverton, an officer of the Royal Naval Volunteer Reserve. Lord Tiverton tackled a wide range of problems, including the choice and vulnerability of targets, the types of bombs required, the facilities required for navigation, and the provision of aircrew training.[4] One especially interesting feature of his work was his use of mathematical reasoning to produce answers to such problems as the probable number and weight of bombs that would be required to destroy a particular type and size of factory from a specified height. His work anticipated by many years the method of scientific research which later became known as operational research. Indeed, it may be said that it was he who first devised this method of investigation. Yet according to the accepted version of air history Lord Tiverton does not even exist.

In view of what has been stated about the approach of the official historians to the work of the Navy, it is not surprising that neither he nor his work are mentioned in *The War in the Air*, but it is a matter of considerable surprise to discover that none of his papers are included in *Documents Relating to the Naval Air Service* (Vol. I 1908–1918), a work commissioned by the Navy Records Society. And most incredible of all is the fact that the official publication *The Origins and Development of Operational Research in the Royal Air Force* (HMSO 1963) does not even mention the man who founded this method of research in the Air Force in 1918.

Lord Tiverton's work should have been continued and developed in the years following the war, and if this had been done, many of the operational difficulties which beset Bomber Command from its formation in 1936 up to the middle years of the war might have been foreseen and the 'trial and error' method of progressing reduced to a minimum. Instead, the Air Ministry files containing his papers were put away and forgotten, and this method of research was lost to the Air Force for nearly twenty years. It came back into use — though quite independently of Lord Tiverton's work — in the second half of the 1930s, when it was applied to the problems of defence against air attack. Bomber Command had to wait a good deal longer, until 1941 in fact, before an operational research section was formed at the command headquarters, and it was not until September of that year that the methods which Lord Tiverton had been working to perfect in 1918 were again used to investigate problems relating to long-range bombing operations.[5]

The effect of the bias shown by the official historians has been to influence the writing of air history ever since. It has come to be accepted that long-range strategic bombing was virtually untried in the First World War, and that, consequently, the failure of the bombing operations in the first half of the Second World War could reasonably be attributed to lack of knowledge and experience. It is true that the operations of the Independent Force, a long-range British bomber force assembled in the Nancy area in the last year of the war, are described in some detail, but the creation of the force is regarded more as a deviation from the established and tried air policy rather than as the logical outcome of the development of air power in the offensive role.

This influence extends even to the official history of strategic operations in the Second World War (*The Strategic Air Offensive against Germany 1939–1945* Webster and Frankland, 4 vols. 1961) whose authors accept without question the assumptions relating to long-range bombing in the First World War as stated by Raleigh and Jones. This authoritative work contains a long introduction dealing with the period 1914 to 1939 (Vol. I, pp. 33–126), and although the narrative covering the years 1919 to 1939 is based on independent research, the section on the First World War is based wholly on *The War in the Air* and follows closely the interpretation of events as set out in that work.

Sir Charles Webster and Dr Noble Frankland were, it is true, successful in disposing of many of the myths which had become part of the history of military aviation for the period 1919 to 1945, but many still remained to distort the writing of history of the years immediately following the First World War. Particularly deep-seated and persistent are the myths concerning the career of Lord Trenchard, who commanded the Flying Corps in France for the greater part of the First World War and was Chief of the Air Staff for the first decade after the war; and for this reason it is vital for an understanding of the period between the wars to establish as far as possible what is fact and what is fiction. It is therefore proposed to set down in outline, first, what may be termed the accepted version of Trenchard's career after he joined the Flying Corps in 1912, and to follow it by what is believed to be a factually more accurate account. The orthodox version would follow roughly along these lines.

Trenchard was a major and aged thirty-nine when he secured a transfer from his own regiment, the Royal Scots Fusiliers, to the Flying Corps. He was quickly recognized as a very able officer and within three months of the outbreak of war he was given command of No. 1 Wing in France. Here he impressed his superiors with his qualities of leadership and the determination he displayed in providing the maximum possible support for the army units at the front; and when the commander of the Flying Corps in France returned to the War Office in August 1915 Trenchard was appointed in his stead with the rank of brigadier-general.

Trenchard was now convinced that the aircraft was essentially an offensive weapon and would be ineffective if used in the defensive role, and guided by this conviction he waged a constant and relentless offensive which carried the fight to the enemy and forced him on the defensive. Losses among the military squadrons were often very high, but this was the price which had to be paid to gain air ascendancy over the battle front.

It was logical to extend the doctrine of the offensive beyond the boundaries of tactical warfare and apply it to operations directed against the German homeland. The operations of the German airships over widespread areas of this country, and, subsequently, the raids made by No.3 Naval Wing against targets in southern Germany, had indicated the potential of such action; but the consensus of opinion of those in authority was that no aircraft could, or should, be spared for this type of bombing so long as the requirements of the squadrons on the Western Front had not been met in full. Then a sudden and dramatic turn of events forced upon the Government a radical change in policy. In late May 1917, a small force of German long-range bombers, operating from airfields in Belgium, began a series of daylight raids against targets in south-east England. London was twice visited by the raiders and civilian casualties were heavy. Public opinion was angered by the ease with which the raiders had been able to operate over England in broad daylight, and there were vociferous demands that the Germans should be given a taste of their own medicine.

The Government responded swiftly to this pressure and proposed that the military and naval air services should be amalgamated to form a single service, the Royal Air Force, and that the new service should give first priority to the formation of a bomber force to attack the German homeland from bases in France. Although many, including Trenchard, doubted the wisdom of creating a new service in the midst of war, the proposal was quickly implemented and the Royal Air Force came into being on 1 January 1918. Trenchard was recalled from France to become the first Chief of the Air Staff, but after failing to agree with the Air Minister, Lord Rothermere, regarding the scope of his authority, he resigned in March 1918. When Lord Rothermere himself resigned the following month, the new minister, Sir William Weir, appointed Trenchard to command the bomber force, subsequently designated the Independent Force, which was being assembled in Lorraine. The planned strength of the Independent Force was never realized, and because of this

Trenchard was compelled to reduce drastically the number of long-range attacks against German targets. As a result, the knowledge and experience gained of strategic operations were so slight as to be of negligible value for future planning.

Soon after the end of the war, Trenchard became Chief of the Air Staff for the second time, and during the early part of his tenure of office he was compelled to fight for the very survival of the Air Force against the demands of the two older services for the return of their air elements. He defended the continued existence of an independent air service by arguing that neither the Navy nor the Army alone would have sufficient resources to equip the type of strategic bomber force which the Air Force had been specifically created to provide.

When relations between Britain and France became so seriously strained in 1923 that conflict between the two nations was considered a distinct possibility, the fact that Britain was virtually defenceless against air attack was forced upon the Government's notice. A urgent review of the situation was carried out, and this resulted in approval being given to a scheme to expand the home-based defence element of the Air Force to 52 squadrons. A number of meetings were held at the Air Ministry in the summer of 1923 to consider the proposed scheme, and during these discussions Trenchard described in some detail his concept of defence by means of the counter-offensive. Believing as he did that the aeroplane was essentially an offensive weapon, he reasoned that the only way to defeat an air attack on this country would be to launch against the enemy nation a counter-attack of sufficient power to force him on the defensive. He had no faith at all in what might be called 'close' defence, being convinced that no matter how many fighters were used in defence the bombers would always get through. From that time onwards, the concept of the counter-offensive formed the basis of Air Force strategic thought, and during the remainder of the inter-war period the bomber force was developed and expanded, though slowly and at times haltingly, to achieve the offensive capability which Trenchard had envisaged.

This then is the orthodox version of Trenchard's career in the flying services and of his influence in moulding air policy during the inter-war years. If, however, a number of little known, or little mentioned, but indisputable facts are incorporated in the account a somewhat different picture emerges. Thus, the amended version would offer the following interpretation of the evidence.

When Trenchard transferred to the Flying Corps he was a major and had almost certainly reached the highest rank he was likely to attain in the peacetime service. He was not a well-educated man either in the general or in the military sense, and he had no scientific or technical background. However, his undoubted ability as an administrator was quickly recognized in the Flying Corps, and in the early part of the war he was given command of No.1 Wing in France. He immediately impressed his military superiors with the unstinted support he gave to the army units at the front, and this was an important factor in his being promoted to command the Flying Corps in France in August 1915.

He was now in a position to intensify the effort in support of the Army, and with his belief that the aeroplane was essentially an offensive weapon and was wasted in the defensive role,[6] he maintained a continuous offensive, carrying the battle at all times into enemy-held territory, regardless of the cost in men and machines. The argument used to justify this action was that it forced the Germans on the defensive and enabled the Flying Corps to secure air supremacy over the battle area. In fact, this relentless offensive achieved neither of these aims. In spite of being inferior in numbers, the Germans were not driven on the defensive, and whenever there was a critical engagement they were able to seize the initiative and inflict heavy casualties on their opponents. Two important factors contributed to the failure of the offensive policy. First, there was the inferior quality of the aircraft used by the military squadrons. In the summer of 1916, for example, almost 50 per cent of the aircraft in service with the Flying Corps in France were of the BE2c type, a machine which was by common agreement poor both in design and performance.[7] Second, the training given to Flying Corps pilots was wholly inadequate, and when Trenchard constantly increased his demands for pilots to replace his growing casualties, the standards of training were further reduced to meet these demands. Thus, the increase in casualties and the lowering of training standards became a vicious circle.[8]

There can be no doubt that the offensive policy was a disastrous one for the Flying Corps, and this conclusion, confirmed soon after the war by German documents which showed that German losses had been only one quarter of those suffered by the British,[9] was reached by many service personnel while the war was still in progress. There were apparently many Flying Corps officers of subordinate rank who in private expressed serious concern about service policy; in general, about the quality of operational aircraft and equipment and the training of pilots and observers, and, in particular, about the wisdom of the offensive policy. These views were widely canvassed, and eventually formed the basis of a number of scathing attacks made against the commanders of the Flying Corps both in Parliament and in the Press. The nature of these charges was so serious − one made in the House of Commons included an accusation of criminal negligence − that the Government gave way to the demands for an investigation and appointed a committee of enquiry under Mr Justice Bailhache. Not unnaturally, the committee showed great understanding of the very real difficulties which faced those who were responsible for developing this novel form of warfare; and since much of their evidence was taken from senior members of the Flying Corps — understandably, few of the junior officers who were critical of service policy were willing to appear before a public enquiry — it is not surprising that they concluded there was no substance in the charges.[10]

Meanwhile, Trenchard continued to increase the scale and intensity of air operations over the Western Front and, as has been shown, was instrumental in frustrating the naval bombing plans. Thus, when the operations of the naval wing were brought to an end in the spring of 1917 this would have meant the end of strategic bombing for the rest of the war if the German daylight raids on London had not provoked the British Government into taking retaliatory action. The Government were determined that the Germans should be made to suffer in the same way that the citizens of London had suffered, but now that the naval wing had been disbanded there was no instrument of retribution at hand. Clearly, major changes of policy would be needed, and General J.C. Smuts, a member of the War Cabinet, was asked to consider what these might be. After a brief investigation, Smuts recommended that the two existing air services should be amalgamated to form an independent air force whose primary function would be to create a strategic bomber force to attack industrial centres in Germany. This recommendation was accepted without dissent, and the necessary measures were at once put in hand to implement it.

Needless to say, Trenchard was as strongly opposed to the formation of the independent air force as he was to the type of bombing it was intended to carry out. There is a strange irony in the fact that the man who in later years was called 'Father of the Royal Air Force' should have been so strongly opposed to its creation; and strange, too, that, in spite of his unconcealed hostility to the new scheme of things, he should have been appointed the first Chief of the Air Staff, and then a few months later placed in command of the strategic bomber force.

Even when he took up his post at the Air Ministry Trenchard was little disposed to accept the changes that were then in being. He continued to regard the Air Force as an army corps separated unnaturally from its parent service, and he had not the slightest enthusiasm for the strategic bombing policy. With this attitude towards the new service, it is not surprising that he soon had serious differences of opinion with the Air Minister, Lord Rothermere, for whom he formed a profound dislike. More than that, he carried his personal animosity towards his minister to the point where his behaviour has, rightly, been described as 'very much like insubordination and treachery, running even to the length of encouraging junior Air Staff officers who were in Parliament to make political trouble for the Minister in the House'.[11] The situation soon became intolerable, and Trenchard took the only course open to him and in March 1918 he resigned. Rothermere followed with his resignation a month later.

Before he left the Air Ministry Lord Rothermere appointed as Chief of the Air Staff Major-General F.H. Sykes, an officer for whom Trenchard had long had a deep hatred, and whose appointment he took as a personal affront. Rothermere's successor, Sir William Weir, therefore had to deal with a morose and unco-operative Trenchard who rejected several posts that were offered to him. Weir then ordered him to take command of the strategic bomber force, and, reluctantly, Trenchard obeyed.[12]

When Trenchard assumed command of the Independent Force in June 1918, a good deal of the work to organize and support the long-range operations had already been done at the Air Ministry, which exercised direct control over the bomber force. Lists of important objectives in order of priority had been compiled and forwarded to the headquarters of the Force and, after that, regular instructions detailing the targets to be attacked were sent. But, to the exasperation of the Air Staff, Trenchard paid little heed to these directives and constantly employed his force against tactical targets, such as railways and aerodromes, in support of the land campaign. Frequent complaints about this practice were made to the Chief of the Air Staff, but he did not possess sufficient authority to bring about a change of policy, and the misuse of the force continued until the end of the war.[13]

In spite of his preoccupation with the concept of air power as a tactical weapon, Trenchard had his own very definite views on the aims and methods of strategic bombing, though these were very different from the views held by the Air Staff. Whereas the Air Staff envisaged the destruction of the major German war industries by attacking specific factories and industrial plants which were manufacturing munitions of war, Trenchard thought that the attacks should be directed against the industrial cities themselves, with the object of breaking the morale of the civilian population. He based his reasoning on the premise that the morale of the civilian population was the most vulnerable element in a nation at war, and believed that if massive air attacks were launched against the centres of population, causing heavy casualties and destroying homes and disrupting public services, the war-will of the people could be broken and the government forced to sue for peace.[14] Trenchard made this concept of air warfare the basis of his policy in the years following the war, and this led the peacetime air staffs to believe that the dropping of large tonnages of bombs on urban areas would present few difficulties. This in turn bred a complacency among the planners, and caused them to underestimate the problems concerned with finding the way to the target area and dropping bombs accurately on a specific objective.

After the war, Trenchard returned to the Air Ministry as Chief of the Air Staff, a post he held for the next ten years. During this time, he was given the opportunity to mould the Air Force in conformity with his strategic doctrine when the 52 squadron defence force was approved in 1923. At a series of meetings held to determine the composition of the projected force, he ruled that the bulk of the force should be bombers, while the fighter component should be set at the absolute minimum. This decision was based on his belief that the aircraft was essentially an offensive weapon and was wasted in defence. In the event of an air attack on this country the bombers would be launched against the enemy's cities in a continuous counter-offensive which, it was claimed, would so weaken the enemy as to force him to suspend his attack against us.[15] In this strategy, Trenchard adhered to the scheme he had outlined in the days of the Independent Force, namely, that the aiming points for the bombers would be the built-up areas in the cities; and although, subsequently, when plans detailing this strategy were circulated outside the Air Ministry they contained references to industrial targets, the basic aim of the bombing remained the same — to break the morale of the civilian population.

From 1923 onwards the concept of the counter-offensive dominated Air Force strategic thought. It was however no more than a concept: it certainly had no contact with the reality of the situation in the Air Force up to the mid-1930s. The squadrons which Trenchard designated for strategic operations were equipped mainly with light day bombers of no great range and capable of carrying only a small bombload. The night bombers had a greater range and carried a greater bombload than the day bombers, but they were few in number and had no means of finding their way in the darkness other than by map-reading. Neither the day nor the night bombers were equipped to fly in bad weather, and the Air Force had no facilities for bringing home safely aircraft overtaken in flight by deteriorating weather conditions.

During the remainder of the 1920s when Trenchard was constantly preaching the gospel of the counter-offensive, aviation was developing rapidly in other countries, notably in Germany and the United States, with new and improved types of radio navigational aids, the introduction of what may be called air traffic control, and the provision of night flying facilities. The financial constraints of this period would certainly have prevented the Air Force from equipping the bomber force with such facilities, though, surely, not from acquiring basic items of equipment for test and research purposes. But, at the very least, Trenchard might have been expected to appreciate the extent to which these developments were transforming aviation, and to realize that they would eventually have to be incorporated in the bomber force if it was to achieve its essential all-weather capability, both by day and night. He might also have given thought to the danger that would face us if we found ourselves at war with a nation which possessed these facilities, and we did not.[16] There is no evidence at all to suggest that he was troubled by such considerations, for when he retired from the Air Force in 1929 the gap between theoretical planning and operational capability, which was already wide, was steadily widening; yet the doctrine of the counter-offensive was preached as fervently as ever.

Finally, there is one important aspect of British air history of the inter-war period which is rarely given sufficient consideration, and that is the serious decline which occurred in virtually every area of British aviation during these years. When the First World War came to an end, the question as to how the aeroplane could be made to serve the needs of peace was raised as one of immediate concern. The majority of the aircraft which had been produced up to that time were intended for military use, but it was felt that some of the larger types might with small modification be employed in some commercial function. In fact, a pointer was given to this possibility when, during the months immediately following the end of the war, service aircraft were used to carry passengers and mail from this country to the continent. Even at this early stage, there were confident expectations in some quarters that the aeroplane would gradually make the world a smaller place by shortening the time scale in travel; and these expectations were seen to be capable of realization when, within little more than a year after the war, Alcock and Brown had flown non-stop across the Atlantic and the first flights had been made to Australia and South Africa. These flights, it is true, were made after careful planning and preparation, and were attended with some element of risk, but they were not conceived as 'once-off' exploits intended primarily to secure a place in the record books, but as pioneer flights blazing the trail for the air routes of the future.

Unfortunately, this vision of Britain's future in the air was not shared by the first post-war Air Minister, Winston Churchill. He did not see it as any part of the Government's responsibilities to assist in the establishment of the civil airlines, and when he left the Air Ministry in 1921 the British companies were losing the battle for passengers in face of the competition from foreign airlines which received generous government subsidies. And so, at a time when Britain possessed what was possibly the most up-to-date aircraft industry in the world, the unique opportunity to exploit that advantage and establish a viable air transport industry was lost, and with it the chance to create markets for our aircraft in foreign as well as in commonwealth countries. Churchill set a precedent for air policy for years to come, and although in 1924 the Government established Imperial Airways as the national airline and provided limited funding, Britain's position as an operator and manufacturer of civil aircraft deteriorated rapidly. The aircraft manufacturers were badly hit by the low level of orders, both civil and military, and as output in the industry was reduced there were many mergers and failures among the companies, and a large body of skilled and experienced personnel was dispersed.

By the early 1930s the United States and Germany were the world's leading manufacturers of aircraft, and the services offered by their airlines were in a class which British airlines could not match. During this period a whole range of new equipment was introduced to make air travel safer and more reliable in all weathers, both by day and night, but none of this equipment was acquired for use in Britain. Thus, both the national airline and the Air Force remained 'fair-weather' operators, unable to fly with safety in bad weather, and rarely flying at night.

Although the civil side of aviation did possess a rudimentary system of air traffic control, the Air Force had no means at all of controlling aircraft in flight; nor had it any organization specially equipped to assist aircraft that were lost or in distress.[17] The effect which a sudden deterioration in weather conditions might produce on aircraft which could obtain no help from the ground was dramatically illustrated by the incident involving seven Heyfords of No. 102 Squadron on 12 December 1936. These aircraft were returning from Aldergrove in Northern Ireland to their base at Finningley, near Doncaster. Soon after crossing the English coast they encountered thick cloud which extended almost to the ground and experienced severe icing conditions. All the aircraft became lost, and only one succeeded in reaching Finningley safely. Three aircraft made forced landings, two near Manchester and one to the north of York, and three crashed, one at Gainsborough in Lincolnshire, one near Oldham in Lancashire, and one at Hebden Bridge in Yorkshire. Three of the crew members of the aircraft which crashed at Hebden Bridge were killed.[18] This incident was unusual only in so far as there were so many aircraft involved at one time, for accidents of this kind were all too common during this period in conditions of bad visibility.

This situation continued unchanged until the second half of the 1930s, when the Air Force began to expand and re-equip with many new and advanced aircraft. This meant that in a short space of time a large number of crews had to convert to aircraft which were more difficult to fly and which involved them in mastering new handling techniques; and this fact, coupled with a substantial increase in night flying, resulted in a large number of accidents. In the years 1936 and 1937 the crash rate increased so alarmingly that the problems of air safety could no longer be ignored; and arrangements were put in hand to set up a number of centres which would be fully equipped to give assistance to aircraft in cases of emergency.

During 1938 eight of these Regional Control Centres, as they were called, were established at airfields extending from St. Eval in the south to Leuchars in the north, each one covering a specified geographical area. Each centre kept a listening watch on W/T (wireless telegraphy) and was equipped with Beam Approach and night landing lights and beacons. A qualified meteorological staff was established at each centre, and current information about weather conditions at all airfields in the area was made available to the Regional Control Officers, who could pass this information to aircraft in flight and arrange diversions to other air-fields when the necessity arose. The centre could also provide homing bearings, courses to steer and controlled approaches. It must however be emphasized that Regional Control was a distress organization, and only came into action when help was requested. There was no intention that it should be used as a means of controlling aircraft in normal conditions.[19]

From the very beginning, these centres were too thinly spread to cope with the rapidly increasing amount of military traffic; and just how inadequate the emergency facilities were in some areas is clearly revealed by an accident which happened shortly before the war to a very experienced pilot who was carrying several important passengers. The aircraft involved, a DH 86 of No. 24 Squadron, was taking the Air Minister, Sir Kingsley Wood, and his party, which included two air marshals, to Belfast. While over the Irish Sea the aircraft suffered an engine failure, and this was followed soon after by a malfunctioning of the blind flying instruments. The pilot then became lost in thick cloud which extended almost to sea level, and, after climbing to 9,000 feet to clear the cloud layer, he decided to return to England. He headed for Manchester, but with no homing facility to assist him − he was forced to rely entirely on wireless fixes − he drifted well to the north of his intended track in re-crossing the Irish Sea. When he descended below cloud he found himself in a hilly area which proved to be in the vicinity of Ulverston in Cumbria. The low state of fuel left the pilot with no alternative but to make a forced landing, and he was able to set the aircraft down on a hillside, fortunately without serious injury to any of those on board.[20]

The aircraft of Bomber Command were, by the nature of their war operations, frequently exposed to the hazards of flying in bad weather and in darkness; and when, early in 1940, there was a general shift from day to night bombing, the number of accidents over this country not attributable to enemy actions rose sharply. The lack of a proper control organization caused heavy losses among aircraft which had returned safely to this country after completing their missions, but were unable to land at their own bases owing to adverse weather conditions. It was no uncommon occurrence for aircraft to fly around (without any direction from the ground) in search of a lighted airfield until they ran out of fuel.[21] This was very different from the situation as Sir Maurice Dean described it. 'From first to last', he wrote, 'the organisation of Bomber Command was superb and coped magnificently with the highly complex task of handling up to 1,000 bombers at night over our tiny island.'[22] In fact, the ability of Bomber Command to exercise safe control over large numbers of aircraft at night was only beginning to manifest itself in the spring of 1942, and not before. In the early phase of the night bombing campaign, during the spring and summer of 1940, though the intensity of operations was relatively low, a conscious effort was made to plan the timing of operations, whenever possible, in such a way as to bring the aircraft back to their bases after daybreak. This tactic was no longer possible during the lengthening nights of the autumn of 1940, and this factor, coupled with the increase in the number of sorties flown, aggravated the problem. The situation deteriorated markedly during the winter of 1940–41, and it was the experience of this first winter of night operations that revealed the manifest inadequacies of the control system and led to the first positive action being taken to equip every operational base with the control facilities which had previously been given only to the Regional Control Centres.[23]

These, then, are some of the most important areas in which this study differs from many of the orthodox histories. This new interpretation of the history of the British bomber force has largely been made possible by the access which the Thirty Years Rule has given to a mass of documentary evidence. This has meant that the official papers relating to the whole history of strategic air policy and practice – from the beginnings in the First World War up to the end of the air offensive in the Second World War – are now open for public inspection. And this is a consideration of the first importance, because there is an essential unity in the history of strategic air power. It is not possible to secure an understanding of any one period in this span of time without a clear knowledge of the whole period. It follows, then, that if a true perspective of the inter-war period is to be gained, it is essential to view it in the context both of the origins of strategic thought and practice in the First World War and of the efficacy of the bombing campaign in the first part of the Second World War; and, for this reason, this work has been based on a detailed examination of the official records covering the years 1912 to 1942.

CHAPTER ONE

BRITISH AIR STRATEGIC THOUGHT AND PRACTICE UP TO 1918

When the First World War came to an end, in November 1918, Britain was the only nation among the belligerents which possessed an independent air force. The Royal Air Force was formed early in 1918, by the amalgamation of the Royal Naval Air Service and the Royal Flying Corps, for the specific purpose of creating a strategic bomber force to strike directly at Germany in retaliation for German aeroplane raids against London. It was intended that the bomber force should be equipped with the surplus aircraft which, it was predicted, would be provided by improved industrial output during 1918; but, in the event, the expected surplus did not materialize, and in consequence the bomber force did not attain more than a fraction of its intended size before the war came to an end.

As soon as hostilities had ceased the bomber force was disbanded and the strategic policy which had inspired its creation was forgotten; yet the Royal Air Force, whose sole raison d'être was the strategic bomber force, survived as an independent service in spite of the determined efforts of the other two services to regain control of their own air formations. Then, some four years after the end of the war, the concept of the strategic offensive was revived in quite a different form in the Air Force — this time as a means of securing Britain from air attack. And it was this new concept of air power, so very different from the original strategic ideas formulated by the Air Staff in the last year of the war, which formed the basis of Air Force doctrine during the inter-war years. It is therefore essential to obtain a clear understanding of the new doctrine and of the influences which moulded it; and in order to do this it will be necessary, first, to trace in outline the history of British air thought from the origins of naval and military aviation up to the formation of the separate air service, and, second, to establish reasons for the wide differences between the strategic policy of 1917–18 and that of the inter-war years.

During the period which preceded the First World War the reluctant

interest shown by the British Government in the flying machine as a
potential instrument of war was stimulated almost entirely by the
advances made in aeronautics by other European countries. In particular, the development of large airships in Germany gave rise to fears
that these machines would be capable of carrying loads of high explosives
direct from their home bases to attack targets in London and in other
parts of the south-east of England. The expression of such fears put
pressure on the Government to discover how real this threat might be,
and in 1908 they appointed a committee under Lord Esher to look into
'the dangers to which we would be exposed on sea or on land by any
developments in aerial navigation reasonably probable in the near
future'. Early in 1909 the Esher Committee reported that such raids
against England were well within the bounds of possibility,[1] and the
Government responded by setting up a special committee, known as
the Advisory Committee for Aeronautics, to undertake a study of the
science of aeronautics, with special reference to the problems of designing
both lighter- and heavier-than-air machines.[2]

The immediate outcome of the committee's deliberations was the
formation in 1911 of a purely military air unit, the Air Battalion
of the Royal Engineers,[3] but when it soon became obvious that any
permanent organization should include provision for naval as well as
military aviation, the whole question of service aviation was referred
to a sub-committee of the Committee of Imperial Defence. This sub-
committee recommended that a British air service, to be known as the
Flying Corps, should be formed, and that it should consist of a Naval
Wing, a Military Wing and a Central Flying School for the training of
pilots of both wings. The task of drawing up detailed plans to implement
this policy was delegated to a technical sub-committee under the chairmanship of the Secretary of State for War, Colonel J.E.B. Seely.[4]

Although it was intended that the recommendations of the sub-
committee should provide for the requirements of both services, the
Admiralty had little sympathy for the idea of a joint air service and the
naval members made virtually no contribution to the work of the sub-
committee. The result was that the sub-committee's report was prepared
under the direction of the senior army representative, Brigadier-General
David Henderson, and dealt almost entirely with the needs of the Army.
Yet even this biased approach does not explain why the report made
no mention of the growing power of the German airship fleet or of the
potential danger to this country from air attack, but concentrated mainly
on justifying the proposal to establish a force of military reconnaissance
aircraft.

The only reasonable explanation is that Henderson did not believe
that there was any danger from air attack and therefore did not consider

the possible employment of aircraft in the defensive role. His main concern was to impress upon the sub-committee that the most valuable use of the aircraft would be as an instrument of army support, with reconnaissance as its primary function. Indeed, he believed that reconnaissance would also be the chief function of the naval aircraft, and these views are clearly reflected in the report which visualized the Flying Corps as a force composed largely of reconnaissance aircraft. From this point of view it was logical to recommend that the force should be so organized as to enable each wing to constitute a reserve for the other, so that in the event of 'a purely naval war the whole of the Flying Corps should be available to the Navy, and in a purely land war the whole corps should be available to the Army'.[5]

Even when the Flying Corps came into being, in April 1912, the Admiralty showed no more interest in the scheme. They organized the naval wing as an independent service and made no use of the joint facilities provided by the Central Flying School for the training of pilots or the Aircraft Factory for the design and production of aircraft. From the beginning naval flying personnel were trained at the naval air station at Eastchurch and contracts for the design and manufacture of aircraft were placed with civilian firms. Nor was the designation 'Flying Corps (Naval Wing)' much used in the service, and even before the outbreak of the First World War the naval wing was generally known as the Royal Naval Air Service.

It was, however, unfortunate for the development of service aviation in Britain that the Admiralty should have chosen to remain aloof both from the deliberations of the technical sub-committee and from the activities of the new air service; for by so doing they permitted the War Office to represent the purely military views as the considered policy of the Flying Corps, when in fact naval and military policy differed in almost every respect.

Military policy was shaped by the concept of the air service as an extension of the cavalry arm, and the officer whose ideas dominated the Military Wing was General Henderson who became the first head of the Aeronautical Department at the War Office. His view of the military aircraft was that of a slow, stable machine making its unhurried (and unhindered) progress over the area of battle; and it was this concept of the reconnaissance aircraft which led to the design and production of types like the BE2 range which by reason of their slow speeds and lack of manoeuvrability were quite useless for operations of war.

The naval aircraft, on the other hand, was from the first developed as an instrument of the offensive, and was intended to provide an active defence against aeroplane and airship raids and to carry out bombing attacks against enemy objectives. A comprehensive programme of trials and experiments was begun in 1912, and this included the firing of machine-guns mounted on aircraft and the dropping of bombs from the air; and when war came two years later the Naval Air Service had already adopted a standard bomb-dropping gear and had issued a simple hand-held bombsight to the squadrons. Efforts had also been made to tackle the problems of navigating an aircraft to a distant target.[6]

On the outbreak of war, all four military squadrons quickly joined the British Expeditionary Force in France, and although air defence was the responsibility of the War Office, not a single operational unit was left in Britain for this purpose. It was indeed fortunate for those who took the decision to transfer the whole of the Military Wing to France that the Germans had made no plans to use their airships against Britain; for although the German airship fleet was numerically too weak to have caused significant damage, the very appearance of these craft over Britain during the period of our reverses in France would have been a shock to the nation's morale. Soon after the departure of the military squadrons, the Admiralty (somewhat rashly) agreed to take over responsibility for air defence, and it was they who bore the full brunt of criticism when Britain's unpreparedness was revealed by the Zeppelin raids which began in the spring of 1915.[7]

During the first year of hostilties, the type of warfare which was evolving on the Western Front had created a new range of air support duties which the military squadrons were ill-equipped to carry out. Much of this work involved the aircraft in lifting extra weight in the form of wireless and photographic equipment, guns, ammunition, bombs and so on;[8] but because of the low horse-power of the aero-engines used in the Flying Corps − General Henderson had ruled that no engines over 100 horse-power should be produced by the Aircraft Factory[9] − the standard aircraft in service could not carry out these duties without serious loss of performance.

By the early autumn of 1915 the failure of the War Office to anticipate and plan for the requirements of the expanding service had led to a difficult and dangerous situation. In particular, this was reflected in the decision to equip an increasing number of squadrons with the general purpose type of aircraft, of which the BE2c was the most notable example. Early in the war, large orders were placed for this slow and over-stable (and consequently highly vulnerable) aircraft, but when, after serious delays in production, large-scale deliveries were eventually achieved in the latter part of 1915, the aircraft was already obsolete. Nevertheless, the BE2c continued to be produced in large numbers, and by the summer of 1916 nearly half the total number of aircraft in service with the Flying Corps in France were of this type.[10]

The first signs of the impending crisis can be discerned in a memorandum which presented an analysis of the bombing results achieved by the three allied air services — the Royal Naval Air Service, the Royal Flying Corps and the French Air Force — during the spring offensive of 1915. The statistical evidence presented in this document, which was prepared by the headquarters staff of the Flying Corps, contained unequivocal proof that the bombing carried out by the military squadrons had been a costly failure.[11] Indeed, it would have been surprising if it had pointed to any other conclusion; for without proper bomb-release gear and bombsights pilots had almost no hope of hitting their targets except by attacking at low level where they were extremely vulnerable to fire from the ground.

But the worst of the setbacks was still to come, and this occurred during the second half of 1915, when the Germans began to arm their aircraft with a machine-gun which fired through the arc of the airscrew. Losses among the military squadrons, which were defenceless against such a massive increase in firepower, began to rise steeply; and so for the first time since the beginning of hostilities one side was able to gain a decisive superiority over the other in the air fighting.

The main cause of these reverses was the failure of the senior Flying Corps officers to appreciate that different types of aircraft and equipment would be needed for different functions; but this was only one element of the fundamental weakness of their approach, which was that they never came to understand the vital importance of technical considerations in all air operations. This caused them to underestimate the advantages to be gained by attaining high technical standards, and, consequently, they failed to recognize the need for a systematic approach in determining the future requirements of the service so far as aircraft, equipment, training facilities and so on were concerned. What was needed was a central organization with responsibility for conducting trials and experiments based on the experience of war, but this was never set up. It would, however, be wrong to give the impression that no work of this type was ever undertaken by the experimental units, because this was not the case; but it was on too small a scale and too unsystematic to produce significant results. In practice, much of the experimental work was left to the individual squadrons, and so, what was done was spasmodic and largely uncoordinated.

The squadrons were also expected to provide the greater part of the training received by pilots and observers. Personnel under training as pilots were given only the most basic instruction at the flying schools before being posted to an operational squadron. In 1916 the newly qualified pilot would have attained perhaps 20 hours flying experience, of which about two-thirds would be solo. For the observer, on the other hand, there was no recognized course of instruction at all before the formation of the Royal Air Force in 1918. It was intended that both pilots and observers should acquire the necessary proficiency in such skills as navigation, bomb-dropping and photography by actual operational experience, supplemented by whatever training the squadron could provide; and for many pilots there was the added burden of learning to fly the type of aircraft with which the squadron was equipped.[12] In such a situation it is hardly surprising that many of the crews did not survive long enough to acquire these skills.

In marked contrast, the training given to a naval pilot was a realistic introduction to operational flying. He received about 24 hours' solo experience at an elementary training school before being sent to an advanced school to complete his flying instruction; and after that he received specialist training in fighting or bombing tactics, according to the type of squadron in which he was destined to serve. The course of training for an observer was of four months' duration.[13]

In contrast, too, was the success achieved by the naval bombing operations. From the beginning of the war naval aircraft attacked a wide range of targets in their campaign against the German airship fleet. Three airships were destroyed and substantial damage was caused to the airship base at Friedrichshafen on Lake Constance.[14] The notable success of these early operations encouraged the naval air staff to seek a wider range of targets for the new naval bomber, the Sopwith 1½ Strutter. High on their list of targets were the bases where German submarines were repaired and re-fitted and factories which manufactured components for submarines.[15]

Meanwhile, the French air staff had been working on similar lines and had, in the spring of 1915, produced a comprehensive plan for attacking enemy industrial targets. The French did not, however, possess an aircraft of sufficient performance to carry out the plan and did not seem likely to produce one in the foreseeable future. Later in the year, the British naval air staff and the French air staff met together to consider the prospects for a joint bombing campaign in the spring of 1916. The two sides were in complete agreement as to the aims to be pursued and the means by which they were to be achieved, but the French were prevented by their lack of suitable aircraft from entering into any firm agreement.[16]

In spite of this setback, the Admiralty were determined that the start of the campaign should not be delayed, and at once plans were made to begin operations from a base in England. The naval air station at Detling, near Maidstone, was chosen as the operational base for the new wing of Sopwiths, but it was soon recognized that the geographical position of the station presented a serious problem. The direct flight from Detling to the main targets lay across Dutch territory, and as plans began to mature it became increasingly evident that no workable precautions could be devised to prevent violations of neutral territory. Then, after much thought had been given to the matter, it was at length decided that the risks were too great, and the plan was abandoned.[17]

Soon after making this decision the Admiralty approached the French with a definite proposal for a joint bombing campaign from a base in France. The French responded with enthusiasm, and preparations were quickly put in train to establish an allied force at Luxeuil, some 25 miles north-west of Belfort. In return for the aerodrome accommodation and other facilities the Admiralty agreed to allocate to the French squadrons one-third of the new Sopwiths delivered to the naval unit and to leave the choice of targets in the hands of the French air staff.

Arrangements to establish the naval bombing force (designated No. 3 Wing) were completed by mid-summer 1916, and just as operations were about to begin the Flying Corps, hard pressed during the Somme offensive, made an urgent appeal for the first deliveries of the 1 ½ Strutters to be allocated to the military squadrons. In response, the Admiralty agreed to give first priority to the supply of 60 Sopwiths to the Flying Corps, and in so doing caused the Anglo-French bombing campaign to be postponed until the autumn, when the weather was already deteriorating. Then, early in 1917, after several months of extremely severe weather conditions, during which operations were greatly curtailed, the Admiralty received more urgent appeals for help from the Flying Corps, and these could be answered only by withdrawing aircraft and personnel from No. 3 Wing. At first the wing was able to maintain its operational efficiency, though with reduced striking power, by internal reorganization; but when further requests for help − supported by the minister responsible for air matters − were received in March 1917, the Admiralty had no alternative but to disband the wing.[18]

The disbandment of the naval wing brought to an end the most original and successful experiment in the use of air power to be attempted during the war. The allied squadrons constituted the first ever strategic bomber force − that is, a force organized and equipped specifically to strike directly at the enemy's war-making capacity as opposed to the units and equipment of his armed forces − and although the actual material damage caused by the allied raids was relatively light, the injury inflicted on the German war effort was out of all proportion to the effort expended by the allies. The raids produced insistent demands from the civilian population for effective anti-aircraft defences, and the German government, moved by the need to maintain a high level of morale among the industrial workers, withdrew or diverted from the Front valuable aircraft and equipment for home defence.[19]

When the naval wing was disbanded the French bombing effort also came to an end, and the Germans were spared the well-nigh impossible task of providing defences for the large area threatened by the allied bombers. The Germans were in fact relieved of the kind of pressure which the Zeppelin raids had exerted on Britain since early 1915, and the initiative in the strategic air war again passed into their hands.

The repeated military requests for naval assistance which made the disbandment of No. 3 Wing inevitable were but one aspect of the calculated opposition of the Flying Corps to any operations which were thought to be competing with the army support squadrons for the limited air resources. It was an unquestioned assumption among the leaders of the Flying Corps that no operations such as those carried out by the naval bombing wing should be permitted until the military needs had been met in full. This was another way of saying that they should never be allowed at all, for the military demands for air material were always greatly in excess of what was available. This conviction was such an important factor in determining air policy during the war that it is essential to find out why it came to be held with such tenacity. This can best be done by tracing briefly the development of military aviation from the early days of the war.

When the military squadrons departed for France in August 1914 almost nothing of the Flying Corps was retained in England. Even General Henderson, the Director-General of Military Aeronautics, left his post at the War Office to take command of the BEF contingent and took with him the majority of his most experienced staff officers. Henderson remained in command in France for almost a year, and during that time the operational duties of the military squadrons were clearly established. This period should therefore have been one of unremitting staff activity to identify and plan for the future needs of the service in the light of actual war experience. Instead, the first year of the war proved to be notable only for the marked lack of activity at the War Office and for the rapidly mounting casualties among the military squadrons. By the summer of 1915 the situation had become so unsatisfactory that Henderson was obliged to return to the War Office and resume control of the Aeronautical Department.

This change proved to be a momentous one, for the officer who succeeded Henderson as commander of the Flying Corps in France, Brigadier-General Hugh M. Trenchard, was to play a decisive part in shaping British air policy for the next 30 years. Trenchard had joined the Flying Corps in 1912, at the age of 39, as a means of escaping from a regimental life which he found dull and unrewarding. His considerable ability as an administrator was quickly recognized in the Flying Corps, and this quality together with his age and experience marked him out for rapid promotion in a service in which the majority of officers were very young men.

Trenchard at once applied his great energy to the task of extending the air support for the BEF, and in spite of his undoubted success in achieving this, he did little or nothing to improve the technical efficiency of the force he commanded. He was in fact ill-equipped both by training and experience to appreciate the essentially technical nature of air operations, and with the approach typical of a regular army officer he placed too much importance on the purely soldierly qualities of discipline, morale and organization, and too little on technical efficiency.

From the outset Trenchard was guided by his conviction that the aeroplane was essentially an offensive weapon and would be effective only if used as such. The worst possible situation he could envisage was one in which the Flying Corps was forced on the defensive by aggressive enemy action, and in order to obviate that possibility he ordered his squadrons to carry the fight to the enemy on every possible occasion, and at whatever the cost. Inevitably, the price to be paid for these tactics was very high, for in addition to the technical superiority which the Germans had already established over the military squadrons, the area of operations on the Western Front, which was small in relation to the number of aircraft deployed there, favoured the defensive tactics which the German Air Force pursued as a matter of deliberate policy.[20]

In these circumstances the offensive policy was a mistaken one and placed an intolerable burden on the Flying Corps. Casualties rose alarmingly, and the War Office organization proved as incapable of providing replacement aircraft in sufficient numbers as it had been of improving the design of aircraft and the quality of flying training. The most obvious response to such a situation would have been to reduce the intensity of operations until some fundamental changes could be carried out in the aeronautical department. Instead, Trenchard maintained the offensive with relentless determination, and even during the costly actions of the Somme offensive he did not modify his tactics, but made urgent appeals for the new naval aircraft to be diverted to the military squadrons so that he could throw an even greater number of aircraft into the battle.

Soon after returning to the War Office, General Henderson had convinced himself that most of the difficulties besetting the Flying Corps were caused by what he considered to be the unfair distribution of air resources. This situation had arisen, he believed, chiefly because the Naval Air Service was engaged in operations over land − long-range bombing, for example − which were properly the function of the Flying Corps. It followed, therefore, that if the naval squadrons could be restricted to operations concerned directly with the war at sea, the Flying

Corps would automatically qualify for a larger share of the available material. He thought that this could best be achieved by seeking an official ruling as to which duties should be undertaken by each service, since he confidently expected that such a ruling would allocate the responsibility for all land operations to the Flying Corps.

Henderson opened his 'campaign' against the Navy early in 1916 when he addressed a paper to the Joint War Air Committee, the body responsible for co-ordinating air policy and the supply of material, asking that the duties of the two services be precisely defined.[21] When this move did not produce the desired result, he resorted to a much more direct approach. In a second paper submitted to the same body, he accused the Admiralty of using unfair methods to secure material for their own service, at the expense of the Flying Corps.[22] The naval air staff answered the charge as bluntly as it had been made. The accusation, they stated, had been made simply to enable the War Office to justify their demands for naval material; for the difficulties in which the Flying Corps found themselves were caused, not by unfair competition for material, but by the failure of the War Office to plan for their future requirements.[23]

The two appeals to the Joint War Air Committee resulted in the transfer of a large amount of naval material to the Flying Corps, but this fell a good deal short of the permanent re-allocation of material which Henderson had set out to achieve. He therefore resumed his attack on the Admiralty, this time with a fierce condemnation of naval bombing policy at a meeting of the Air Board (the body which replaced the Joint War Air Committee) in the autumn of 1916. It was the firm conviction of all the military leaders, he stated, that the naval bombing operations were of minor importance compared with the operations of the military squadrons and should not be continued as long as the air service supporting the BEF was below the strength asked for by Sir Douglas Haig, the Commander-in-Chief. The naval members of the Air Board countered this by pointing out that the naval operations were in fact supporting the land campaign by compelling the Germans to withdraw air units from the Western Front, but Henderson replied that there was no evidence at all to support this claim.[24]

It was a foregone conclusion that Henderson would carry his point, for the Air Board never questioned the validity of military policy. Nor did they ever express any doubt as to whether the vast expenditure of air resources on the Western Front was essential to the successful conduct of the war. While the Air Board was considering what action should be taken, Sir Douglas Haig added the weight of his great authority to the attack on naval policy. On the advice of Trenchard, he addressed a letter to the War Office protesting against the use of air resources on operations which he considered to be irrelevant to the task of defeating the enemy. He concluded with the warning that if the Admiralty persisted with their plans to increase the scale of their bombing campaign, future military operations might well be placed in jeopardy through lack of essential air support.[25] Haig's intervention proved to be decisive. Great pressure was brought to bear on the Admiralty, and within a short time the bombing was brought to an end and the naval wing at Luxeuil disbanded.

Then, in the spring of 1917, a new and wholly unlooked for development occurred in the air war. At the end of May, enemy aircraft made the first of a number of daylight raids against targets in the south-east of England. The Germans opened this campaign with a new bomber, the Gotha G.IV, which possessed the range to reach many important objectives in this area from airfields in Belgium. On 13 June the Gothas made their first daylight attack on London. No warning of their approach was received in the capital, and only when the first bombs began to fall was it realized that a raid was in progress. The streets of the City were crowded when the attack began, and the resulting casualties, 162 killed and 432 injured, were the highest of any single raid on Britain during the whole of the war.[26]

The first reaction of the Government was to ask why the air defence organization, the responsibility for which had been returned to the War Office in February 1916, had not only failed to give prior warning of the raid but had also been unable to engage the enemy bombers effectively during their considerable flight over the English countryside. An emergency meeting of the Cabinet was held within a few hours of the raid, and, though there was much confusion of thought, it was finally agreed that the weaknesses in the defence system could reasonably be attributed to shortages of aircraft and equipment. The shock caused by the raid produced a swift response, and within 24 hours of the meeting approval had been given for a substantial increase in the strength of each of the air services.[27]

A little over three weeks later, on 7 July, the Gothas appeared over London in daylight for the second time, and again the defences were ineffective. Although the number of people killed and injured, 54 and 190 respectively, were far fewer than in the first raid, the impact on the nation was much greater. A wave of indignation swept through the country when it was learnt that enemy aircraft had once again been able to attack London in broad daylight and return to their bases virtually unscathed.[28] There were vociferous demands for an overhaul of the nation's air defences and for retaliatory raids against German cities, but the Prime Minister, David Lloyd George, declined to take any action until he had received advice from an impartial enquiry. He therefore appointed Lieutenant-General J.C. Smuts, the South African soldier and statesman who was a member of the War Cabinet, to conduct an enquiry into two important aspects of the air problem: first, the arrangements for defence against air attacks, and second, Britain's air policy and organization at the highest level.[29]

General Smuts carried out his task with great energy and by the middle of August had submitted both reports to the Cabinet. The second of these reports, which dealt with policy and organization, was of fundamental importance, for it recommended the creation of an independent air force whose primary function would be to strike directly at the enemy's war-making capacity.[30] General Smuts had himself been present in London during the raid of 7 July and was greatly impressed by this demonstration of aircraft flying from distant bases to strike directly at the homeland of the enemy. This experience, perhaps more than any other single factor, convinced him of the immense potential of strategic bombing, so that he foresaw a time in the not so distant future 'when aerial operations with their devastation of enemy lands and destruction of industrial and populous centres on a vast scale may become the principal operations of war, to which the older forms of military and naval operations may become secondary and subordinate'.

For the immediate future, he predicted that by the summer of 1918, 'while our Western Front may still be moving forward at a snail's pace in Belgium and France, the air battle-front will be far behind on the Rhine, and ... its continuous and intense pressure against the chief industrial centres of the enemy as well as on his lines of communication may form an important factor in bringing about peace'. This vision led him to press for the immediate establishment of a independent air force; for this was deemed to be the essential preliminary to the creation of the strategic bomber force and the air staff to plan and direct its operations.

This recommendation was received with little enthusiasm in official circles, where it was felt that if such a reorganization were undertaken in wartime the work of the two air services would be seriously disrupted. There was also the more serious objection, expressed by many who were well qualified to judge, that Britain did not possess the industrial capacity to produce the extra aircraft needed to equip the bomber force. Strangely, General Smuts did not consider either of these problems to be a serious obstacle to the fulfilment of his plan, and in view of his immensely realistic approach to his investigations it is of some importance to discover why this was so.

The answer to the first point is to be found in the influence exercised by General Henderson, whose advice and assistance General Smuts had constantly sought during the course of the enquiry. Henderson saw the proposed amalgamation of the two air services as a unique opportunity of the military service to exert a decisive influence on air policy; for in the event of an independent air service coming into being the majority of the senior posts in the new service would be filled by officers from the Flying Corps, which was by far the larger of the two air services. In this way the influence of the Naval Air Service both as an originator of unwelcome ideas and as a competitor for air material would be reduced to insignificance. He encouraged Smuts to persist with his scheme for an independent air service, giving him firm assurances that the necessary reorganization could be accomplished without impeding the work of the two services.[31] There can be no doubt that Smuts accepted this judgement unreservedly and placed great reliance upon Henderson to direct the reorganization. Events were soon to show that this trust was not misplaced, for when the Government finally gave consent to the change Henderson worked with impressive skill and energy to bring about a smooth transition to the independent service.

Smuts was not so fortunate in the advice he received on the question of aircraft supply. His chief adviser was Lord Cowdray who, as President of the Air Board, was well placed to make an assessment of the future supply situation. Lord Cowdray anticipated that production in 1918 would yield a considerable surplus of aircraft after the requirements of both the Navy and the Army had been met in full; and he suggested that this 'Surplus Aircraft Fleet', as he called it, should be used to build the long-range bomber force.[32] The importance of this forecast in influencing the conclusions which Smuts reached can hardly be exaggerated; for it is virtually certain that without the promise of a substantial number of surplus aircraft in 1918 he would not have recommended the formation either of a strategic bomber force or of a separate air force. Unfortunately, Lord Cowdray's estimates were soon shown to be based on a complete mis-reading of the supply prospects, but by the time this discovery was made the question of the independent air force had become the centre of a major political issue.

Initially, the Government had supported the scheme for reorganization, but when it became clear that the German aeroplane raids were proving to be a less serious threat than had been feared, they became increasingly unwilling to undertake the onerous task which the reorganization would involve. By the early autumn the Cabinet were on the point of deciding against both the independent air service and the bomber force; but public opinion was now so strongly in favour of the reorganization that the Government had no alternative but to yield to the pressure. A bill giving sanction to a separate air force was quickly drafted and presented to Parliament, and by the end of November it had received the Royal Assent.[33]

Several weeks before the Air Force Bill became law, Trenchard was instructed to make preliminary arrangements for the reception of the new bomber force in France, and after protracted negotiations with the French authorities he was able to secure a base at Ochey, near Nancy. Then, early in October, after receiving instructions to begin operations, he formed the 41st Wing and allocated to it one naval and two military squadrons. This was the nucleus of a force which was scheduled to expand to 37 squadrons by the end of October 1918.

The first Air Council came into being in January 1918. Lord Rothermere was appointed Secretary of State for the Air Force and Trenchard was brought from France to become the Chief of the Air Staff. Within a few weeks it was obvious that the two men could not work together, and before the end of April both had resigned.[34]

The second Air Council, in which Sir William Weir was Secretary of State and Major-General F. H. Sykes the Chief of the Air Staff,[35] gave greater priority to the expansion of the bomber force. In May 1918 the first reinforcements were sent to Ochey, and on 6 June this force became known as the Independent Force and was placed directly under the control of the Air Ministry. But there was little that could be done to maintain the planned growth of the force for, as had been foreseen, the large surplus of aircraft did not materialize, and when the war came to an end the strength of the Independent Force had reached only nine operational squadrons.

During the few months which elapsed between the acceptance of the Smuts Report and the formation of the Air Council, the responsibility for determining the employment of the bomber force rested with the Air Board, which began its work by seeking the advice of a number of service officers who had had experience of long-range bombing operations. One of the first to be consulted was Viscount Tiverton, an officer of the Royal Naval Volunteer Reserve, whose contribution to air thought during the war was one of outstanding originality. Though a barrister by profession, Lord Tiverton possessed a considerable knowledge of mathematics and science and this enabled him to make a scientific study of strategic bombing, a type of bombing he was convinced could be fashioned into a weapon of great power, provided its essentially technical character was both recognized and understood.

After serving briefly as Armament Training Officer in the Air Department of the Admiralty, Lord Tiverton was appointed Armament Officer of No. 3 Wing at Luxeuil in 1916, and during this tour of duty he was able to gain first-hand knowledge of the nature of strategic operations. By the summer of 1917 he was well advanced with his research and had formed an estimate of the requirements of a bomber force in terms of aircraft, equipment, training and research. The results of this work, which were embodied in a paper submitted to the Air Board, presented an analysis of strategic operations which the history of the following 25 years has shown to be an extremely accurate one.[36] In particular, he emphasized the great technical difficulties involved in navigation, target identification and bombsighting, and these areas of his work have a special relevance to the early bombing operations of the Second World War.

It should be noted that the success which Lord Tiverton achieved was to an important degree the result of his method of work, which anticipated by many years the method of scientific investigation later known as Operational Research. Perhaps his most impressive application of this method is to be found in his calculations to ascertain the probable number of bombs required to destroy various kinds of targets.

When Lord Tiverton was invited by the Air Board to submit a paper on long-distance bombing, he was instructed to base it on three main assumptions: first, that the strength of the bomber force would be 2,000 aircraft; second, that the principal aim of the offensive would be the systematic destruction of the German munition industry; and third, that the base of operations would be located either in the Verdun–Toul area or near Ostend. In view of the stated aim of the offensive, Lord Tiverton had no hesitation in choosing the Verdun–Toul area as the base for operations, since all the industrial centres which he nominated for attack were within range of that area, whereas only half of them could be reached from Ostend.

Having settled the question of the operational base, Lord Tiverton then turned to consider in detail the preparations required to establish the bomber force. Among these, he thought that the provisions for navigation and weather forecasting should be given the highest priority. If the bomber crews were to find their way to the targets, their training should include a course of map-reading specially designed to give them a thorough knowledge of the territory over which they were to operate. The weather, too, would present its problems, and these were particularly acute in the Verdun–Toul area. The operations of No. 3 Wing had shown that even during the same period of time weather conditions in that area were often very different from those to be found in the Rhine valley, where many of the industrial targets were located. If therefore the effects of the weather were to be reduced to a minimum, an efficient meteorological service must be established at the operational base so that up-to-date weather information would always be available.

Lord Tiverton was convinced that the key to success in these operations lay in concentrating every available aircraft on one objective on the same day, for it was vital to strike with as much power as possible on the very limited number of days when weather conditions would allow

attacks to be carried out against the distant targets. It was his intention
to select an important industrial unit — the chemical works at Ludwigshafen, for example — and subject it to continuous bombardment for
several hours until the main parts of the plant were destroyed and the
morale of the workers broken. He believed that if destruction on this
scale could be repeated at other industrial centres the German government might well be forced to seek terms.

Some weeks later Lord Tiverton submitted a second paper to the Air
Board. This dealt exclusively with the vulnerability to air attack of a
cross-section — nearly a hundred in all — of German factories manufacturing war material.[37] In it he described the characteristics of each
factory under a number of headings — the area of the site, the type
of manufacturing activity, the proportion of the area occupied by
buildings and plant vulnerable to bomb attack, and so on — and using
this information in conjunction with a mean bombing error twice as
great as that experienced in practice bombing in England (to ensure that
due allowance was made for the reduction in accuracy which inevitably
occurred during actual operations) he calculated, among other things,
the percentage of bombs likely to fall within the factory area and the
percentage of bombs likely to cause effective damage. The results of
these calculations pointed to the same conclusions as his experience and
previous research had suggested: first, that it was essential to mount
large-scale attacks if worthwhile damage was to be caused; and second,
that large factories were easy to hit but difficult to destroy, whereas
small factories were easy to destroy but difficult to hit.

Towards the end of 1917, the Air Policy Committee, the body set
up to advise the Cabinet on air matters until the establishment of the
Air Council, produced an operational plan which advocated a bombing
policy very different from the one suggested by Lord Tiverton.[38] In
this plan the German cities themselves were named as the actual targets,
and the principal aim of the bombing was to destroy the morale of the
civilian population. There is no doubt at all that the originator of this
plan was Trenchard, and this may be confirmed by comparing the plan
prepared by the Air Policy Committee with a memorandum entitled
'Long Distance Bombing' which was prepared by Trenchard's headquarters in 1917.[39] The two documents set out identical views (in
certain places even the wording is identical) concerning the aims of the
bombing campaign and the tactics to be employed.

This was perhaps the earliest bombing plan to embody the philosophy
upon which Trenchard founded his strategic policy in the post-war Air
Force. In the post-war plans the aim of that policy (that is, the terrorization of the civilian population) was to be achieved by selecting targets
that were located in densely populated industrial areas, so that all the

bombs which failed to hit the aiming points (ostensibly industries supporting the enemy war effort) would strike at the morale of the civilian population by destroying their lives and homes and disrupting the services (transport, gas, water and so on) on which they depended. This type of bombing seemed to the Air Staff of the inter-war years to offer a means of attack by which every bomb could be made to count. In consequence, they formed an exaggerated notion of the destructive power of bombing and this led them seriously to underestimate the need to develop and improve equipment and operational techniques.

When the Independent Force came into being Trenchard, who was still without employment after resigning as Chief of the Air Staff, was invited to take command of it. It is not surprising that he was most unwilling to accept the post, for he had long been opposed to independent bombing operations; and it was only when the Air Minister put great pressure on him to accept that he reluctantly did so. It must be assumed that the Air Minister believed that Trenchard, once having accepted the responsibility of command, would support the strategic policy of the new Air Council, but in fact he did not do so. He constantly disregarded Air Staff instructions concerning the choice of targets and directed the greater part of his attacks against tactical objectives such as railways and aerodromes. It is true that he was under some pressure to hold the Independent Force at the disposal of the Allied Supreme Commander, General Foch; but, on the other hand, he showed no reluctance to provide support for the land forces (however dubious its value) whenever he was called upon to do so.[40]

Even the limited number of strategic operations which were carried out were handicapped by Trenchard's disregard for the advice and assistance given by the Air Staff. This attitude is clearly revealed by his failure to provide adequate facilities for meteorology and navigation. From the beginning the Air Staff had pressed for the establishment of a meteorological service, yet no attempt was made to comply with this instruction, and the bomber force operated without a meteorological section throughout its existence. The weather reports used by the squadrons were obtained from a centre outside the Nancy area and all too frequently were not relevant to the period of time during which the flights would take place or to the height at which the bombers would operate.

To meet an important operational need the Air Staff provided a course in navigation (together with an element of bombing) which was completed by all personnel who were to fly in the long-range bombers; yet none of the squadrons of the Independent Force were ever provided with even the basic navigational instruments which would have enabled the crews to profit from this training. This meant that they had no accurate means of determining wind velocity, that is, the direction and strength of the wind, a basic requirement of air operations, and were forced to rely almost entirely on forecast winds for both navigation and bombing.[41]

In spite of these setbacks, the Air Staff continued their efforts to improve the efficiency of long-range bombing, but in the face of Trenchard's indifference to their work they made little progress. As soon as peace returned, the Air Staff papers dealing with the independent bombing operations were consigned to the discarded files of the war, and to oblivion. And so, when the concept of a bomber striking force was revived in the mid-1920s this vital staff work, which should have been the starting point for the development of a peacetime strategic policy, was already irretrievably lost; and during the reconstruction of the bomber force the very existence of the problems which the Air Staff of 1918 had begun to tackle had long since been forgotten.

In spite of much evidence to the contrary, it is still widely believed that no significant knowledge of strategic operations was acquired before the Bomber Command offensive against Germany in the Second World War, and for that reason alone it is important to place on record just how clear an understanding of long-distance operations had been achieved by the Air Staff of 1918. This can best be done by considering the three aspects of operations – navigation, target identification and bomb-aiming – which were generally agreed to have presented some of the greatest difficulties. As has been seen, much of this work was done or inspired by Lord Tiverton, the officer responsible for bombing plans at the Air Ministry, and it is in the papers written by him that Air Staff thought and policy are most clearly reflected.

Perhaps the most common theme in these papers relates to the difficulties experienced by the crews in finding their way to the target. Lord Tiverton believed that in a campaign of the type in which the Independent Force was engaged – one in which the flights were to a limited number of target areas, over territory containing many prominent features – these difficulties could in large measure be overcome by giving the crews a special course in map-reading relating to the operational area, so that they would become familiar with the features along the routes to the main targets.

Once the target area was reached the crews were faced with the problem of identifying the actual objective, which was often a single factory located in a built-up industrial area. Lord Tiverton suggested that training in target recognition should be made an integral part of the bombing course and should be combined with practice in approach and bombing techniques. He recommended that full-size outlines of important German factories should be marked out on Salisbury Plain, each one being so orientated that the pilot would approach it on the same compass course as he would steer for the actual target, and that simulated day and night attacks should be made against these outlines with practice bombs having the same 'fall' characteristics as the bombs in operational use.[42]

Ultimately, however, the success of a bombing raid would depend upon the accuracy of the bomb-aiming and the effectiveness of the bombs. The first of these was determined mainly by the efficiency of the bombsight, and in the summer of 1918 the Air Staff were making preparations to introduce into squadron service the last of a number of important sights designed by naval personnel. This was the course-setting bombsight designed by Lieutenant Commander H. E. Wimperis, which enabled the aircraft to approach the target from any direction, and not merely up-wind or down-wind as with previous sights.[43] Emphasis too was placed upon the need to investigate other factors which affected the accuracy of bombsighting – the height from which the bombs were dropped, the method of attack, the type of aircraft used, and so on – and Lord Tiverton and Lt.Cdr. Wimperis constantly stressed the importance of collecting as much data as possible relating to them.

Lord Tiverton was perhaps the first of the planners of air warfare to base his work on the assumption that the bomb (and not the bomber) was the vital element in air bombardment. For him the aeroplane was essentially the carrier of the missiles, and should therefore be designed specifically to deliver the most effective bombs to the most desirable objectives. This approach was quite different from that adopted by the planners in the inter-war years, when aircraft were often built without any consideration of the targets they would have to reach or of the bombs they would be required to carry. Lord Tiverton was very conscious of the fact that little was known of the nature of the damage caused by bombs of different types and sizes, and he pointed out that since no experiments had ever been carried out to discover these facts, a start could be made by establishing the nature of the damage that had been caused by the various types of German bombs dropped on London.

Another aspect of this problem was the need to discover which type of bomb would cause most damage to a particular kind of target. From his research into the vulnerability of different German factories Lord Tiverton had concluded that the design of a high explosive bomb should be determined by the layout, structure and manufacturing activities of the factory against which it was to be used. He believed that the best way of acquiring this information would be to set up a number of committees of expert advisers, under the Director of Aircraft Armament. He suggested that the committees should undertake as a matter of first priority the task of recommending the best types of bombs for use against the main kinds of factories.[44]

The bomber force which operated in the Nancy area during the last year of the war was in every respect a makeshift one, yet it achieved a remarkable degree of success. An Air Ministry commission which was sent to Germany soon after the war proved this beyond any doubt.[45] And when the Germans carried out their own investigations a few years later they reached the same conclusions.[46] Though the raids caused only light material damage, they produced a serious effect on the morale of the civilian population which was already dispirited and war-weary. Industrial production, too, was severely affected and this was caused mainly by the frequent air raid warnings, for it was the German practice to sound alerts throughout the whole of the area in which the bombers were operating.

But the most serious handicap which the bombing imposed on the Germans was that it compelled them to maintain a large defence force — comprising guns, searchlights and aircraft — to protect the threatened areas. These resources could be provided only by withdrawing or withholding material from the Front; and this placed a great strain on the German military units, and especially on the fighting squadrons of the air service. The effect on the air service may be judged by the fact that at the end of the war 330 first-line fighting aircraft were stationed on the Alsace, Lorraine and Verdun fronts to oppose the Independent Force which at its greatest strength did not reach 130 aircraft.[47]

The squadrons of the Independent Force operated with that marked advantage over the defending forces which characterized all the strategic operations of the First World War. The day bombers flew in formation at about 15,000 feet — above the effective height of anti-aircraft gunfire — and had little difficulty in defending themselves against opposing fighters, except when they were heavily outnumbered. There was no co-ordination between the ground and air defences, and so the fighters, usually operating singly or in small groups, were compelled to search a wide area in their efforts to intercept the bombers. In this type of action they operated at a great disadvantage, since their performance was only marginally better than that of the two-seater day bombers. And even if they did succeed in making contact with the raiders, they were likely to be outgunned by the bombers flying in formation.

The night bombers of the force had little to fear either from gunfire or from fighters and flew as high or as low as was operationally desirable, usually between 2,500 and 8,000 feet. They were large, slow aeroplanes designed principally as weight carriers, and owing to the fear among service commanders of collisions at night, they operated singly and at several minute intervals. These tactics produced unlooked for but not unwelcome results. They caused an increase in the number of air raid warnings that were sounded and intensified the effects which the alerts produced both on morale and industrial output.

As soon as the war came to an end, Trenchard handed over the command of the Independent Force to the air commander in France and returned at once to England. There is no doubt that the haste with which he rid himself of this unwanted command was intended to serve as a reminder that in spite of his involvement with the Independent Force he had in no way abandoned his opposition to strategic bombing. Yet, less than five years later, Trenchard, who was again holding the post of Chief of the Air Staff, had imposed on the Air Force a policy which depended for its implementation on a powerful strategic bomber force. Unfortunately, his radical change of mind was not based upon a reassessment of wartime experience, but came about because he applied to the peacetime air defence problems his long held but erroneous belief that in air warfare all the advantages lay with the attacker. At first this new concept did not win unqualified approval in the Air Force, but because of his unrivalled personal authority Trenchard was able to defeat all opposition to his policy, and when he retired from the Air Force in 1929 his doctrine was accepted without question throughout the service.

CHAPTER TWO

THE NEW STRATEGIC POLICY
1919–33

At the end of the First World War the Royal Air Force was the most powerful and modern air force in the world. It not only bore witness to the immense progress that had been made in aviation during the years of war, but also pointed to the great possibilities which lay in the future. Both the Air Minister, Lord Weir, and the Chief of the Air Staff, General Sykes, recognized the great potential of aviation, especially in the virtually untried field of civil transport, and were conscious of the need for immediate and decisive Government action if Britain was to maintain her lead in the air. During the second half of 1918 they gave considerable thought to the needs of aviation in the post-war era, and at the end of the year presented comprehensive but realistic plans for both service and civil aviation.

Fundamental to their thinking was the belief that the development of service and civil aviation would follow along similar lines for the foreseeable future, and so they suggested that the two sides of aviation should be linked together in the Air Ministry. They placed great importance on the systematic investigation of the future requirements of aviation and planned to establish a section concerned with research and experiment. They intended that this section should be placed under the control of the civil department, their reason being that since first priority ought to be given to research into the needs of civil transport – a field about which so little was known – it was preferable that the programmes of research should be drawn up by those who were responsible for the direction of civil aviation.[1]

Unfortunately for the future of British aviation, Lord Weir did not remain at the Air Ministry long enough to present his plans to the Government. If he had done so, it is likely that the high reputation he had acquired among his ministerial colleagues would have enabled him to win approval for the main recommendations in his plans. Instead, he was determined to return without delay to his work in industry and, in spite of the efforts made by General Sykes to persuade him to remain in office for a further six months to see the establishment of a new organization, he refused to do so and resigned his post in January 1919.[2]

The departure of Lord Weir presented the Government with a far from unwelcome opportunity to reconsider its policy concerning a separate Air Ministry and an independent Air Force. The way in which Government thought was moving was quickly made plain when, on 14 January 1919, Winston Churchill, the Secretary of State for War, was given the Air Ministry as a secondary responsibility. Not unnaturally, this action was seen by many as the preliminary step towards the abolition of the unwanted third service, and although it is certain that no firm decision had been made at this stage, the Government left no one in any doubt as to how little importance it attached to post-war aviation.

It need hardly be stated that the post of War Minister was a particularly onerous one at that time and Churchill was much preoccupied with the tasks of demobilizing large numbers of servicemen and of providing troops to occupy the various territories for which Britain assumed responsibility after the war. He could therefore devote only a fraction of his time to the affairs of the Air Ministry, yet it is certain that the decisions he made as Air Minister were calculated ones and showed what little importance he attached to aviation in peacetime. Sykes recalled that Churchill's 'old enthusiasm for the needs and possibilities of the air seemed to have evaporated. He appeared now to regard the R.A.F. merely as a useful adjunct to the two older Services and as an economical auxiliary for police work in the less civilized parts of the Empire.'[3]

Lord Weir and General Sykes had stressed the importance of research and experiment to the development of aviation; and although they believed that this work could be organized most effectively in the civil division of the Air Ministry they recognized that it would benefit both military and civil aviation. But Churchill attached little importance to this work, and the policies he initiated seriously inhibited progress in the design of aircraft and equipment for many years to come.

As a preliminary move, Churchill recalled Trenchard to be Chief of the Air Staff and moved Sykes to the newly created post of Controller General of Civil Aviation. He rejected the plans submitted by Lord Weir and supported Trenchard's proposals for a minute though independent air force.[4] He allocated all but a tiny fraction of the available funds to the military side and placed the department of research under service control.[5] In return, Trenchard relieved the War Office of a considerable financial burden by allocating a sizeable proportion of his small force for the policing of certain difficult areas, mainly in the Middle East.

Trenchard had by this time acquired a high reputation as an air commander, yet in spite of his long experience in directing the powerful air force in France he never seemed to show any understanding of the importance of technical efficiency in air operations. During his long tenure of office as Chief of the Air Staff he constantly preached the doctrine of the air offensive, but he never made plans for a bomber force capable of fulfilling the demanding requirements of that policy by being able to fly to distant targets in all weathers. Indeed, it is doubtful whether he realized that such operations presented any special difficulties.

When he retired from the Air Force in 1929, he left behind him a bomber force which had improved little in operational capability since its formation in 1923; and even more significant for the future, he consigned the responsibility for developing the Air Force to a group of officers who, like himself, believed that the success of strategic operations would be dependent almost entirely upon the morale of the bomber force and the fighting spirit of the aircrews. During the remainder of the inter-war period, the research department of the Air Ministry made little contribution to the operational development of the bomber force; and in spite of the significant advances which had been made in flying techniques in Europe and in America, even as late as 1938 the Commander-in-Chief of Bomber Command was compelled to admit that his force was a 'fair weather flying corps' incapable of operating effectively at night and in bad weather.[6]

On the other hand, Churchill showed complete indifference to civil aviation, his views being summed up in his dictum 'Civil aviation must fly by itself'.[7] He was strongly opposed to the provision of financial assistance for the newly formed airlines, and the fate which overtook the companies operating a service across the English Channel was inevitable. The converted bombers used by both British and French companies were inefficient and expensive to operate as passenger aircraft, but the French companies were given generous government subsidies to enable them to maintain their services without financial loss. Churchill, however, continued to reject the idea of government aid, and it was only when the British airlines suspended their services to Paris, after losing the battle to compete with their French rivals, that he agreed to the granting of temporary subsidies.[8]

Even at this early stage it was clear that unless the Government was prepared to give some kind of permanent financial backing to the airline companies, civil aviation in Britain would soon cease to exist. The action which Churchill finally agreed should be taken by the Cross-Channel Subsidies Committee was merely a palliative. Nothing had been resolved and the decision as to whether or not Britain needed the civil airlines had only been postponed. The inevitable reckoning came less than two years later, and in the outcome the Government decided to amalgamate five existing companies to create a national airline which was called Imperial Airways.[9]

The establishment of the national airline in 1924 presented the Government with a timely opportunity to make a fresh appraisal of the nation's (and the Empire's) air needs and to promote a policy which would enable the airline to develop and expand its routes and to exploit all possible operating techniques. Unfortunately, those who were responsible for establishing the national airline suffered from the same lack of imagination and foresight as had characterized Churchill's approach to civil aviation. There was in fact no one in authority of sufficient vision to appreciate the great potential of air transport and to grasp the importance of government support in its development. Consequently, during the years leading up to the Second World War, when many foreign airlines − aided by various types of state subsidies − went from strength to strength, Imperial Airways, which lacked the essential political and financial support, slid into a position of insignificance among the world's major airlines. Complaints of inefficiency were persistently directed against the airline, and in 1937 the Government responded by appointing a committee under Lord Cadman to investigate these allegations and at the same time to make recommendations concerning the future of British civil aviation.[10]

Sir Frederick Sykes later commented on the situation in Imperial Airways.

> We were operating with obsolete machines of inferior speed, and British air transport became the laughing-stock of the world .... Australian and Canadian airlines were equipped with foreign machines. Our West Indian possessions were served by American companies, and we paid France and Germany £100,000 annually to carry our mails to South America.[11]

It may be objected that Sykes, who in 1922 had resigned from his post as Controller General of Civil Aviation after failing to achieve what he considered to be a fair deal for his department, could hardly be expected to express an impartial judgement, yet the statements which he made are to be found in exact detail in the papers relating to the investigations of the Cadman Committee.[12]

The refusal of the Government to provide any financial aid beyond what was absolutely necessary to prevent the demise of British civil aviation had an adverse effect on the development of aviation generally in Britain; and this in turn retarded its development in the Air Force, and particularly in the bomber force. In the first place, the aircraft manufacturers could not expect to receive sizeable orders from the civil side and so had to depend almost entirely upon the small orders for military aircraft to maintain their factories in production. For the most part they existed from hand to mouth and were prevented by lack of funds from undertaking adequate research to improve the design of aircraft. If the Government had encouraged the growth of a healthy air transport industry at home immediately after the war, Britain could have played a leading part in developing civil aviation in many parts of the world, and in so doing would have been assured of orders for British aircraft on a scale large enough to enable our manufacturing industry to maintain the leading position it had attained during the war.

In the early post-war period neither Germany nor the United States, the two countries which dominated the world's civil aviation in the late 1920s and throughout the 1930s, could have competed on equal terms with Britain; the former because of the restrictions placed upon her aircraft industry by the peace treaty, the latter because she was slow to appreciate the potential of aviation for developing communications. Unfortunately, Britain did not take this unique opportunity of securing for herself a leading place in post-war aviation, and by the beginning of the 1930s she had yielded place both to Germany and to the United States which had by then become the major suppliers of aircraft to the world's airlines.

Second, the drive and efficiency which inspired the German and American airlines constantly to extend their services encouraged them to improve their ability to fly in the dark and in bad weather. The lighting of aerodromes, the siting of beacons to light the routes along which the aircraft operated, and the use of radio navigational aids and blind landing devices were all common features of operations in Europe and North America, while in Britain virtually nothing was done to combat the hazards of darkness and bad weather.[13] It is worthy of note that during the 15 years of its existence, from 1924 to 1939, Imperial Airways did not operate any night services, although night schedules had been flown on a regular basis by German and American airlines since the mid-1920s. In fact, it was not until July 1936 that a regular night service was flown by any British company. This was a night mail service operated by British Airways, an independent airline, from London to Cologne and Hanover. And so, Imperial Airways, like Bomber Command, was very much a 'fair weather flying corps', and when war broke out in 1939 Britain had no pool of experience in all-weather and night flying upon which the Air Force could draw to improve its own performance.

The immediate post-war years were difficult ones for the Air Force. The Government was determined to reduce drastically the spending of the service ministries, and when Winston Churchill suggested at a cabinet meeting on 5 August 1919 that service estimates should be based on the assumption that there would be no major European war for the following five or ten years, the Prime Minister, David Lloyd George, accepted this as the basis of a proposition that service estimates should be framed on the assumption that 'the British Empire will not be engaged in any great war during the next ten years'.[14] The effect of this 'ten year rule' on the Air Force, which possessed almost no permanent accommodation or training facilities, was most severe; for although the Air Force received all but a small fraction of the funds allocated for air expenditure, this was quite inadequate for a service which had almost nothing on which to build. Trenchard was therefore under some pressure to spend a considerable proportion of his annual grant on permanent buildings, and in consequence he had little to spare for new aircraft and for the facilities which were needed to improve the operational capability of the service. There seemed to be little prospect of creating the independent Air Force which Trenchard had, in 1919, predicted 'will grow larger and larger and become more and more the predominating factor in all types of warfare'. In fact, the tendency was in the reverse direction; and less than a year after this statement was made the strength of the Air Force had been reduced to 20 squadrons, of which only two were based at home.

A further effect of the ten year rule was to create great competition for the meagre funds allocated to the service ministries, and both the Admiralty and the War Office made strenuous efforts to get rid of the unwanted rival. They began to press for control of the air wings which were designated for co-operation with their respective services, and urged that the Air Force should make use of the training facilities already existing in naval and military establishments, instead of creating new ones as Trenchard planned to do. Trenchard countered these attacks by arguing that the strategic bomber force which the Air Force had been specifically formed to organize and direct could be created only by an independent air service. He supported his case by showing that if the existing air material and personnel were divided between the two older services neither would possess sufficient resources to provide for the bomber force.

However, the Government was far from being convinced of the need for a strategic bomber force, and Trenchard's claim that the possession of such a force was the best form of defence against air attack commanded little support. It was not unnaturally asked against whom such protection was needed, and it was not until Britain's relations with France had become seriously strained, following differences of opinion concerning the payment of reparations by Germany and the occupation of the Ruhr by French troops in 1923, that the question appeared to be anything but an academic one.

The deterioration of Franco-British relations induced the Government to appoint a committee under Lord Salisbury 'to enquire into the co-operation and correlation between the Navy, Army and Air Force from the point of view of National and Imperial Defence generally'. The committee was also given the specific task of determining the strength of the Air Force required for home and imperial defence. When Trenchard was invited to give evidence he had little difficulty in persuading the committee that Britain, with only a handful of aircraft in the home-based squadrons, was defenceless against the French Air Force which was estimated to have at least 600 aircraft capable of operating against England, and which was still expanding. Lord Salisbury took a serious view of the situation described to him and recommended that the disparity in strength between the British and French air forces should be redressed as a matter of urgency.[15] The Government acted speedily on this advice, and on 20 June 1923 the Cabinet gave approval to a scheme to expand the home defence element of the Air Force to 52 squadrons, a force that the Prime Minister, Stanley Baldwin, told the House of Commons was intended to be 'of sufficient strength adequately to protect us against air attack by the strongest air force within striking distance of this country'.[16]

Soon after the expansion programme was approved, Trenchard held a number of meetings at the Air Ministry to decide the broad lines on which the expansion was to proceed, and during the course of these meetings he formulated a policy which was based on his own special interpretation of home defence.[17] Fundamental to this policy was his doctrine, first enunciated in a memorandum of September 1916, that the only way to use air power effectively was in the offensive role.[18] The result of applying this doctrine to air defence was to establish the concept of a defence force in which bomber aircraft predominated. It was intended that an air attack on this country would bring upon the aggressor a swift response in the form of a counter-offensive, in the first place to reduce the scale of his attack, and then when that had been achieved, to throw him on the defensive. And it was this doctrine which was to find embodiment in the 52 squadron force, in that it was to have 35 bomber as against 17 fighter squadrons.[19]

The Air Ministry meetings of July and August 1923 were attended by some of the most experienced officers in the service. Among these were Air Vice-Marshal J. F. A. Higgins, Commander of the Inland Area, the home command responsible for, among other things, home defence; Air Commodore H. R. M. Brooke-Popham, Commandant of the R.A.F. Staff College; Air Commodore T. C. R. Higgins, Director of Training and Staff Duties at the Air Ministry; and Squadron Leader C. F. A. Portal, a member of the Air Ministry Directorate of Operations and

Intelligence, who was destined to hold the post of Chief of the Air Staff for the greater part of the Second World War.

As was to be expected, Trenchard dominated these meetings, and from the outset he left no room for doubt about the principles which were to determine future policy. There was, he stated, a tendency to tackle the problem of air defence in the wrong way, in that provision was made for the purely defensive element without first taking into account the needs of the offensive. The correct way to deal with the problem was, first, to decide the proportion of the force that would be required for attack, and when that had been settled, to allocate the rest for defence. It was not intended that this statement should be open for discussion, and when Air Commodore Higgins ventured to suggest that a strong defence was important because 'every enemy machine that got a bullet in the radiator was out of the war', Trenchard retorted that 'equally every machine that was not used against the enemy was out of the war'.[20] Squadron Leader Portal received an equally curt response when he suggested that efforts should be made to discover the correct proportion of bomber to fighter aircraft. Trenchard replied that there was no such thing as a correct proportion; the idea was to have as many bombers and as few fighters as the circumstances would permit.[21] Later, he extended the scope of this policy by ruling that no long-distance fighter squadrons should be provided for bomber escort[22] and that there should be no special aircraft for night fighter work.[23]

Throughout these discussions Trenchard was consistent in advocating that the counter-offensive would be the most effective means not only of defending the nation but also of winning the war. His thinking was summed up in the following statement.

> Would it be best to have less fighters and more bombers to bomb the enemy and trust to their people cracking before ours, or have more fighters in order to bring down more of the enemy bombers. It would be rather like putting two teams to play each other at football, and telling one team they must only defend their own goal, and keep all their men on that one point. The defending team would certainly not be beaten, but they would equally certainly not win, nor would they stop the attack on their goal from continuing. I would like to make this point again. I feel that although there would be an outcry, the French in a bombing duel would probably squeal before we did. That was really the final thing. The nation that would stand being bombed longest would win in the end.[24]

Indeed, the question of morale, affecting both service personnel and the civilian population, but especially the latter, was a theme to which Trenchard often returned.

C.A.S. said he agreed that a high casualty rate would have a greater effect on the morale of the French pilots than it would on ours. Casualties affected the French more than they did the British. That would have to be taken into consideration too, but the policy of hitting the French nation and making them squeal before we did was a vital one — more vital than anything else. The question had been asked at Camberley 'Why is it that your policy of attack from the air is so different from the policy of the Army, whose policy it is to attack the enemy's Army, while yours is to attack the civil population.' The answer was that we were able to do this while the Army were not, and go straight to the source of supply and stop it. Instead of attacking a machine with ten bombs we would go straight to the source of supply of the bombs and demolish it, and the same with the source of production of the machines. It was a quicker process than allowing the output to go on. The Army policy was to defeat the enemy Army — ours to defeat the enemy nation.[25]

There was general agreement concerning the role of the bomber force, but there was much less certainty about its composition; and this led to considerable discussion as to what proportion of the force should be day bombers and what proportion night bombers. Air Vice-Marshal Higgins believed that anti-aircraft gunfire was becoming progressively more accurate and would take a heavy toll of the bombers. Squadron Leader Portal, on the other hand, thought that the effectiveness of gunfire was much overrated and that large formations of aircraft flying by day would confuse the gunners.[26] Air Commodore Higgins suggested that because of their inability to locate small targets during the hours of darkness the night bombers should be used for attacking larger targets while the day bombers should be assigned to the smaller targets. Trenchard did not however accept this argument and stated that his own experience led him to take a different view. He agreed that the day bombers were usually able to reach the vicinity of the target without much difficulty, but pointed out that they were forced by gunfire to fly at such high altitudes that they were in general no more successful in locating small targets than the night bombers. On the other hand, the night bombers were able to locate small targets on clear nights, for the difficulty which the crews experienced in seeing in the dark was in part compensated for by the low altitudes at which they could operate with safety.[27]

In spite of differing views on the merits of each type of bombing, the officers whom Trenchard consulted were agreed that the force should be able to operate effectively both by day and by night. They were also agreed that the greatest material damage would be done by night. This opinion was based on the belief that the night bombers, being less vulnerable to anti-aircraft defences, would suffer lighter casualties than the day bombers. This comparative immunity would yield two signal advantages: first, a larger proportion of the night bombers would always be available for operations; and second, the night bombers would have less need for defensive armament than the day bombers and could therefore carry a higher proportion of their lifting capacity in bombs. And for Trenchard these were considerations of the first importance, since he believed it was necessary to cause substantial damage if the attack on civilian morale was to be successful.

> C.A.S. stated that material damage was very important. On material damage at times rested the moral damage. If there was no material damage in many cases the moral damage would be nil. He quite agreed that the greatest amount of damage could be done by night.[28]

There was however less agreement concerning the types of aircraft with which the force should be equipped, though it was generally believed that the day and night squadrons would, because of the different nature of their work, require different types of aircraft. Nevertheless, there was some support for the view, stated by Air Commodore Brooke-Popham, that a type of aircraft capable of carrying out both day and night operations should be sought. Trenchard agreed that it was an ideal to be aimed at but did not believe it was a feasible proposition at that time.[29]

At the last of this series of meetings Trenchard gave a tentative ruling that of the first 24 bomber squadrons to be formed 12 should be day and 12 should be night squadrons; but he thought that the final proportion should be in the region of 22 day to 13 night. At the same time, he recorded his view that, with the exception of a few specialist day bomber and night bomber squadrons, the main body of the striking force would ultimately be equipped with aircraft capable of operating both by day and by night.[30]

These then were the concepts which underlay the creation of the home-based bomber force which was brought into being in 1923 and which was to become the very essence not only of the air defence system but also of the Air Force as a whole. The decisions taken by the Chief of the Air Staff during the summer of 1923 established without doubt that the primary function of the Air Force was to carry out independent operations in the air defence of Britain. This function was to be fulfilled by means of a bombing offensive which would be planned and executed as a campaign separate from the operations being conducted concurrently by the other two services.

Perhaps the clearest and most convincing statement of the doctrine of the strategic offensive as a means of securing Britain from air attack was made by Squadron Leader J.C. Slessor in an article written in 1931:

> Purely passive self-protection, that is to say waiting for an enemy's attack and then attempting to repel it, has never been the British conception of national defence, and it is peculiarly ineffective in the three-dimensional battlefields of the air .... It must therefore be apparent that to afford us any sort of protection against air forces that could now be directed against us, we should require a force of fighters immeasurably greater than we can afford in peace. And even then we should not be secure. So the policy is to provide the essential minimum of fighters for close defence in co-operation with the ground anti-aircraft defences, and to concentrate the bulk of our resources on the maintenance of a formidable striking force of bombers, the positive proportion of the defences, to enable us to launch a counter-offensive if we are attacked.[31]

As has been stated, Trenchard's unrivalled prestige and authority enabled him to secure unquestioned support for his new policy throughout the Air Force. He also won complete acceptance for his views from Sir Samuel Hoare (later Viscount Templewood) who was Air Minister for most of the period 1922–29. In his memoirs, written many years later, Lord Templewood recalled his great admiration for Trenchard:

> Whilst Trenchard spoke, I felt myself in the presence of a major prophet. My mission was to be the prophet's interpreter to a world that did not always understand his dark sayings. Thenceforth for nearly seven continuous years, I was destined to play the interpreter's part. Whether it was in the Cabinet, in the Committee of Imperial Defence, or in the country, my task was to explain the doctrine of the independence of the air in its many ramifications. Trenchard's mind and mine, though very different, worked well together. In nine cases out of ten he would start some new idea, and I would interpret it in words that the politicians and the public could understand.[32]

Unfortunately, Trenchard's concept of defence by means of the counter-offensive paid little attention to the realities of strategic warfare, being based partly on unsupported assumptions and partly on misinterpreted war experience. In the first place, his mistaken belief in the supremacy of the offensive directed Air Staff thinking towards policies that were beset with dangers, especially in view of the signal advantages which modern weapons confer on the defensive. Indeed, the ascendancy attained by the defensive was one of the most marked characteristics of the fighting during the First World War, and the battering-ram tactics employed on the Western Front by the British Army — and by the air units supporting it — resulted in casualties which were out of all proportion to the gains achieved. The constant offensive which the military squadrons waged against the enemy air force has been estimated to have cost them four times as many casualties as were suffered by the Germans.[33] The argument which was advanced to justify these tactics was that the British operations forced the German Air Force on the defensive and so reduced drastically the support it could give to the German Army. There is, however, little evidence to support this contention. It is known that the Germans pursued their defensive tactics as a matter of deliberate policy, and there is much evidence to show that they actually gained supremacy in the air during many crucial engagements.

Second, Trenchard profoundly misunderstood the significance of long-range bombing in relation to air defence in the First World War. He wrongly attributed the success of the small-scale bombing operations and the relative failure of the defences to the natural superiority of attack over defence. The truth is that the air defences were ineffective mainly because neither side was prepared to make a genuine effort to improve them so long as the bombing raids presented no serious threat to the nation's war effort. It is true that large numbers of anti-aircraft units were mobilized (at great cost in manpower and material) both in Britain and Germany, but this was the price, it was accepted, which would have to be paid to sustain the morale of the civilian population. It was not until the last year of the war, when the extension of the bombing by both sides had provoked unprecedented outbursts of protest from the civilian populations exposed to the raids, that air defence became a matter of serious concern either in Britain or Germany; but by that time it was too late to do anything more than tackle the most glaring deficiencies.[34]

It is obvious that such limited experience of air defence would yield few trustworthy lessons for the future. It is equally obvious that the Air Staff, with their bias towards the offensive, would be particularly prone to misinterpret this evidence. Not surprisingly, they reached the conclusion that there could be no certain defence against a determined bomber attack and ignored in their planning the possibility of an increase in the efficacy of air defence and the effect that such an improvement might have on the conduct of a bombing campaign.

During this period the doctrine of the offensive hardened into the dogma that was to find its most famous expression in Stanley Baldwin's statement that the bomber would always get through.[35] But when the offensive policy was put to the test of war it failed. Events were soon to prove that the effectiveness of air defence had been seriously under-estimated, while the power of the offensive had been equally seriously overestimated; and for much of the first half of the Second World War the bomber force was defeated in its aims by the opposition of ground and air defences working in co-operation.

Another weakness in Trenchard's approach to air strategy was his tendency to confuse the very real distinction between bombing designed to break the morale of the enemy by means of attacks against the civilian population, and that intended to deprive him of the means to wage war. He often stated that whenever there was material damage there would also be damage to morale, and this led him to believe that the two objectives could be achieved simultaneously. But this was true only in a limited way, since the two types of bombing were essentially different and required for their execution different equipment and techniques. There was a significant difference between the type of operation which sought to drop as great a weight of bombs as possible on the populous areas of cities, and that which was concerned with the identification and destruction of relatively small targets such as power stations, bridges, oil refineries and railway marshalling yards. It was obviously a matter of the first importance to determine which of the two was to be the primary function of the bomber force; for upon this would depend the types of aircraft required, the nature of aircrew training, and the kinds of tactics to be employed. The result of this confusion of thought was that it led the Air Staff to regard strategic bombing as a double-edged weapon and encouraged them to believe that if the attacks against a nation's war-making capacity should prove too difficult or impossible there remained the equally effective way of winning the war by breaking a nation's morale, and thereby its will to resist.

The Government was greatly influenced by Air Staff thinking because it corresponded closely to the widely held public belief − fostered by predictions contained in a wide variety of writings − that massive air attacks against the centres of population would be an inevitable feature of a future war. Though some of these predictions were considered to be wildly exaggerated, many differed little in essential detail from those contained in Air Staff papers and in official enquiries carried out independently of the Air Ministry. In later years the Air Staff were often criticized for having presented an exaggerated account of the destructive power of air bombing, and one of the most forthright complaints on this score was expressed by Winston Churchill in a minute sent to Sir Charles Portal, the Chief of the Air Staff, in October 1941.

Before the war we were greatly misled by the pictures they [the Air Staff] painted of the destruction that would be wrought by Air raids. This is illustrated by the fact that 750,000 beds were actually provided for Air raid casualties, never more than 6,000 being required. This picture of destruction was so exaggerated that it depressed the Statesmen responsible for the pre-war policy, and played a definite part in the desertion of Czecho-Slovakia in August 1938.[36]

The Air Staff were frank in their reply to this criticism. They admitted that the 'Estimation of casualties before the war was largely crystal gazing', but pointed out that they had based their estimates on the only relevant information available to them, namely, the experience of the German air raids on this country during the 1914—18 War.[37]

In fairness to the Air Staff, it should be noted that Churchill himself had in the pre-war period used the same evidence to issue some grim warnings of the dangers of air attack. In July 1936, for example, he made this statement to Stanley Baldwin, the Prime Minister.

Germany has the power at any time henceforward to send a fleet of aeroplanes capable of discharging in a single voyage at least five hundred tons of bombs upon London. We know from our war statistics what the destruction of lives and property was per ton dropped. One ton of explosive bombs killed ten people and wounded thirty, and did £50,000 worth of damage.[38]

The earliest of the Air Staff papers dealing with the dangers of air attack were produced during the period of deteriorating relations with France. A typical paper of this period was one, dated 24 May 1924, which contained, among other things, estimates of the casualties that Britain was likely to sustain in the opening phase of a war with France. It was assumed for the purpose of the calculations that for the first 24 hours the attackers could operate with 100 per cent of their bomber aircraft, during the second 24 hours with 75 per cent, and during every subsequent 24 hours with 50 per cent. The probable casualties for the three phases of the attack, in numbers of killed and injured, were estimated to be, respectively, 1,700 and 3,300, 1,275 and 2,475, 850 and 1,650. It is of significance to note that the Air Staff expected the duration of the third phase to be determined almost wholly by 'the strength and efficiency of the counter-offensive of our bombing aircraft'.[39]

The Government was greatly disturbed by predictions such as these, and in 1924 it appointed an Air Raid Precautions Committee, under the chairmanship of Sir John Anderson, the Permanent Under-Secretary of State at the Home Office, to consider how best the nation could be protected in the event of an air war. In the course of his long association with the committee, Sir John Anderson became the acknowledged authority in this field and, in 1938, during the uneasy period which

preceded the outbreak of the Second World War, he was given a place
in the Cabinet, as Lord Privy Seal, to organize civil defence. Later, in
1939, he became Home Secretary, and his work in home defence was
acknowledged when his name was given to a small air-raid shelter which
was erected in the gardens of many thousands of homes in the early
part of the war.

Soon after its formation the Air Raid Precautions Committee heard
evidence from Trenchard and was greatly impressed by his view that
it would be a well-nigh impossible task to prevent hostile bombers from
reaching their targets.

> Sir Hugh Trenchard was so emphatically of the opinion that an
> increase of the defence forces beyond a certain proportion would
> not secure greater immunity from attack, that we felt we had no
> alternative but to continue our investigations with a view to
> mitigating, so far as possible, the evils attendant upon aerial
> bombardment. We think that the extent of the menace to which
> this country, especially London, is exposed and the difficulties of
> combating this menace are not generally appreciated.

The committee was equally impressed by Trenchard's solution to the
problems of air defence, and signified their agreement with it in the report.

> In our opinion the most effective reply to an attack from the air
> is the provision of a strong attacking force wherewith to carry the
> war to the enemy's country.[40]

The committee continued its work during the remainder of the 1920s,
and the picture which it formed of the likely effects of air attacks,
especially where poison gas was involved, was depressing in the extreme.
In September 1930, Sir John Anderson attended a meeting of the Committee of Imperial Defence to comment on the report in which his
committee had recommended that a specially trained military unit,
numbering between 4,000 and 5,000 men, should be established as a
stand-by force to assist the civilian organizations in dealing with the
effects of air bombing. This proposal related primarily to London, since
it was clear 'from the mass of information which his Committee had
accumulated, that the maintenance of the economic life of that city was
of the very first importance'.

He pointed out that the type of work which the personnel of such
a force would be required to undertake would not be in any way comparable to police work, but would involve such duties as the repairing
of roads damaged in bombing attacks and the decontamination of areas
affected by gas. In any case, in the type of situation which he envisaged
it would be necessary to establish martial law in the capital.

London would, in effect, be in very much the same position as occupied territory. The only difference being that, instead of the land being occupied, the air – according to the picture painted for them by the Air Ministry – would be very fully occupied; and under these conditions ... it would be an extremely difficult task to persuade civilians to get on with the work. It would be very dangerous to assume that it would be possible to rely implicitly on civilian labour to carry out the work under the same conditions, practically speaking, as might be expected of soldiers in the front line of battle. It was, therefore, essential to have as a standby disciplined forces which could be called in if conditions became such that it was impossible for the civilian organisation to carry on. If this was not done, he had little doubt that such a state of panic would be produced as might bring about the collapse, certainly of the community in London, if not of the whole country.[41]

These then were the impressions which Sir John Anderson's committee formed of an air war of the future. Without question, it was Trenchard who influenced them most on aerial bombing in general, but in the specialized area of poison gas, the type of warfare which caused them the greatest anxiety and dominated their investigations, it was the work of the Earl of Halsbury (formerly Viscount Tiverton) which made the deepest impression.

At the end of the war, Lord Halsbury returned to his practice at the Bar, but continued to make a serious study of strategic air power. His early research suggested that since neither the bomber nor the missiles it carried were likely to improve much in effectiveness in the immediate future, aircraft might well become the instrument by which poison gas – a weapon which had become many times more deadly since it was first employed on the Western Front in 1915 – could be used on a large scale against civilian populations, both to kill and incapacitate.

Lord Halsbury believed that the gases which became available soon after the war were so powerful and so relatively easy to transport by air as to render unnecessary the specialized aircraft, equipment and techniques that would be essential for long-range bombing with explosive and incendiary bombs. All that was needed to use this deadly weapon was the requisite propensity for evil, a quality which seemed to Lord Halsbury to be all too common among the leaders of the world in the post-war age. Lord Halsbury expressed his fears of what might happen in the future in a novel, entitled *1944*, which was published in 1926.[42] The story, the main action of which was set in the year 1944, described a massive air attack against Britain with lethal gas. The effect of this onslaught, which began with a devastating raid on London, was to bring civilized life in Britain to an end.

It is important to note that although the story was set almost 20 years in the future the scale of destruction imagined to have been inflicted on this country could well have been caused by the aircraft and weapons which were in existence when the novel was written. This was a point which Lord Halsbury was at pains to emphasize in the preface to his novel.

> I suppose that any reader of the following pages might well form the opinion that the whole idea is purely fantastical and that such an attack upon the centres of civilization as I have ventured to suggest is and always will be an impossibility. To him I commend the writings of such world wide authorities as M. Michelin and Captain Brifaut. Let him take such comfort as he may from the fact that these experts do not suggest that with *weapons of today and the armaments of today* more than one centre such as London, Paris or Brussels could be destroyed within, say, *twenty-four hours.* Mr. J. B. S. Haldane is more optimistic, but not on the ground that a gas of extermination is impossible, but on the ground that one which causes temporary paralysis is more economic, more humane and more practical − in any case for open warfare. For the above consideration, I have been at pains, so far as the attack itself is concerned, to limit myself strictly to the weapons of today and not to rely for any offensive upon some new invention which may or may not be forthcoming. Further, I have over-estimated and not under-estimated the material necessary.

In depicting the horror and inhumanity of gas warfare, Lord Halsbury had two principal aims in mind: first, to show that the aeroplane could be used as a carrier of death and destruction with weapons other than high explosive and incendiary bombs; and second, to present a case for the abolition of chemical weapons by international agreement. And the many perceptive reviews of the book suggest that he was remarkably successful in achieving both these aims. *1944* was widely read and its theme attracted considerable attention, but its main impact on the public did not come until some two years after it was first published.

In May 1928 the actual effect that poison gas would produce on a populated area was seen on a miniature scale when a small quantity of phosgene gas was accidentally released from a chemical works at Hamburg in Germany. *The Times* of 22 May contained the following report.

> The invisible gas quickly spread over the adjoining district. Passing through the streets and over a tract of land much used by holiday-

makers, it reached the open country, leaving a trail of victims in its wake. Its effects are stated to have been felt up to six miles away. Many cattle were overcome by it and have since had to be slaughtered. The danger, however, is not over, for phosgene, which is heavier than air, keeps to the ground level, and there are many 'pockets' of gas still hanging about the district. The best thing that could happen now would be a heavy fall of rain, which would neutralize it, but a change of wind might redistribute it and produce further disaster.

A report in *The Times* of the following day completed the picture of the incident.

Four of the more seriously affected patients poisoned by the escape of phosgene gas at Hamburg on Sunday have died since yesterday. This brings the total number of deaths up to eleven. There remain some 250 persons under treatment, and inhabitants of the stricken area have been alarmed to learn that cases at first slight have become more serious, and that one or two persons, who for more than a day had apparently remained in perfect health, have had to be removed to hospital today. This characteristic accompaniment of gas poisoning has, according to reports received in Berlin, given the scene of the disaster something of the appearance of a plague-stricken area, where men and women, haggard from sleeplessness, walk about haunted by the fear that they will yet be victims of the invisible peril.

When this industrial accident was reported in the British press public feelings were at once deeply aroused. Phosgene was vividly associated in the minds of the British people with a type of gas which had been used by the Germans against allied troops on the Western Front. The first conclusion to be drawn from these reports was that the German government was secretly maintaining stocks of war gases in violation of the peace treaty. It was not generally realized that phosgene was used in many industrial processes or that it had long since been superseded by more effective war gases.

Even when it was established that there was no sinister motive behind the storage of the phosgene, public discussion on the subject of gas warfare, to which the Hamburg incident had given rise, continued to be a focus of attention for some time afterwards. There was an immediate revival of interest in *1944* and the ideas which lay behind it, and because of this Lord Halsbury was given the unique opportunity of explaining his views, through the medium of the press, virtually to the whole nation.

Lord Halsbury's case was based on the assumption that in a major war of the future there would 'not merely be armies engaging armies but whole nations mobilised against nations'. Thus, the old distinction between soldier and civilian would disappear completely.

> The girl filling a shell at a factory is just as much part of the machinery of war as the soldier who fires it. She is much more vulnerable and will certainly be attacked. It is impossible to say that such an attack would be unjustified. The matter does not end with mere munition workers. The central organisations essential to modern warfare are carried on in 'open towns' and largely by civilians. An attempt to paralyse them would be perfectly legitimate. *The first conclusion, therefore, that emerges is that an attack will be made upon the civilian population.*[43]

An enemy would therefore seek the most effective means of striking at the great centres of population, and of all the weapons that could be used poison gas was by far the most deadly as well as the most economical.

The devastating effect of gas had been amply demonstrated on the battlefields of the Western Front. What still remained to be proved was whether it could be used with equal effect against targets at long distance. Lord Halsbury believed that it could be and supported his judgement with calculations of the effort that would be required for a full-scale attack against the centre of London. He took as his illustration an attack with phosgene − a gas he described as being as much out of date as the blunderbuss for purposes of war − on a triangular area defined by Chalk Farm in the north, Clapham in the south and the docks in the east. The amount of gas that would be required 'to produce a level atmosphere over the whole of that area up to forty feet' would be less than 2,000 tons. In view of the much improved weight-carrying capacity of aircraft since the war, this would by no means be an impossible amount for a powerful enemy, especially since the transport and dropping of gas containers would not require special aircraft or equipment. However, the gases which had been developed in recent years were many times more effective than phosgene and were easier to carry and discharge, so that the 2,000 tons of phosgene would be reduced to 40 tons of a modern gas.

Britain's obvious vulnerability to this kind of attack, Lord Halsbury emphasized, should point to the necessity of taking immediate steps to protect the nation against the ravages of poison gas. At the same time we should make every effort to secure international agreement banning its use in future wars; for there was no security to be found in arming ourselves with these weapons so that we could retaliate if we were attacked. 'It is poor consolation', he reasoned, 'that the only answer we can find to the destruction of half civilization is that we should be able to destroy the other half.'[44]

There can be no doubt that Lord Halsbury's arguments had a profound influence on political thinking. His belief that the quantity of gas required to paralyse a large city could easily be transported by air appeared to be supported by compelling evidence; and if this contention were accepted, it would also be necessary to accept that 'at the present moment London is at the mercy of any nation that is close enough and evilly disposed enough to come and obliterate it'.[45] The influence of his arguments was further strengthened by the fact that the action which he suggested – the organization of passive defence measures until the use of poison gas could be banned by international agreement – was very much in line with the thinking of all British Governments during the inter-war years. Indeed, it was widely held by members of all political parties that war itself, as well as the more barbarous means of waging it, could be banished by the efforts of nations working in concert; but so long as the attainment of this aim remained no more than a remote prospect, successive governments gave first priority to the search for direct protection against all forms of air attack, in spite of their commitment to the counter-offensive strategy.

It was this political tendency more than any other single factor which caused the limited material and manpower resources to be diverted from the bomber striking force into the various schemes of defence. Its effect is most clearly seen in the measures that were taken to provide a defence against chemical warfare. No effort was spared in the endeavour to find means of protecting the nation against poison gas; and this work reached its culmination in the year before the outbreak of war, when 35 million respirators were issued to the civilian population.[46]

In 1928 Trenchard decided that the time had come to produce a written statement for the Chiefs of Staff Committee laying down 'explicitly the doctrine of the Air Staff as to the object to be pursued by an Air Force in war'; and he did this in a memorandum, dated 2 May, which contains the clearest statement of his philosophy on air warfare to be produced during his time as Chief of the Air Staff. This memorandum is a document of the first importance and will repay careful study, but before examining in detail the policy which it sets out it is essential to have a clear understanding of the assumptions on which it is based.

As has been shown, the stated aim of Britain's air strategic policy was to bring about the systematic disruption of the enemy's war economy. Such a policy would have to be based on a precise knowledge of the war industries to be attacked, yet the Air Staff had little or no intelligence concerning French industry and no organization for collecting it. In fact, it was not until 1929 that the Committee of Imperial Defence created the machinery for gathering and evaluating this kind of information relating to foreign countries; and a further two years were to elapse before a research department, known as the Industrial Intelligence Centre, was established on a full-time permanent basis. And even then, the reports produced by the centre did not cover France, the very country against which the striking force was intended to operate.

It may reasonably be argued that after 1925 war with France was not considered even a remote possibility. Even so, the assumption that France was the most likely enemy should have been used by the Air Staff as a means of creating and perfecting the machinery necessary to plan for the counter-offensive. The fact that this was not done points to the same conclusion as is indicated by other evidence, namely, that the real purpose of the bombing was to attack the morale of the civilian population and not the enemy's war industry. As has been shown, Trenchard never drew a clear distinction between 'economic' and 'morale' bombing, but there is not the slightest doubt that of the two he considered the latter to be the more effective. Indeed, he frequently expressed the belief that bombing possessed the necessary power to depress the morale of the civilian population to such an extent that a government would be compelled to sue for peace. It indicates that his thinking in regard to a war with France had not progressed beyond the idea of dropping the greatest possible weight of bombs on Paris and other centres of population within range of his aircraft, with the object of demoralizing the civilian population.[47]

Trenchard's belief that 'the moral effect of bombing stands undoubtedly to the material effect in a proportion of 20 to 1' gained strength with time;[48] and this is reflected in numerous Air Staff documents of the period. An example of this is to be found in a memorandum of 1924 which stated that the most effective employment of an air force was to 'bomb military objectives in populated areas from the beginning of the war, with the object of obtaining a decision by the moral effect which such attacks will produce and by the serious dislocation of the normal life of the country'.[49] Implicit in this statement is the conviction, which was stated explicitly in an earlier paper, that 'the morale of an enemy nation' is 'the true object of all war'.[50] Perhaps the most unequivocal expression of this view is to be found in a speech which Trenchard made before the Dominion Premiers in 1926:

> Can air power be used as a means of shortening wars either with or without the co-operation of other forces? Will not the threat of air power be capable − to quote Foch − of 'impressing public opinion to the point of disarming the Government, and thus

becoming decisive'? If we can show air forces in greatly pre-
ponderating strength over those which an enemy can bring into
a particular theatre, the moral effect may be such as to make the
theory put forward by Foch a recognised fact.[51]

For the most part, however, the Air Staff were at pains to emphasize
that the primary function of the striking force would be to attack
the basis of the enemy's war-making capacity, and the reason for
this is obvious. If they had openly proclaimed their object to be the
terrorization of unarmed civilians, they could not have hoped to secure
approval for their policy either from the Government or from the other
two services. In any case, there was no need for them to invite certain
opposition to their policy when they could easily camouflage their
intentions by extending the scope of economic bombing to the point
where it was indistinguishable from bombing designed to break the will
of the civilian population.

In fact, this point had been reached in the policy set out in the
memorandum which Trenchard submitted to the Chiefs of Staff
Committee.[52] In it, he stated that the object to be pursued by an air
force in war was 'to paralyse from the very outset the enemy's production
centres of munitions of war of every sort and to stop all communications
and transportation', maintaining that it was not unlawful to bomb any
military objectives, wherever they were situated:

> Among military objectives must be included the factories in
> which war material (including aircraft) is made, the depots in which
> it is stored, the railway termini and docks at which it is loaded
> or troops entrain or embark, and in general the means of communi-
> cation and transportation of military personnel and material. Such
> objectives may be situated in centres of population in which their
> destruction from the air will result in casualties also to the neigh-
> bouring civilian population ... The fact that air attack may have
> that result is no reason for regarding the bombing as illegitimate
> provided all reasonable care is taken to confine the scope of the
> bombing to the military objective. Otherwise a belligerent would
> be able to secure complete immunity for his war manufactures and
> depots merely by locating them in a large city, which would, in
> effect, become *neutral* territory — a position which the opposing
> belligerent would never accept. What is illegitimate, as being
> contrary to the dictates of humanity, is the indiscriminate bombing
> of a city for the sole purpose of terrorising the civilian population.

In spite of his assurance that the civilian population would not be
the primary target for attack, he included in his list of objectives

virtually every industrial activity carried out in towns and cities, so that, in practical terms, the civilian population would be as much the target for attack as the enemy's war economy. With a list so comprehensive that it included 'the enemy's great centres of production of every kind of material, from battleships to boots, his essential munition factories, the centres of all his systems of communications and transportation, his docks and shipyards, railway workshops, wireless stations, and postal and telegraph systems', it is easy to see that the distinction between 'economic' and 'morale' bombing ceases to exist. Trenchard did in fact emphasize that such attacks would produce a significant effect on morale, but he represented this as an advantage to be secured from economic bombing rather than as an object to be pursued for its own sake.

When this memorandum was presented to the Chiefs of Staff Committee it caused the strongest objections to be raised by the heads of the other two services. Both Sir Charles Madden, Chief of Naval Staff, and Sir George Milne, Chief of the Imperial General Staff, rejected the doctrine on which the Air Staff based their future air strategy, and gave almost identical reasons for doing so.

The aspect of the doctrine they found most difficult to accept was the implication that the accepted principles of war did not operate in the case of air forces. Sir Charles Madden summed up this objection.

> For this purpose [the defeat of the enemy nation] the Navy and the Army concentrate their attention primarily upon the opposing armed forces. With the air force, however, it is claimed that air power can dispense with the intermediate step, can pass over the enemy navies and armies, and penetrate the air defences, and attack the centres of production, transportation and communication from which the enemy war effort is maintained.
>
> In the paper of the Chief of the Air Staff it is simply stated that new methods consequent on the introduction of air warfare have caused a change, that with air forces it is no longer necessary to consider the opposing armed forces as barriers which must first be broken down. The reason for this is not fully explained in the paper. Presumably it is for tactical reasons that air fighting forces do not present barriers to air bombing forces.

Sir George Milne thought it was a grave mistake to assume that no effective means of defence against air attack could be devised. Experience during the last war had shown that the development of one weapon created the incentive to discover a way of countering it. 'Indeed it is difficult to see', he wrote, 'how in the end the issue will not be determined by the superiority of one air force over another just as fighting on the ground is determined by the superiority of one army over another.' Nor did he believe that it would be possible to achieve the degree of air superiority that would be necessary to produce the effect described by the Air Staff.

> Turning to the last phase of the Great War during which the Air Forces of the Allies had reached their maximum development, I find that ... there were on the western Front in November 1918 approximately 2,000 British and 3,000 French aeroplanes of various types. At the same time the Germans possessed 1861 machines. Even with this vast air superiority there is nothing to show that the necessary paralysis was obtained, and, in point of fact, there is no precedent to show that this has ever been achieved.

As was to be expected, the all-embracing nature of the targets nominated in the memorandum evoked strong objections, on the ground both of humanity and of expediency. Sir George Milne pointed out that there were factories in every town producing some article or other that could be regarded as war material.

> If factories that produce every sort of military material are to be regarded as legitimate military targets ... the result in practice would be that, though the objective might be a given boot factory, the actual target would be the town in which the factory happened to be located, and the victims would be its unarmed inhabitants. It is ridiculous to contend that the dropping of bombs has reached such a stage of accuracy as to ensure that the bombs would hit only so-called military targets.

He believed that the acceptance of the Air Staff doctrine would mean 'that we are advocating what might be termed the indiscriminate bombing of undefended towns and of their unarmed inhabitants'. He conceded that 'the air action envisaged by the Air Force may be forced upon us if similar action is employed by our enemies', but thought that this was 'a very different matter from publishing to the world at large that we intended to employ these methods from the outset of a war'.

He questioned the wisdom of this policy also on the score of expediency, stressing the fact that no other European country was so vulnerable to air attack as Britain and none possessed a central objective of comparable importance to London. Sir Charles Madden was of the same opinion, believing that such a bombing policy would ultimately work to our disadvantage. He drew attention to the situation in the First World War when arguments almost similar to those used for air bombardment of factories were used by the Germans when they decided to adopt a 'sink-at-sight' policy, which was aimed at our resources and the morale of our merchant seamen. The policy reacted against Germany in every sphere of the war. It did more than anything else to bring America in on our side. It did not weaken our morale, but tended to stiffen it.

These reasoned and perceptive arguments made no impression on the Air Staff and did nothing to shake their faith in the doctrine of the counter-offensive. They continued to regard as unassailable the two basic tenets of their dogma: that the bomber would always get through and that the success of air bombardment would be assured by the selection of targets which were located in areas of dense population. They did not consider it even a remote possibility that in a future war the day bomber might be prevented from operating over enemy territory by the action of defending fighters, or that the night bomber might be forced by the accuracy of anti-aircraft gunfire to fly so high as to be unable to locate its target in all but the most favourable weather conditions. For this reason they made virtually no effort to discover how the bomber would fight and navigate to its objective and what tactics it should employ against the various kinds of targets; and in consequence the answers to these and similar problems of first importance remained as obscure as ever.

CHAPTER THREE

THE EXPANSION OF THE BOMBER FORCE 1923–33

The nature of the role accorded to the bomber force necessitated that it should be capable of striking at the enemy swiftly and with great power immediately on the outbreak of hostilities. Thus, it would have to be maintained in a high state of readiness, and this could be achieved only by regular units; yet the 52 squadron programme was drawn up to include at least a quarter of non-regular squadrons. Even so, this would not have created so serious a problem if the non-regular squadrons had been allocated both to the bomber and fighter elements of the force, but in fact this was not done.

Soon after the approval of the expansion scheme, severe financial restrictions compelled the Air Staff to introduce widespread economies, and it is hardly surprising that these were directed mainly against the more costly bomber squadrons. Two measures in particular were responsible for seriously retarding the development of the striking force. In the first place, it was decided that all the non-regular squadrons (seven reserve and six auxiliary) were to be bomber squadrons, so that even when the programme was completed the first-line bomber force would never be 35 squadrons, but only 22.

Second, many of the new squadrons were to be made responsible for their own flying training, both at elementary and advanced levels. The effect of this decision on the operational readiness of the force was immediate, for during the first two years of a new squadron's existence little would be accomplished other than the training of aircrews. Under this scheme, the first 18 of the 39 projected regular squadrons were to be trained in the normal way at the schools of flying training, but of these 18 only nine were bomber squadrons, so again it was the bomber force which suffered most. The effect of this change in policy was that 26 of the 35 bomber squadrons, as against only eight of the 17 fighter squadrons, would be subjected to the delays imposed by the scheme; and of those 26, 13 would never in peacetime be more than cadre squadrons.[1]

From the very beginning, the task of creating the bomber force was hampered by the restrictions of finance, and these became increasingly severe during the decade following the approval of the expansion programme. Nevertheless, plans for the home-based force were pressed forward, and in 1925 a new command, the Air Defence of Great Britain, was formed. The officer appointed to command this new formation was Air Marshal Sir John Salmond, an officer of great experience and ability, who had recently returned from an active command in Iraq. He held this appointment for five years before succeeding Trenchard as Chief of the Air Staff. It was intended that all 52 squadrons of the expansion programme were to become part of this command which was to comprise three bombing areas and one fighting area. Ultimately, the three bombing areas, designated Wessex, Oxford and East Anglia, were each to consist of a group of aerodromes in a geographically defined area.[2]

By this time, good relations between Britain and France had been restored; and, in addition, a period of better understanding between the European nations seemed to have been inaugurated by the treaties which were signed at Locarno in 1925. The most significant provision of the Locarno Pact was the guarantee of the frontiers of Germany, France and Belgium by those three powers, with Great Britain and Italy as guarantors, and the perpetual de-militarization of the Rhineland. All five powers pledged themselves to go to war against any nation which broke the agreement. Britain therefore entered into a specific agreement to take military action against France or Germany in the event of either country committing an act of aggression; and by so doing committed herself to maintain armed forces of sufficient strength to fulfil that agreement. The British Government, however, believed that the Pact itself was a sufficient guarantee of peace, and so far from taking such action, actually decided on a reduction in the existing military plans, including the very modest air expansion programme. In 1925 the completion date of the 52 squadron programme was postponed from 1928 to 1935, and in 1928 it was again postponed, this time until 1938.[3]

During the second half of the 1920s there was a marked deterioration in the world economic situation. Britain did not escape the effects of this depression and the Government was compelled to make drastic reductions in spending. As ever, the financial allocation for defence was one of the first to be cut; and during this period there was no sterner advocate of economy in defence expenditure than Winston Churchill, who was Chancellor of the Exchequer from 1924 to 1929. During his period of office he rigorously enforced the rule — originally suggested by himself in Cabinet in 1919 — that the service ministries should frame their estimates on the assumption that there would be no major war for ten years. The repeated (i.e. yearly) renewal of this rule, which has been accurately described as being 'worse than useless as a long term basis for strategic planning, since it begged the question which strategic planning is called upon to answer',[4] was one of the major causes of Britain's unpreparedness to meet the dangers which were created by Hitler's advent to power in 1933. Yet Churchill was prepared to tighten the screw even further, for in July 1928 he re-affirmed the ten-year rule in an even more restrictive way, laying down that the ten-year period should begin anew each day; and in this strengthened form it remained in force until 1932.[5]

During this period, too, the League of Nations was still widely believed to be the only instrument by which the hard won peace could be safeguarded. As early as 1925 a commission of the League had met to consider means by which armaments could be reduced and limited by international agreement, but progress in framing positive proposals was painfully slow. For its part, Britain was prepared to support the limitation of air armaments and the abolition of air bombardment provided workable proposals could be agreed upon. In 1931, the British Government, under the leadership of Ramsay MacDonald, who was dedicated to the belief that world peace could be secured by means of disarmament, took the lead in calling a conference, although there was still little agreement as to what definite proposals should be submitted. In spite of the fact that the prospects of success were far from encouraging, Britain showed her goodwill by accepting an armaments truce (which came into effect in November 1931) in the hope that this action would create a favourable climate for the Disarmament Conference which was due to assemble at Geneva in February 1932.

The main aim of the Conference was to find an acceptable formula for the limitation of arms, but when this proved impossible to achieve, efforts were made to secure the abolition of those weapons which were of a purely offensive nature. One weapon in particular – the bomber aircraft – was by common consent deemed to be the offensive weapon par excellence, and it was specifically against the bomber that a new set of proposals was designed. Throughout the lengthy discussions which followed, Britain showed herself willing to support any reasonable proposals, although the acceptance of a ban on bomber aircraft would have compelled the Government to disband a large part of the home-based force which had been formed purely for defensive purposes.

The Air Staff took a different view. They were strongly opposed to the proposals, not merely because they were unwilling to support a policy which would undermine Britain's air strategy, but also because they were convinced that it would be impossible to devise a practical means of enforcing the ban. They believed that any country could manufacture civil aircraft which were so designed as to be easily converted into bombers. This concern proved to be well-founded, as the subsequent revival of the German Air Force was to show. Among the first-line bomber aircraft in service with the Luftwaffe at the outbreak of the Second World War, two of the standard types, the Heinkel 111 and the Dornier 17, both had their origins in civil aircraft. In the event, however, the proposals to abolish the bomber raised serious difficulties and were finally dropped. The main disarmament talks were continued into 1933, but the victory of the Nazi party in Germany in that year virtually put paid to any hopes of an agreed reduction of armaments.[6]

The armaments truce continued in force until the end of March 1933, and during the period of its operation no new bomber squadrons could be formed. The expansion of the defence force was almost brought to a halt, but more serious, the very existence of the service whose raison d'être was its bomber striking force was called into question. The prospect of an agreement at the Disarmament Conference hung like a cloud over the Air Force, as Lord Londonderry, the Air Minister during this period, later described.

> There was ill-disguised discontent in the Air Ministry. Everybody was dissatisfied and many were positively apprehensive of the future. It was felt that the Government was prepared to sacrifice the Air Force without even examining the pros and cons of the case. This, of course, was not actually correct, but by no means the least of my difficulties was maintaining the spirit of the R.A.F., both active and administrative, when proposals for the abolition of Air Forces were continually appearing in the newspapers.[7]

When the armaments truce came to an end, the bomber element of the home-based defence force was numerically very weak. Although 28 of the 35 bomber squadrons had already been formed, this figure gives no indication at all of the effective strength of the force. Of the 28 squadrons, 20 were day bombers, and of these only ten were regular squadrons. But of these ten, two were skeleton units engaged on experimental work, and two were designated as the Air Force element of the Expeditionary Force and would almost certainly be despatched overseas as soon as hostilities began. Thus, there were six regular squadrons operationally ready for immediate war service. The remaining ten squadrons were made up of Auxiliary Air Force and Special Reserve squadrons, and none of these could be brought up to first-line standard during the opening weeks of a war.

The night bomber squadrons, on the other hand, were better prepared

Viscount Tiverton   1918

The Vimy crew which made the first flight to Australia in 1919 are (left to right) Keith Smith, Ross Smith, Sgt J. W. Bennett, Sgt W. H. Shiers. Here they are standing in front of an RAF Vimy, not the aircraft in which they made the flight

for war, five of the eight squadrons being regular units; but this was of no practical significance, since the night squadrons represented such a small proportion of the bomber force. It had originally been intended that the expanded force should have 15 night and 20 day bomber squadrons, so that in the same ratio the 26 squadrons should have comprised 12 night and 16 day: instead, there were only eight night to 20 day squadrons. Thus it will be seen that the true first-line strength of the bomber force at the end of March 1933 was six day and five night squadrons, and behind these were the ten day and three night squadrons of the Auxiliary Air Force and Special Reserve.[8]

In the context of operational readiness, it is important to draw a clear distinction between the auxiliary and reserve squadrons on the one hand and the regular squadrons on the other. The personnel of the auxiliary and reserve squadrons were part-time volunteers and reservists who flew at the weekends and during a two-week period at a summer camp. For the convenience of their members, the squadrons were formed near the centres of population and not on the stations from which they would operate in war. Normally, the auxiliary squadrons possessed only two training and two service aircraft, the remainder being held in store until such time as mobilization was ordered. The organization of the reserve squadrons was similar, except that one of the three flights was manned by regular Air Force personnel and possessed a full complement of aircraft and equipment. Both the auxiliary and reserve squadrons were therefore no more than cadre units. They would not be fully manned and equipped or moved to their operational stations until the order for mobilization was issued, and would not be in a state of readiness to play any part in the vital opening phase of the war.[9]

The small size of the defence force was in itself a severe handicap, since there were too few squadrons to take part in realistic exercises; for peacetime training is of very limited value if it cannot be related to the probable scale and conditions of war operations. It is certain that one of the most harmful effects caused by the frequent delays in completing the expansion was that it prevented the service from undertaking the kind of training that would have shed light on the problems of war. When, in 1928, Winston Churchill told the Committee of Imperial Defence of his intention to apply the ten-year rule more stringently, he countered the protests of Sir Samuel Hoare, the Air Minister, by stating that this action 'would not in any way hamper the development of ideas but would check mass production until the situation demanded it'.[10] This judgement could not have been wider of the mark. The development of ideas in the service depended to an important degree upon the squadrons being able to acquire an adequate amount of operational flying experience, and this in turn depended

BSAP–F

upon their possessing sufficient resources of material. In fact, it was the very lack of these resources which prevented them from gaining this essential experience, and in consequence inhibited the formulation of future requirements in aircraft and equipment.

Churchill was also in error in assuming that whenever the necessity arose the aircraft industry could without difficulty increase its output of aircraft quickly and efficiently. Nor did he appreciate the important part that the aviation industry itself would have to play in translating service requirements into new aircraft and equipment. A healthy aviation industry was essential to the development of military aviation, as indeed it was to the development of civil aviation. And a healthy aviation industry was the very thing that Britain did not possess. In spite of the constant 'mergers' which occurred within the industry, the firms which did survive were compelled by lack of orders to reduce their staffs and production facilities to the point where they did little more than remain in business. The process was one of continual deterioration. As the orders for both military and civil aircraft became smaller and smaller, so the capacity of the industry to produce large numbers of aircraft by mass production methods declined in proportion.

Soon after Hitler's accession to power in Germany, Churchill, who was then out of office and was to remain so until the outbreak of war, began his campaign to exhort the Government to speed up the nation's defence preparations in the face of German rearmament. He concentrated mainly on the menacing growth of German air power and related it to Britain's extreme vulnerability to attack from the air. He spared nothing of his great gift for language to paint a picture of the horrors which might well befall Britain, and especially London, in an air war of the future. He insisted that the air rearmament programme (lately approved by the Government) was sighted to achieve too little, too slowly. Later, he expressed concern regarding the slowness of both the Air Force and the aviation industry to meet the demands of what he considered to be the very modest aims of subsequent expansion programmes: the one, to introduce modern aircraft into service and to increase the number of operational squadrons; the other, to produce up-to-date aircraft by mass production methods.[11] If he can be judged by the opinions he expressed during this period, it is evident that he was quite unaware of how seriously British aviation generally had declined since the end of the First World War, or, for that matter, of how great was his own responsibility for that decline.

It is important to appreciate that the numerical weakness of the bomber force was not in any way compensated for by the quality of the aircraft in service. In the immediate post-war period the squadrons were equipped with aircraft developed during the war; and it was not until the mid-1920s that the last wartime aircraft were withdrawn from regular squadron service, although one wartime aircraft, the DH9a, continued to be used by the auxiliary squadrons until 1930. It must not, however, be assumed that the post-war aircraft were necessarily much improved in design and performance compared with the wartime machines. Air Ministry specifications, set out in terms of speed, bomb load, endurance and so on, reflected the pressure of economy and the needs of the overseas 'police' squadrons rather than the operational requirements of the counter-offensive force. This method of procuring new aircraft replaced the wartime system by which the aircraft manufacturers had been given virtually a free hand to design what they considered to be the most effective aircraft of the particular type required. Mr C.R. Fairey, head of the Fairey Aviation Company, believed that this new system worked against the production of efficient aircraft types — a view that found much support within the aviation industry itself.

> The technical knowledge of building aircraft during the war had grown largely because the designers were allowed to produce the best kind of aircraft which the service required. After the war specifications were laid down too rigidly by the Air Ministry and this led to less careful design of the aircraft as a whole. When the DH9a was to be replaced, a greater military load was required but the Air Ministry specification asked for some 6 m.p.h. less than the existing type. The result was the 'Fawn' which was an inferior type.[12]

This 'inferior type' was one of the new post-war day bombers, and remained in regular squadron service from 1924 to 1929.

The night bomber squadrons were better equipped for their operational role than the day squadrons, but that is not to say that they constituted an effective force. The mainstay of the night squadrons between the wars was the Vickers Virginia, which entered service as a replacement for the Vimy in 1924 and was not withdrawn from service until 1937. The Virginia underwent several important modifications in design during this period, but even the final variant, the Mark X, with a cruising speed of well under 100 m.p.h. and a range of 985 miles, fell far short of meeting the requirements of the force. The indifferent performance of the Virginia emphasized the need for a four-engined heavy bomber of greater endurance, the 'Giant' type of aircraft for which Trenchard had, in 1923, stated a firm requirement.[13] In the event, this type of aircraft was passed over in favour of the twin-engined machine which was cheaper to produce and more economical to operate, but which lacked a really long range. And so, when the Handley Page V1500 was withdrawn from service at the end of the First World War the Air Force had to wait until 1941 before its next four-engined aircraft, the Stirling, came into service.

Although the Air Staff never wavered in their belief in independent air action, strict government economy and the strong tradition inherited from the Flying Corps induced them to favour the light, two-seater bomber of limited range. The squadrons were therefore equipped with aircraft which did not possess the capability of fulfilling the task for which they were intended — the bombing of strategic targets in France. None of the light day bombers was capable of carrying more than a small bomb load beyond the northern parts of France. The Hawker Hart, for example, the most successful light bomber of the 1930s, could carry only four 112 lb bombs or two 230 lb bombs to objectives no more distant than 230 miles from its base. Operating from the regular aerodromes at the rear or on the flanks of the home defence system, it could just reach Paris and the industrial area of north-eastern France around Lille. The industrial areas of Lorraine, of central and southern France, most of the ports and naval bases on the Britanny coast and all of those on the Mediterranean were well out of range of the day bombers. The night bombers could have reached at least a few of these targets, but they were too few in number to cause damage of any significance.

It will be seen that the bomber force could not fulfil the role for which it was intended. The question of equipping the squadrons with aircraft which precisely matched the operational needs of the force had been raised by Air Vice-Marshal J.F.A. Higgins at one of the Chief of the Air Staff's meetings in the summer of 1923.

'We must', he said, 'design our future machines in accordance with our strategical and tactical policy, which we are now in a position to do, and so obviate the necessity of modifying our tactics and strategy to suit the machines available'.[14]

This was sound advice, but there were at that time, and for many years to come, overriding considerations of a different kind which led the Air Staff to equip the squadrons with aircraft which were irrelevant to the requirements of the counter-offensive.

The need for economy and the strength of inherited tradition have already been mentioned. Another important factor was the nature of Air Force operations in the Middle East. As has been shown, part of the price paid by the Air Force for retaining an independent existence was its contribution to the work of maintaining law and order among the unruly inhabitants of such countries as Iraq, Transjordan and Aden. The lack of good communications and the scarcity of facilities needed to keep an aircraft in the air set a premium on the light aeroplane which was easy to handle and maintain and which could operate from primitive

A Handley Page 0/400 of Handley Page Transport 1920

A DH 9 of KLM 1920

Vickers Virginia

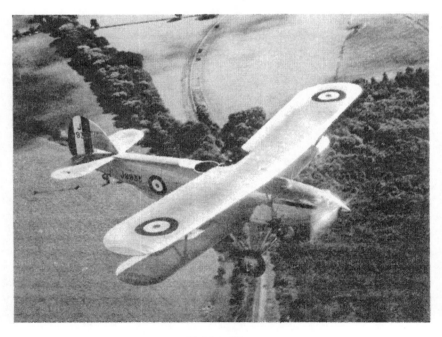

Hawker Hart

aerodromes. The obvious choice was the light bomber. Since there was not enough money to provide suitable aircraft both for the home and overseas squadrons, precedence was given to the requirements of the overseas units, with the result that the 'police' operations of the Middle East influenced to an unrealistic degree the aircraft and equipment produced for the Air Force as a whole.

None of these, however, are sufficient by themselves to explain the profound ignorance of strategic operations which existed in the Service at that time. Undoubtedly, the crucial factor was the indifference shown by the Air Staff to the scientific and technical elements of aviation. They neglected that area of planning which was concerned with research and experiment, for they were convinced that their knowledge of air operations must of necessity increase with experience. The methods which Lord Tiverton had devised for tackling operational problems during the war did not survive the transition to peace, and the major decisions affecting the development of the post-war striking force were based on the opinions and judgements of a few senior officers, all of whom were dedicated believers in the gospel of the offensive.

Most of the little that was done by way of trials and experiments originated at squadron level, and an example of this was the night flying trials carried out by No. 58 Squadron at Worthy Down in 1926. The officer commanding this squadron was Squadron Leader A. T. Harris, who was destined to lead Bomber Command during the latter half of the Second World War. He carried out various night flying trials, but the main theme of his work was to investigate the practicability of formation flying at night. He pursued his investigations with great thoroughness, and, as he later wrote, 'the squadron did more night flying at that time than all the rest of the world's then existing air forces put together'. He set down his findings, together with various recommendations concerning improvements in night flying techniques and equipment, in a report which was forwarded to the Air Ministry in June 1926. His suggestion that formation flying should be practised regularly by the night bomber squadrons was strongly supported by the squadron and flight commanders, but it received a less than enthusiastic reception at command level. However, an important concession to the idea was made when the Chief of the Air Staff approved an amendment to the Flying Training Manual permitting a limited amount of training in formation flying at night.[15]

It is hard to form an impression of the Air Force in the 1920s other than that of a service created in the image of the peacetime British Army, with each station as much concerned with ceremonial, parades and customs as with flying. Churchill was accounted by many to have been responsible for allowing the service to develop in this way, and this was

the essence of the severe criticism of his tenure of office at the Air
Ministry which appeared in *The Times* in April 1921:

> Gold braid and metal polish, acres of cantonments, establishments
> aping the Army, these are the fruits of his well-meaning and
> laborious, but wholly inadequate rule at the Air Ministry. He leaves
> the body of British flying well-nigh at its last gasp, when a military
> funeral would be all that would be left to it.[16]

Evidence of the trivialities which seemed to be inordinately important
in service life at that time is to be found in a wide range of sources.
Sir Philip Joubert de la Ferté recalled the unprofitable time he spent
at the Air Ministry when 'for rather more than three unhappy years
I picked files out of the "in" tray, wrote a trenchant phrase or two on
vital matters as to whether Air Force officers should carry a cane or
not, and placed them in the "out" tray'.[17] At squadron level, the same
kind of picture emerges, as the history of No. 9 Squadron records.
'For all cross-country flights, even very short ones, razors had to be
carried and officers had to carry their walking-sticks so that, should
a forced landing be made, the aviators could set out as if for parade.'[18]

In the absence of any real pressure of work on the Air Staff during
these years, it is remarkable that no call was ever made for a systematic
study of the strategic operations carried out by both sides during the
First World War, with the object of seeking to discover what lessons
could be learned for the future. If such a study had been made, it would
have pointed to the many serious problems inherent in long-range
operations. In particular, it would have revealed the extreme difficulty
of navigating accurately at night. And this was a factor of the first
importance, since it was intended that nearly 40 per cent of the bomber
force would eventually be composed of night squadrons, with a bomb-
carrying capacity much greater than that of the day squadrons.

It is therefore of interest to ask what benefit the Air Staff might have
derived from such a study. It is true that the available evidence was
uneven in value, but no great insight would have been required to identify
the types of operations which were carried out in conditions similar to
those in which the home-based bomber force would have to operate
against a continental enemy. British night bombing was confined to the
Naval Air Service raids from Dunkirk and the operations of the Independent Force from Nancy; while the principal German operations were
carried out against Britain, first by Zeppelins operating from bases in
northern Germany, and later by the Gothas based in Belgium.

Even a brief glance at the nature of these operations would have been
sufficient to establish the points of coincidence and difference. On the
British side, the raids carried out by the naval squadrons involved flights

of relatively short duration and were in the main made along the Belgian coast where an aircraft's position could easily be identified from the low altitudes at which the night bombers were able to operate. In addition, the bases used by the naval squadrons lay in what might be termed the same 'weather zone' as their main objectives, so that weather conditions at base and over the target would usually be similar during a given period of time — an important factor in the planning and execution of operations. Obviously, none of these features would apply to the operations of home-based aircraft against targets on the continent. In particular, the weather conditions over Britain are frequently very different from those over continental Europe, so that when conditions are favourable at base they may well be adverse over the target, and vice versa.[19]

The squadrons of the Independent Force operated under a similar 'weather' handicap, for only rarely were weather conditions in the Nancy area and over the proposed targets favourable on the same day. On the other hand, the area in which the Independent Force operated was relatively small and contained many easily identifiable landmarks, so that navigation presented few difficulties, either by day or night.

On the German side, the Gotha raids would have provided no guidance at all for the future. They were directed almost entirely against London which, because of its size and nearness to the continent, was easy to locate. The airship raids were, however, of a very different kind. The Zeppelins operated at long range against targets in many parts of Britain and were compelled by their vulnerability to anti-aircraft defences to fly at altitudes at which it was expected that bomber aircraft would have to operate in a future war. These then were the identical features which would characterize the operations of the home-based force in a bombing campaign of the future.

If the evidence, both German and British, relating to the Zeppelin raids had been studied, it would have provided a clear pointer to the problems of long-range night operations. One fact above all others would have emerged from such a study, namely, that the airship commanders experienced the greatest difficulty in finding their way over the blacked-out countryside of Britain and frequently dropped their bombs many miles from their intended targets. Two narratives of Zeppelin raids will serve to illustrate this point.

On the night 9–10 August 1915, the Zeppelin L.10, commanded by Oberleutnant Wenke, was one of five German airships which set out to attack targets in England. The airship crossed the coast at Aldeburgh at about 9.40 p.m. and steered for London on a south-westerly course. After maintaining this course for some time, Wenke changed to a south-easterly course, and shortly after midnight he made his attack in poor visibility on what he thought were the London docks. He was in fact some 30 miles to the east of the capital and his bombs fell, not on London, but on the Isle of Sheppey, at the mouth of the Thames. Of the other four airships taking part in the raid, only one, the L.9 commanded by Kapitänleutnant Loewe, succeeded in reaching the area in which his target lay. Loewe crossed the English coast a little to the south of Flamborough Head and was soon forced to make a number of rapid changes of course to evade the naval aircraft which were sent up to intercept him. He then set a south-westerly course towards the Humber, his designated area, and in spite of the persistent ground mist he successfully located the river. Shortly afterwards, he attacked a town which he identified as Hull, but in fact his bombs fell on Goole which lies some 20 miles to the west.[20]

Early in the following year, on the night of 31 January – 1 February 1916, a force of airships was despatched from the bases at Nordholz, Tondern and Hage to attack the Midlands and the west coast of England. All the airship commanders were instructed to make a special effort to locate and attack Liverpool. One of these commanders was Kapitänleutnant Dietrich of the L.21. The airship crossed the Norfolk coast a few miles south-east of Cromer and steered a westerly course. Dietrich passed to the north of Derby, which he identified as Manchester, and after altering course to the south-east, he dropped the majority of his bombs on the urban area between Birmingham and Wolverhampton, believing he had sighted Birkenhead and Liverpool. On the return flight he dropped the remainder of his bombs on a town which he took to be Manchester, but was in fact Thrapston in Northamptonshire, more than 100 miles south-east of Manchester.[21]

It is clear that Dietrich had followed a path across England which was very different from the one which he thought he had made good, and the same can be said of the other commanders who took part in the raid. The comment of the British official historian is worthy to be quoted in full.

> The detailed account in the German official history of the movements and doings of the airships is of small value as a check on our own observations that night. The German historian admits the difficulties and uncertainties of navigation during this raid. What is clear, is that the airship commanders, for the most part, came in much farther south than they thought they did and this initial mistake continued to confuse their subsequent navigation. Broadly stated, the Germans were under the impression that they bombed Sheffield three times in succession, Immingham and Yarmouth once each, Manchester by two airships simultaneously,

Liverpool twice at short intervals, and Goole and Nottingham once each. Of the nine airship commanders, four, it is claimed, reached the west coast although only two bombed there, but both of these were emphatic that their bombs had fallen on Liverpool. In fact, no bomb fell on any one of these towns. Nor did any airship get near the west coast, the most westerly point reached being Shrewsbury.[22]

Evidence such as this should have shown that unless significant advances were made in navigational equipment and techniques British aircraft carrying out attacks against targets on the continent would operate under even more severe handicaps than the German airships had done; for the airships had operated under circumstances far more favourable than the British aircraft could hope to experience. In the first place, the airships were equipped with instruments for determining position by means of direction-finding wireless and astronomical observations and were commanded by officers who had received a far superior training in navigation than was given to the post-war air force crews. Second, it was in general easier to navigate from the continent to Britain than in the opposite direction. An airship making its landfall on the coast of Britain could reasonably expect to obtain an accurate indication of its position before starting the final stage of its flight, whereas a British aircraft would cross the coastline of the continent in the early part of its flight and would have to cover the greater distance to the target over unfamiliar countryside. Finally, the slow speed of the airship and its ability to remain stationary in the air in order to fix its position over the land conferred upon it an advantage which would not be enjoyed by the bomber aircraft with a speed at least twice as great as that of the airship.

In the post-war Air Force map-reading continued to be the standard method of navigation both by day and night, as in the days of the Flying Corps, and although this is the simplest and most accurate means of position finding, it is effective only when the ground is clearly visible from the air. It is therefore successful only in conditions of good weather, and uniformly good weather is seldom found over a wide area in western Europe either by day or night. During a long flight in bad weather or in darkness, or a combination of the two, the navigator might be unable to see the ground for long periods of time. If he had no navigational aid other than his maps he might drift so far from his intended track as to be unable to locate his position again; for the more an aircraft drifts from its track the greater the area on the map the navigator has to search, and the less chance he has of identifying the objects over which he is passing. An added problem of map-reading at night is that even in good weather objects on the ground become increasingly difficult to identify as aircraft operate at greater altitudes. This would apply not only to the landmarks used to navigate the aircraft to the target, but also, and perhaps more importantly, to the targets themselves, and especially the smaller ones, such as power stations, oil refineries, and specific factories and plants. It was accepted in the Air Force that improved anti-aircraft defences would force the night bomber to fly at much higher altitudes than it had operated in the First World War, but no work was ever undertaken to discover by practical experiment just what could and could not be seen from these greater altitudes.

During the whole of the inter-war period it was taken for granted that direction-finding (D/F) wireless would be used as an auxiliary aid to map-reading, and many statements to this effect are to be found in the Air Staff papers.[23] Wireless equipment was carried by the night bombers – it was too bulky and heavy to be fitted in the day bombers – but the practice which was carried out with this navigational aid was somewhat perfunctory. It would seem that bearings were taken more to fulfil a training requirement than to obtain information which could be used to navigate the aircraft; and they were in the main obtained from transmitters at short range, so that results of reasonable accuracy could be expected.

Although it was assumed that D/F wireless would prove to be a valuable aid on war operations, little was known of the extent to which its accuracy and reliability would be affected by such factors as the distance from the transmitter, weather conditions and the hours of darkness. In any case, the system as it was organized in peacetime had obvious disadvantages for use in war. Under the normal procedure, an aircraft seeking aid in the form of a bearing or a position was required to transmit its callsign followed by a continuous note to enable the ground station or stations to measure the direction of the incoming signal. In wartime, one obvious disadvantage of this procedure would be that the enemy could also pick up the transmission and fix the aircraft's position; and for this reason there would probably be some pressure to limit its use in certain circumstances, as for example when aircraft were still over enemy territory. However, a much more serious defect would be the time lapse between the request for aid and the receipt of the information. A ground station could provide information for only one aircraft at a time, so that in the event of several aircraft seeking help at the same time, there would be a considerable lapse of time before all the aircraft could be dealt with. Such a delay might have serious consequences for an aircraft that was damaged, or short of fuel, or lost.

There was also the possibility of an aircraft being given information which was intended for another aircraft, and this could easily occur when several aircraft were working on the same frequency, especially if reception was poor. This kind of error was doubtless made on numerous occasions, but for many obvious reasons the details were rarely placed on record. One exception to this is to be found in the Operations Record Book of No. 9 Squadron under an entry dated 2 January 1927. A Virginia of that squadron lost its way in thick cloud during a flight from Spitalgate near Grantham to its base at Manston in Kent. The pilot called for aid from a D/F station and, having been given a bearing intended for another aircraft, he changed to an easterly course and finally landed at Oosterhout in Holland.[24]

A new technique, which was introduced during the rearming of the bomber force in the second half of the 1930s, was intended to reduce the dependence of aircraft upon the ground D/F stations. This involved fitting the new twin-engined aircraft with a special directional aerial, known as a loop aerial, which would enable the wireless operator to establish the direction from which a signal was received from any transmitter. If two or three such bearings were obtained simultaneously from wireless beacons whose positions were known, the navigator could determine the position of the aircraft by plotting the bearings on his chart and marking the point at which they intersected. Unfortunately, bearings obtained by this method were subject to very considerable errors, especially during the hours of darkness, but the nature and extent of these errors were never fully appreciated until the equipment had been tried on war operations.[25]

Another navigational aid which received sporadic attention during the inter-war years, but about which very little was known, was celestial or astro-navigation. One of the earliest references to this subject is to be found in an article written soon after the First World War by Air Commodore H. R. M. Brooke-Popham, who suggested that the more accurate methods of sea navigation should be adapted for use in the air. He thought that one area in particular, that of astro-navigation, offered great scope for development, and advocated that trials should be made with a new type of sextant which had been designed specifically for use in the air. The new air sextant was lighter and less bulky than the marine sextant, and was fitted with a simple spirit level which enabled the navigator to level the instrument without the necessity of taking a sight on the horizon.[26]

During the following years several types of air sextants were produced, but none of them was ever tested in the Air Force. Nevertheless, it was accepted that astro-navigation would be a practicable aid on long-range bombing operations – a judgement which was perhaps influenced by the known success achieved by the highly professional crews of the civil airlines. It was not, however, until 1937 that the decision was taken to include an element of astro-navigation in the training given to the bomber crews. Large orders were placed for an improved type of sextant, and special astronomical tables were compiled for use in the air.[27] Unfortunately, the air sextant proved to be a difficult instrument to use, and the degree of skill required to achieve results of acceptable accuracy was rarely attained by the average navigator in the bomber force. But this discovery lay very much in the future, for, as was the case with D/F wireless, the serious practical difficulties inherent in this method of position-finding remained unsuspected until long after the war had started.

The lack of adequate provision for navigational training in the Air Force can in part be explained by the belief that navigation was a skill to be acquired by practice rather than by formal instruction. From this point of view, the most important way of raising standards in navigation was to ensure that the crews were given as much flying practice as possible. Although all members of the crew played their part in determining the aircraft's position by map-reading, the responsibility for navigation rested with the pilot, who was expected to perform this duty in addition to flying the aircraft. On the ground, he was responsible for preparing the flight plan before takeoff, and in the air, for determining changes of course and checking ground speed, and so on. And this could hardly have been otherwise, since the pilot was the only member of the crew to receive any systematic training in navigation. Indeed, he was the only crew member who was employed on flying duties on a full-time basis. The other personnel who made up the crews – the gunners, wireless operators and observers – were ground tradesmen who received little specialized training for their aircrew duties and flew only when they were required to do so. The requirement for a member of the crew who would be trained specially to undertake the responsibility for navigation was never appreciated during the years when the light bomber dominated the scene and was only vaguely realized after the advent of the new long-range bombers in the period immediately preceding the war.

This unsatisfactory state of affairs was a reflection of the lack of direction at the Air Ministry, for although there were Air Ministry departments dealing with engines, instruments, armaments, and so on, there was no department responsible for navigation. As late as 1937, Air Commodore A. T. Harris, who was then commanding No. 4 Bomber Group, could still complain of this deficiency. 'The present organisation', he wrote to the Commander-in-Chief of Bomber Command, 'does not in my opinion provide any responsible department and head whose business it is to keep pace with these "practical flying" requirements. The only navigation is attached to "Training" whereas there should be a Deputy Director of Navigation and Practical Airmanship.'[28] In view of this neglect of navigation it is hardly surprising to find that very few officers of the General Duties (i.e. flying) Branch — all of whom were trained as pilots — sought to obtain specialist qualifications in navigation. The fact that there were so few posts for specialists in navigation deterred most officers from seeking extra qualifications in this field. The Air Force List of January 1933 contained the names of 1,346 officers of the General Duties Branch between the ranks of Flight Lieutenant and Group Captain (both inclusive), and of these only 38 had passed the ordinary specialist course in navigation. And even during the vital period between the rearming of the bomber force in 1938 and the beginning of the night offensive against Germany in the spring of 1940 the position had not shown a significant improvement. In the Air Force List of May 1940 there were 2,742 officers in the category indicated above, while the number of those who had qualified on the specialist navigation course had risen to 109 — hardly an adequate increase in view of the fact that there were still no officers in these ranks who were trained solely as navigators.

The picture to be obtained from an examination of the Operations Record Books is that little systematic training in navigation was undertaken by the regular squadrons. This was chiefly because the day bombers, which formed the greater part of the force, were required to concentrate on improving their standard of map reading, the method of navigation they were intended to use on war operations. Nevertheless, there was a valid case for developing more advanced techniques for the night bombers, for there was less certainty as to how these aircraft would locate their targets in the dark. Yet the squadron records show that their training differed little from that of the day bombers. There was the usual round of duties — endurance flights, the annual Bombing and Gunnery Camp, exercises in conjunction with the anti-aircraft defences and the Observer Corps, and the Air Defence of Great Britain exercises — but these included very little long-distance flying at night. It seems that the flights of long duration were for the most part made during the hours of daylight, and in favourable weather conditions, while the shorter flights were made at night. Inevitably, map-reading was the principal method of navigation, though wireless bearings were occasionally obtained.[29]

There is no doubt that the squadrons themselves could have made an important contribution to the development of navigational techniques during their routine training flights; but unfortunately the staff departments which should have been responsible for planning and authorizing the trials and, later, for interpreting the results that were obtained, did not exist. The few experiments which were carried out were organized in response to some particular need of the moment rather than as part of a planned schedule. In 1932, for example, it was decided to investigate the navigational problems of flying in cloud, and No. 12(B) Squadron was selected to carry out the work. A programme of flying trials was called for and as soon as this had been completed the experiments were brought to an end.[30] The results of this work were not subjected to any kind of scrutiny or analysis and no further trials were ordered; so that although the flights were far from being unsuccessful, the overall gain in knowledge was negligible.

In contrast with their failure to appreciate the importance of navigation, the Air Staff were keenly aware of the need for accurate bombsights and effective bombs, but, as was so often the case, their bombing policy was ill-conceived because it was based upon haphazard opinions and not upon scientifically based judgements. For instance, they believed, correctly, that the standard of bomb-aiming had steadily improved since the war; but this was not to be explained, as was suggested, by some inevitable process, but by the fact that the peacetime crews were better trained and received more constant practice than their wartime counterparts and operated in less rigorous conditions than those which had obtained in war. The belief that a higher standard of bomb-aiming was being achieved was fostered not only by the relatively accurate bombing results obtained by the home-based squadrons, but also by the outstandingly successful results claimed by the overseas squadrons. 'We were informed by the Chief of the Air Staff', stated the report of a committee on Coast Defence, 'that the accuracy of aim has improved so much that on the North-West Frontier of India aircraft are able to bomb a house of a particular sheikh'.[31] Such operations were carried out at very low level, without effective opposition, and in excellent weather conditions – in short, in conditions which made the bombing results quite irrelevant so far as operations in the European area were concerned – yet these considerations did nothing to diminish the importance which the Air Staff attached to these claims.

The Air Staff made the mistake of regarding the improvement in bomb-aiming as an isolated fact, instead of judging its significance in relation to the changes that would be brought about by war. They should have questioned whether the improvement was great enough to compensate for the more difficult conditions of war operations; and if they had done so, they would almost certainly have concluded that it was not. Instead, they persisted in the belief that bombing skills would continue to increase in absolute terms, and the result of this was to obscure the need to develop a more advanced bombsight. And so, the course-setting bombsight, which was introduced into service immediately after the First World War, remained the standard sight throughout

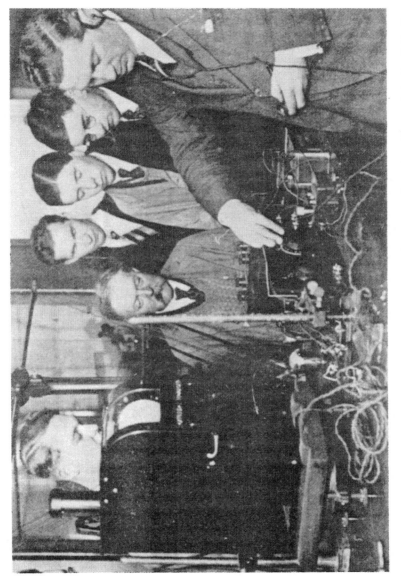

E. V. Appleton (far right) Wheatstone Professor of Physics, University of London. His work in the field of radio provided the knowledge which was essential to the development of radar

The old generation — Handley Page HP 42 *Hannibal* of Imperial Airways 1931

The new generation — Douglas DC-2 *Uiver* (Stork) of KLM 1934. This aircraft was entered for the MacRobertson Air Race and came first in the handicap section, while achieving second place in the speed section which was won by the DH 88 (Comet)

the inter-war period and during most of the first half of the Second World War.

So much of the evidence of this period points to the wide gap which existed between theory and practice and this is nowhere shown more clearly than in the formulation of tactics for the bomber force. The various methods of bombing and the targets against which they could most effectively be used were described in considerable detail in a number of Air Force documents, but the experience which the squadrons were able to gain in these methods was so limited as to be valueless. For example, bombing at high and low level was described, but neither method was ever practised. Most of the bombing runs were carried out at medium heights, never above 14,000 feet, from which it would have been dangerously low to attack defended targets. On the other hand, it was not possible to carry out genuinely low level bombing because the standard bombsights were not calibrated for heights below 3,000 feet.

Much less thought was given to night operations, since it was assumed that the tactics evolved during the First World War would, more or less, still be valid. In fact, the tactics employed by the night bombers had scarcely changed since the war, in spite of the fact that the danger from anti-aircraft defences was acknowledged to have increased greatly since that time. The aircraft still made their approach to the target singly and at low level, and it is hardly surprising that the night squadrons were able to achieve results of reasonable accuracy at their annual bombing and gunnery camp. In 1933, for example, the average bombing errors of No.58 Squadron and No.9 Squadron were, respectively, 75 and 139 yards from 6,000 feet.[32] However, when it is borne in mind that the targets were illuminated and that the bombs were dropped from a low altitude, it is clear that such results would in no way be indicative of the accuracy that might be expected in the more difficult conditions of war.

In the provision of bombs, too, the rift between theory and practice had widened but, strangely, this did not happen until near the end of the period under review. During the years when Trenchard was Chief of the Air Staff a wide range of bombs was produced and tested, but the decision to restrict this to small and medium types was dictated by the need for economy and not by operational policy. From the beginning, Trenchard had recognized the need for very heavy bombs and at one of his meetings in the summer of 1923 had stated that a bomb as large as 4,000 lb should eventually be produced.[33] Subsequently, he continued to insist on the need for the large type of bomb[34] and, in 1930, soon after his retirement from the Air Force, a new 1,000 lb bomb was undergoing tests and the requirements for 3,000 lb and 4,000 lb bombs were being considered.[35]

At the same time, however, there was an influential group at the Air Ministry who believed that the range of bombs should be restricted to small and medium types, their theory being that a group of small bombs dropped in a salvo would cause more damage than one large bomb of equivalent weight. Needless to say, this theory was merely an opinion and was founded neither on the experience of war operations nor on practical experiments carried out since the war. Indeed, virtually the only relevant evidence that did exist related to the operations of the Independent Force, and this pointed clearly to the opposite conclusion. Nevertheless, the support for this view increased rapidly after Trenchard's departure from the Air Ministry and finally the Chief of the Air Staff, Sir John Salmond, gave it official sanction. In July 1932 he ruled that no bomb heavier than 500 lb should be produced, and this ruling remained in force until long after Germany appeared as a real potential enemy.[36]

The formation of the Air Defence of Great Britain Command in 1925 permitted the holding of defence exercises on a larger scale than had been possible before. In July 1927, the first of these exercises was organized, in this case, to test the air defences of London. Unfortunately, no attempt was made to analyse the results of this or of subsequent exercises, so that the broad conclusions reached in the Air Ministry reports did little more than confirm the Air Staff's belief in the invincibility of the bomber. The 1927 exercises could not have provided them with more convincing testimony. During the whole period of the exercise thick cloud helped the bombers to approach their targets undetected and seriously hindered the work of the defending fighters. The Air Staff conceded that the bad weather frequently prevented the bombers from locating their exact targets, but insisted that it would not have prevented them from dropping their bombs in the London area. In any case, they expected that the capability of the bomber to operate in poor weather conditions would continue to improve. They believed that when D/F wireless was fully developed, this navigational aid, used in conjunction with the automatic pilot, would 'enable bombers to make even more use of cloud when approaching their objectives, in which case weather which is normally considered adverse from the flying point of view may be highly favourable to bombers. In these circumstances the difficulties of the defence will be greatly increased.'[37]

As might be expected, the evidence provided by these exercises strengthened the Air Staff's belief that the night bomber, using the cover of darkness to evade interception, would continue to enjoy a large measure of immunity.[38] The statistics for the exercises of 1931 and 1932 showed that the defences had failed to intercept 40 per cent of the night raids, as compared with only 25 per cent of the daylight raids.

Thus, the Air Staff presented a far from optimistic picture of the chances of defending Britain, and especially London, from air attack, and this gloomy view was reflected in much that was written by informed commentators during the following years. A typical example of this is to be found in an article, written by Major C. C. Turner, which appeared in the November 1931 issue of the *Royal United Service Institution Journal*. Major Turner, the Air Correspondent of *The Daily Telegraph*, was convinced by the report on the 1931 exercises that the task of defending London effectively from air attack, especially at night, would be a well-nigh impossible one. Although he thought that the figures given for the weight of bombs which might have been dropped on London during the exercises − 54 tons of high explosive and 1¼ tons of incendiary bombs − were probably exaggerated, he was nevertheless convinced that it would be 'inevitable that in the event of war with a first-class continental Power, one of the first measures to be taken would, of necessity, be the removal of the seat of government to Manchester or to Liverpool'.[39]

It is clear that these exercises did little or nothing to promote a greater understanding among the Air Staff of the nature of strategic operations. They were designed primarily to test the defences of London and, because of this, they tended to point to conclusions which had long since been accepted, namely, that the task of warding off an air attack by means of close defence (i.e. fighters and anti-aircraft guns) would be a formidable one. On the other hand, they had nothing to offer in the way of identifying the problems which the offensive element of the defence system (i.e. the counter-striking force) would have to overcome in making retaliatory raids against a continental enemy such as France. It was acknowledged that enemy aircraft operating from the continent would have little difficulty in finding London, because of its great size and proximity to their bases, even in bad weather conditions; but this could not be said of the targets against which the British bombers would have to operate. Their main targets would be moderately sized towns scattered over a wide area in the north-east of France, and the success of their attacks would depend greatly upon the correct identification of the targets. There was no single objective in France comparable to London in size, vulnerability, and importance. Not even Paris occupied a position of importance comparable to that of London in Britain; and in any case, the French capital lay at the very limit of endurance of the British day bombers.

The success of the counter-offensive would therefore depend to an important extent upon the ability of the bombers to navigate accurately to their targets in all conditions of weather. Such a capability, however, the bomber force did not possess, and this was not only because the standards of navigational training and equipment were inadequate, but also because none of the service aerodromes was equipped with the new scientific devices for bringing aircraft back safely to their bases and assisting them to land in bad weather and poor visibility. This weakness stood in marked contrast to the capability of many American and continental airlines to operate in all weathers. In 1934, Sir Robert Brooke-Popham, who was then commanding the Air Defence of Great Britain Command, admitted that the night-flying capability of his bombers was inferior to that of Lufthansa, and he cited the example of the German airline's Cologne to Croydon service which had missed only four night flights during the previous twelve months.[40] Yet in spite of such an authoritative warning, the serious nature of this weakness was still not grasped by the Air Staff; and even as late as March 1938 the Commander-in-Chief of Bomber Command was compelled to express his deep concern that the bomber force had not even begun the task of converting itself from a fair-weather into an all-weather flying corps.[41]

It will be seen that there was, at the end of this period, a wide gap between strategic planning and the production of bomber aircraft. The Air Staff had designed their plans for a bomber force capable of carrying out powerful and sustained attacks against distant targets, but the light bombers with which the force was equipped in 1933 were capable of reaching only the most northern parts of France with an insignificant bombload. It was assumed that the design of aircraft would continue to improve until operational performance matched strategic requirement, but there was no very clear idea as to what this performance would mean in terms of range, bomb-carrying capacity, defensive power, and so on.

It was also assumed that the ascendancy which the light bomber had established over the fighter during the second half of the 1920s and in the early part of the 1930s would be maintained when the next generation of aircraft came into service. This ascendancy began with the introduction of the Fairey Fox, a two-seat day bomber which had incorporated in its design the new streamlining techniques used by American manufacturers for racing aeroplanes. When this aircraft came into service with No. 12(B) Squadron in 1926 it was capable of outstripping the fastest Air Force fighters. At the beginning of the 1930s the situation was virtually unchanged, and the influence which this exerted on Air Staff thought is clearly shown in a memorandum, written in March 1930, by Squadron Leader J. C. Slessor (later Marshal of the Royal Air Force Sir John Slessor). In it he compared the performances of two modern aircraft — the Bristol Bulldog, a single-seat fighter, and the Hawker Hart, a two-seat bomber which could also be used as a fighter. He showed that in most respects the Hart, used either as a bomber or a fighter, was superior in performance to the Bulldog. In fact, only in its rate of climb did the fighter aircraft have the edge on the bomber; and it was for that reason alone that Squadron Leader Slessor thought:

> we shall very likely always have to have single-seat fighters for our one specialised problem, the defence of London, where the time factor is everything. This I believe is the sole reason for their existence; the French — no one else, in fact, except possibly some day Germany with the Ruhr — have the same problem, and I believe that very soon the single-seat fighter will die in France.[42]

It is of interest to note that this judgement — reflecting as it did Air Staff thought on the future development of military aircraft — was made on the very threshold of a revolution in aircraft design which was to improve performances beyond all recognition, and which was in a little more than five years to lead to the production of a fighter aircraft, the Hawker Hurricane, which was in every respect incomparably superior in performance to the most modern bomber.

The views expressed by Squadron Leader Slessor were in accord with Air Staff thought, and for this reason were seldom called into question by serving Air Force officers. One of the rare occasions when the orthodox thinking was challenged by a serving officer was in the pages of the *RUSI Journal* of November 1931. The writer was Squadron Leader J.O. Andrews, a staff officer and a specialist in armaments, who complained of the tendency deliberately to underestimate the effectiveness of air defence in order to strengthen the case for the offensive. 'We must bear in mind', he wrote,

> that the doctrines of the use of air power are at present, and until proved by war, speculative. Resting largely on a theoretical basis, the doctrine that air forces must be used primarily in an offensive role has had much influential support and appears well on the way to becoming sacrosanct. Consequently the approved policy is one of aggression, with the development of the maximum strength of bombing aircraft. As a corollary, defensive commitments tend to be regarded with disfavour, and air forces allocated to play a strategically defensive role are reduced to the minimum.

Squadron Leader Andrews believed that this was a dangerous policy in view of London's great vulnerability to air attack; for he could not imagine any country that would suffer greater devastation than Britain in the event of a war in which unrestricted bombing was practised. The unfavourable view that had been formed of the defending fighter, he pointed out, was based largely on experience derived from the First World War; but, owing to the advances made in aircraft design since

1918, this was no longer valid. In his view, the essential pointer to the effectiveness of the contemporary fighter against the contemporary bomber was to be found in the statistics relating to the increase in the speed of the bomber compared with the increase in the fighter's rate of climb since the end of the war. The figures showed that while the speed of the fast modern bomber had increased by only 25 per cent, the rate of climb of the fast modern fighter had increased by 40 per cent; and this fact alone, Squadron Leader Andrews believed, could well mean that the day bombers would not be able to reach their targets without suffering heavy losses.[43]

In 1933 the Air Force bore no visible signs of the revolution in aircraft design which was soon to inaugurate a new era in military aviation. The aircraft then in squadron service were all biplanes and differed little from those which had equipped the Air Force since 1923. There was an overall improvement in aircraft performance, but this was brought about mainly by the development of engines of greater power, for progress in aerodynamics had generally been slow. Air Staff thought was still dominated by the idea of the light bomber capable of operating both by day and night. The qualities required for this all-round type of aircraft − speed and defensive power combined with a reasonable bombload − were most nearly realized in the Boulton Paul Sidestrand which came into service in 1928; but the range of the Sidestrand was little better than that of the Hart. And even when a specification (P27/32) for an aircraft to replace the Hart was issued in the summer of 1933 the requirements were again for a light bomber of limited range.

However, even before specification P27/32 was issued, the Air Staff had taken the important step of preparing a specification for a long-range heavy bomber. This specification (B9/32) was issued in the early part of 1933, and although the change in policy which it seemed to herald was not discernible in Air Staff thought for some time to come, it provided the basis on which the re-arming of the bomber force was founded. The two aircraft which were built to this specification, the Wellington and the Hampden, were the first effective weapons in the armament of the striking force, and these, together with the Whitley, bore the brunt of the air offensive against Germany in the early years of the Second World War.

CHAPTER FOUR

THE EARLY EXPANSION PROGRAMMES, 1934–5

The creation of the new German Air Force, the Luftwaffe, is commonly regarded as part of the rearming of Germany which followed Hitler's advent to power. This, however, is only partly true, for the foundations of the new service had been established many years before. It is in fact more accurate to state that Hitler made possible the resurgence of German air power by providing massive support for a force already in being.[1]

Under the terms of the Treaty of Versailles, Germany was specifically forbidden to maintain an air force, but was not prohibited from possessing or manufacturing civil aircraft. It is true that some restrictions on the size and number of civil aircraft she could produce were later imposed, but these were removed by the Paris Air Agreement of 1926. The Germans were quick to realize that this freedom gave them an excellent opportunity to re-establish their military air power; and they set out to achieve this by developing civil and commercial flying, and by encouraging the expansion of the German aircraft industry. This clandestine military activity was greatly aided by the fact that the Germans had been allowed to retain a Ministry of Defence, and with it the nucleus of a General Staff.

If any one person can be given credit for founding the new German Air Force, that must surely be General Hans von Seeckt, who became Chief of the Army Command soon after the war. Von Seeckt was a dedicated supporter of air power and believed that the air force should be an independent branch of the armed services. During his tenure of office at the Defence Ministry he gathered together a group of air-minded officers, and to these he entrusted the task of preparing for the eventual revival of German military aviation.

One of von Seeckt's first objectives was to gain administrative control over civil aviation, which began to expand rapidly after the war; and in 1924 he took an important step in this direction when he secured the appointment of his own nominee as head of the Civil Aviation

Department at the Ministry of Transport. From then on, he was assured of the close co-operation of the civil authority in forwarding his plans. This enabled him to make use of the civil flying schools to train military aviators in secret, and in so doing, to evade the restrictions of the Paris Air Agreement which severely limited the number of military personnel who were permitted to receive flying instruction. In addition, he had the facilities provided by the Soviet Union to train regular officers at an airfield near Lipetsk, some 200 miles south-east of Moscow.[2] This concession was in part a mark of recognition by the Soviet government of the vital part which German civil aviation played in establishing air transport in the Soviet Union.

In 1921, Deruluft, a company sponsored mainly by German interests, undertook a series of proving flights to link the major cities of eastern Germany and Russia, and within a year had established a regular service between Berlin and Moscow, via Danzig and Königsberg. By 1926 part of this route was lighted − this was the first airway in Europe to be operated at night − and the journey from Berlin to Moscow could be completed in one day. In 1921 the Junkers company opened a factory near Moscow and undertook extensive surveys to establish air routes in both European and Asiatic Russia. Within a few years many of the major centres in the Soviet Union had been linked by air, and the companies which operated these routes were equipped mainly with German aircraft.[3] Co-operation between the two nations in this field continued to be close throughout the 1920s, and on the Russian side this included the provision of air training facilities at Lipetsk. The first group of German officers arrived there in 1925 and the last course to pass through the school finished their training in 1932.[4]

In 1926 the structure on which the 'undercover' air force was being built was greatly strengthened when the major German independent airlines were amalgamated to form the national airline, Deutsche Lufthansa. The purpose of this reorganization was to accelerate the development of aviation generally by channelling the resources of the whole aviation industry into one major airline. Lufthansa enjoyed a monopoly in civil aviation and received generous subsidies from the government; and under the able direction of Erhard Milch, who was later to play an important part in the re-building of the German Air Force, it attained a level of efficiency which was equalled by few airlines in the world. During these formative years virtually all the operational activities of Lufthansa had some contribution to make to the future development of German air power; but perhaps the most significant were the programmes of research and experiment which were designed to improve the techniques in all-weather flying, blind approach, and long-range navigation.

On 1 January 1933 Hitler became head of the German state, and from that time onwards the pace of air expansion was quickened. In the following April he sanctioned the establishment of an air ministry and appointed Hermann Goering, his associate since the early days of the National Socialist Party, to take control of it. This was only the first step, for Goering was already marked out to head the new German Air Force when it should come into being; yet in spite of his distinguished war record as a pilot he did not possess the requisite knowledge or experience of aviation to fit him for such wide-ranging responsibilities. Moreover, he was compelled by his high position in the Nazi party to be much involved in purely political affairs, and in consequence he was not able to give more than a fraction of the time and effort which should have been devoted to his ministerial duties. He was therefore compelled to delegate much of his authority to his deputy, and he was indeed fortunate that the man appointed to be his deputy was the outstandingly able Erhard Milch.

Milch embarked on his new task by giving first priority to the expansion of Lufthansa, for it was from the national airline that he intended the secret air force should receive most of its aircraft and trained aircrews; and to this end he worked to expand the resources of the aircraft industry both by enabling existing companies to increase their productive capacity and by providing the incentives for companies outside the industry to undertake the manufacture of aircraft and aircraft components. At the same time he created an air ministry organization capable of dealing with both civil and military aviation. In 1934 the first military aircraft went into production, and among these were the He 51 biplane fighter and the He 46 monoplane reconnaissance fighter. Soon after that, bomber aircraft such as the Ju 86 and the He 111 came into service, though these two aircraft were first supplied to Lufthansa as civil transport types. At this stage, however, Milch gave high priority to the production of training aircraft; for he rightly judged that the considerable expansion of German military aviation which would be called for in the following years would need to be based on a sound training organization.

In March 1935 Hitler repudiated the military restrictions imposed on Germany by the Treaty of Versailles, and among the measures he announced to re-establish Germany's military position was the creation of the new German Air Force. It is certain that he placed his main reliance upon a powerful army to secure his ultimate objectives, but it is equally certain that he believed that the possession of an effective air arm — a force which could be created in a fraction of the time needed to re-build the army and the navy — would be a formidable weapon to support his demands for further revisions of the peace treaty. Indeed, subsequent events were to show that his assumption was correct; for it was the fear inspired by the power of the German bomber force − a power exaggerated by Nazi propaganda, but nonetheless formidable − which was an important factor in enabling him to gain his early objectives without striking a blow. Soon after Hitler had announced the re-birth of German air power, the various clandestine flying units were received into the new service with the kind of ostentatious display at which the Nazis excelled, and Hitler himself was present at many of the ceremonies. The new air force came into being with 1,888 aircraft and some 20,000 officers and men; and although it possessed at that time only a limited offensive capability, within the next few years it was destined to grow into a force of unequalled striking power and versatility.[5]

The immediate effect in this country of Hitler's advent to power was that it compelled the Government to re-examine the assumptions on which its defence policy was founded. Up to that time, France had, somewhat academically, been regarded as Britain's only potential enemy in Europe; but since the likelihood of a conflict between the two former allies was not considered even remotely possible, no plans had ever been drawn up for a war with France. Now, however, events in Germany had brought about a complete change in the situation, and for the first time since 1918 there seemed a distinct possibility of a war in the near future. The rise of an aggressive German nationalist party, following upon the obvious failure of the Disarmament Conference, forced the British Government to reconsider the whole question of home defence and to draw up plans based upon the assumption of a conflict with Germany. In 1933 and 1934 a series of discussions took place at the highest levels to re-assess Britain's defence needs in the light of recent events in Europe; and during these discussions the future policy of the Air Force, and in particular of the bomber striking force, was drawn in broad outline; and this policy not only guided the expansion of the Air Force up to the outbreak of war but also determined the main types of air operations carried out during the early stages of the war.

The British Ambassador to Germany, Sir Horace Rumbold, quickly took the measure of the new German government, and in his dispatch to the Foreign Office, dated 25 April 1933, he warned that Hitler's actions were creating a potentially dangerous situation in Europe. Sir Robert Vansittart, Permanent Under-Secretary of State at the Foreign Office, wholly agreed with this assessment, and in the yearly review of foreign affairs which the Foreign Office prepared for the Chiefs of Staff he conveyed this warning clearly and forcefully. The paper stated that 'the completely crude and unbalanced administration of Herr Hitler ... will proceed to the building up of formidable armaments on land and especially in the air' and that this course of action 'would plunge continental Europe into a bitter competition in armaments, and eventually into war'. In consequence, the movement of events might well lead to a situation in which Britain would be called upon to fulfil her obligations under the Locarno Pact to maintain the territorial status quo on the German frontiers with France and Belgium and to preserve the de-militarization of the Rhineland. The inescapable conclusion to be drawn from this evidence, the Foreign Office believed, was that the low level of armaments which Britain had accepted since the war was no longer adequate in view of the changed situation in Europe.[6]

The Chiefs of Staff, however, took a much less pessimistic view of the European situation than did the Foreign Office. Although they were in general agreement with the opinions expressed, they did not believe that the danger posed by a re-arming Germany was imminent. They estimated that Germany would need several years (at least three and probably five) to build up her military strength to the point where she would be in a position to challenge the major powers, and on the basis of this assumption they concluded that Britain still had time to make good her military deficiencies, provided the task was taken in hand without delay.[7]

Of the two appreciations, the one prepared by the Foreign Office assessed more accurately the seriousness of the threat posed by the reckless policies of the Nazi government. It is true that in 1933 the naval and air forces in Britain were still incomparably more powerful than those of Germany, yet the military resurgence of Germany was creating a situation potentially more dangerous for this country than that which had existed at the outbreak of the First World War. In the period before 1914 Britain's ties with Japan, Russia, France and Italy had enabled her to concentrate most of her forces in north-west Europe; but such a concentration would not have been possible if a similar type of crisis had occurred in 1933, for, with good reason, both Japan and Russia were then regarded as potential enemies. If Germany were added to the number of hostile nations, Britain might find herself threatened simultaneously from several quarters; and considered in this context, the revival of German militarism appeared even more menacing.

In October 1933 Hitler withdrew Germany both from the Disarmament Conference and the League of Nations, and the hopes of a lasting peace in Europe received a severe setback. It was now clear that a re-examination of Britain's defence needs could no longer be postponed; and as a first step the Cabinet appointed a committee under their secretary, Sir Maurice Hankey, to decide which of our deficiences were the most serious. The Defence Requirements Committee, whose members included the three Chiefs of Staff and the Permanent Under-Secretary of State for Foreign Affairs, Sir Robert Vansittart, was set up on 15 November 1933 and produced its report for the Ministerial Committee on Disarmament at the end of February 1934.[8]

The Defence Requirements Committee based their recommendations on the assumptions that the greatest danger lay in Europe and that Germany was 'the ultimate potential enemy against whom our "long-range" defence policy must be directed'. Since this was the case, first priority should be given to the re-building of our home defences against a possible German attack, and the nature of our defence requirements should be determined by the scale and speed of German re-armament. However, our island position and great naval strength rendered us virtually immune from direct attack except from the air, and so the most pressing need was to increase the strength of the home-based air force. The committee believed that this task should be taken in hand without delay and should begin with the completion of the 52-squadron programme.

In general, the committee kept well within their brief to deal only with the worst deficiencies, but so serious a view did they take of the threat from the air that they felt justified in taking it upon themselves to suggest what should be done to provide for something more than the barest minimum of security. They included in their report a strong recommendation that a Field Force, together with an air component, should be made ready for despatch to the continent within one month of the outbreak of war. They envisaged that such a force, used in conjunction with a continental ally to secure the Low Countries against invasion, would be well placed to establish a chain of air defence units as a first line of defence for London.

Indeed, the need to maintain the integrity of the Low Countries – a point on which the Chiefs of Staff were unanimous – had a special significance for the Air Staff. They realized that if the Germans were able to occupy the Low Countries they could establish air bases and an anti-aircraft defence system well in advance of their own frontier. This would place them in a position of great strength, for the short range of their bases from targets in south-east England would considerably increase the effectiveness of their attack. They would also be well placed to check a British counter-attack. If, on the other hand, our bombers were able to operate from bases in the Low Countries they would be within easy range of many industrial targets in Germany.[9]

Meanwhile, the Chiefs of Staff had devoted much attention to the many defence problems raised by the possibility of a war in the not too distant future. They were agreed that Germany would probably begin with an offensive in eastern Europe, while remaining on the defensive in the west; but it was their first responsibility to plan for the eventuality of an attack in the west, since this represented the more dangerous situation for Britain. If the Germans intended to strike in the west, it seemed likely that they would pursue one of two broad strategic plans. They might direct the main weight of their land and air forces against the Low Countries, with the object of defeating the French Army and of establishing air bases within short range of south-east England; or they might launch a massive air attack against Britain to prevent her from intervening on the continent.

There was, however, a sharp difference of opinion between the War Office and the Air Ministry as to which course the Germans were more likely to pursue. The War Office thought it would be the former. Their information led them to believe that the German Air Force was being developed primarily as a tactical weapon and that in a future war it would be used mainly to support the land forces. The Air Ministry on the other hand were convinced that the assault would begin in the air. They believed that German military thought was moving towards the view that air power would be a decisive factor in the next war and that in a war with France and Britain the latter should first be knocked out from the air before the final assault was delivered against France.[10]

In spite of these differences of opinion, the Chiefs of Staff were unanimous in believing that the most dangerous situation for this country would arise from an attempted 'knock-out blow' from the air; and since no detailed assessment of the nature of this threat had been made since the resurgence of German air power, the Chief of the Air Staff, Sir Edward Ellington, was invited by his colleagues to prepare a paper on this subject. This paper, which was presented to the Chiefs of Staff Committee on 12 June 1934, was the first major statement of air staff policy related precisely to the situation created by a re-arming and aggressive Germany.[11]

Sir Edward Ellington introduced his paper with a brief statement of air staff doctrine relating to a war with a major European power. In the event of a conflict with Germany, Britain would stand at a severe disadvantage owing to her great vulnerability to attack from the air; and in consequence we should be unwise to place any reliance upon defending aircraft to prevent the enemy bombers from reaching their targets. Our main hope lay in creating a more powerful bomber force than the enemy possessed and in striking at him with even greater force than he could direct against us; for the war would almost certainly be won by the side which was able to inflict the greater amount of punishment. We should lose no time in making our preparations, both by building up in peacetime large reserves of pilots and aircraft and by laying plans for the rapid wartime expansion of the industries vital to the offensive. It was important, too, that the civil population, who would inevitably suffer in a war of this type, should be able to withstand the demoralizing effect of air attacks; and this could best be done by giving them an understanding of what air warfare of the future would mean, and by making adequate preparations to protect their lives.

The Chief of the Air Staff believed that the Germans would begin the war with an air offensive against Britain, but he did not believe that they would be able to achieve a decisive result in this way provided we had built up an adequate force of first-line aircraft and had made the necessary preparations to defend the civil population. The Germans would not, he thought, be able to develop the full weight of their attack until they had advanced their bases into the Low Countries; but even if they were able to secure such bases, their peak attacks would be followed by lulls as reserves were used up. Our greatest test would come in the opening phase of hostilities, but provided we were able to withstand the initial period of raids, there was every chance that we should be able to expand and develop our air forces at least as quickly as the Germans.

The Chief of the Air Staff then reviewed the figures prepared by the Air Staff relating to the probable expansion of the German Air Force during the following eight years. It was thought that the first target for which the Germans were aiming was one of 480 first-line aircraft, to be achieved by the second half of 1935, and that this would be followed by two further periods of expansion, each one of which would provide 480 more aircraft; so that by 1942 the number might reach 1,440 first-line aircraft, of which perhaps 1,230 would form the striking force. A further expansion might subsequently raise this figure to 1,800 aircraft, with a striking force of 1,640. However, he warned against reading too much into these estimates, which obviously could not take into account Germany's undoubted capacity to accelerate her air expansion programme. There was in fact much evidence to suggest the feasibility of such an acceleration, and in the light of this evidence it was certain that 'Germany could, if she wished, build up rapidly in peacetime to a force of 2,000 aircraft, and that the preparations which she is now beginning to make may within, say, five years enable her to maintain such a force at practically its full strength in war'.

The Chief of the Air Staff then considered the kinds of targets that the Germans would be most likely to attack in order to achieve a 'knock-out blow'; and his approach to this question was clearly determined by the Air Staff's unquestioned belief that the morale of the civilian population was the most effective objective for strategic bombing. He acknowledged that the south-east of England offered a wealth of important and tempting objectives, such as airfields, munition works, aircraft factories, and the centres of government in London; but he thought that the Germans might well consider that an all-out attack against the morale of the civilian population would be a more effective means of achieving a quick and decisive result. If this supposition were correct, the attack would probably be directed against London and certain areas of central England: against targets such as the ports on the Thames, Humber and Mersey (which together handled nearly 70 per cent of the foodstuffs and 60 per cent of the total tonnage of shipping entering the United Kingdom) and against centres of communications, gas works and electricity generating stations, all of which provided facilities and services of vital importance to the well-being of the nation.

This brought the Chief of the Air Staff to the very crux of the problem. There was no hope, he stated, of defeating an air attack of the scale and intensity he had described by purely defensive measures: the most effective means of thwarting the enemy's designs would be to launch a counter-offensive. This would have a twofold aim: first, to reduce the scale and frequency of the German raids by means of attacks on aerodromes, supply depots and aircraft factories; and second, to compel the Germans to employ a significant part of their air resources in the defensive role by attacking important war industries in such areas as the Ruhr and the Rhineland.

Finally, Sir Edward Ellington examined the various situations in which Britain might find herself at war with Germany and considered how the outcome of the air war might be affected in each case. In essence, the nature of the situation, i.e. whether it would be favourable or unfavourable to Britain, would in the main be determined by the positions taken by France and the Low Countries. The most dangerous situation for Britain would arise if France remained neutral and the Germans were able to operate from bases in the Low Countries. In this case the Germans would be able to launch heavy and sustained attacks against Britain with little or no warning. The British bombers, on the other hand, would operate under a severe handicap, since they would first have to fly long distances over territory held by the enemy in order to reach their targets in Germany. Losses in the bomber force would inevitably be high and the power of the counter-offensive would be much reduced.

Even with France as our ally, our position would still be serious if the Germans were able to operate from the Low Countries. They would still be able to deliver heavy and frequent attacks, and with a striking force of 1,230 aircraft they would probably drop an average of 150 tons of bombs each day on Britain for the first two or three weeks of the campaign. British and French bomber forces would naturally retaliate with an offensive from French bases; but if Britain failed to sustain the heavy losses which would be inevitable in air fighting conducted at such close quarters, the success of the campaign might well be placed in jeopardy.

In a straight fight between Britain and Germany, with both sides respecting the neutrality of the Low Countries, the result would almost certainly be a stalemate. The Germans would have to operate at very long range and the weight of bombs they could drop on this country would probably be reduced to about 75 tons a day. The British counter-offensive would also be much less effective. The only route open to our bombers would be across the short and heavily defended north coast of Germany, and in consequence the number of feasible targets would be seriously reduced.

If Britain and France were allies and the Low Countries remained neutral, the daily tonnage of bombs which the Germans could drop on Britain would probably be reduced to 50 tons. A combined British and French bombing campaign carried out from French airfields would further reduce this amount, and might eventually force the Germans on to the defensive. Finally, the most favourable situation would occur if Britain and France were allies and our striking force could operate from bases in the Low Countries. The Chief of the Air Staff pointed to the advantages we should gain if such a situation should exist: 'The German air menace to this country will be substantially reduced if we can count upon France as an ally and would no longer constitute a serious danger to this country if, in addition, we could hold at least the western half of the Low Countries'.

The other chiefs of staff considered the paper to be altogether too alarmist. They raised strong objections to it at a meeting of the Chiefs of Staff Committee on 27 June 1934, and did not send it forward either to the Ministerial Committee on Disarmament or to the Committee of Imperial Defence.[12] Sir Edward Ellington replied to these objections in a second paper, dated 11 July 1934, and in it he explained that he had concentrated on what the Germans rather than on what the British could achieve in an air war, since it had been his intention to point to the most serious dangers that Britain might have to face.[13] At the same time, he emphasized that he had not in any way modified the views he had expressed in the first paper. Nevertheless, the second paper was more optimistic in tone than the first one, and this was reflected in the Chief of the Air Staff's views on the prospects for the future. 'I would like to record my opinion', he wrote, 'that if this country and France maintain adequate air forces and make every possible preparation in peacetime to permit of the rapid replacement of our casualties in war, and if Germany realized that she cannot attack one without the other, she is unlikely to undertake an air campaign against us'.

The Ministerial Committee on Disarmament did not receive an official copy of Sir Edward Ellington's paper, but they had been informed of its contents and were in sympathy with the views expressed in it. They had in fact already resolved to give first priority to the needs of the Air Force, and they put this intention into effect by calling for an immediate expansion programme (later known as Expansion Scheme A) to enable the Air Force to be 'ready for war in 5 plus three (8) years'. The stated purpose of this expansion programme was to provide a deterrent to Germany as the potential aggressor.[14]

The Ministerial Committee recommended that the Metropolitan Air Force should be expanded to 84 squadrons by 1939, but that only the most essential reserves should be provided during this period. It was intended to postpone the provision of full reserves until the period 1939–1942, and two reasons were given for this decision. First, Germany would need several years to build up her air strength and so the most obviously effective deterrent would be provided by increasing the number of squadrons as rapidly as possible. Second, in view of the revolution in aircraft design which was then taking place, it would be folly to create large reserves of aircraft types which would have a very limited operational life. Nevertheless, the Ministerial Committee recognized that there were obvious risks in creating new squadrons without the necessary reserves, 'putting all our wares in the shop window', as they described it. If the Germans should discover that our air strength was merely a façade, the effectiveness of the deterrent might be lost; and to guard against the possibility of this happening the committee warned that 'the reserves must be provided before an outbreak of war becomes imminent'.[15]

The introduction of Expansion Scheme A in July 1934 marked the beginning of a new and more clearly defined stage in the development of Britain's air power. Under the provisions of the new scheme the Air Staff were charged with the task of preparing for a war which might break out in as little as five years. This task involved the formulation of defence plans to meet a danger that was clearly defined, as opposed to the rigid theorizing about the counter-offensive strategy which had been the substitute for planning up to that time. The Air Staff were as deeply committed as ever to the doctrine of the counter-offensive, but they were now compelled by the practical demands of the situation to make concessions regarding the most hallowed of their principles, that concerning the proper ratio of fighters to bombers.[16] Ever since Trenchard had made his pronouncement in 1923 that the fighter provided no real defence against the bomber, the Air Staff had kept the number of fighter squadrons to the absolute minimum; but the requirements of the new expansion scheme called for a higher proportional increase in the fighter squadrons as compared with the bomber squadrons.

The reason for this change of emphasis was that the emergence of Germany as a potential enemy had considerably increased the number of areas in Britain vulnerable to air attack. The existing defences had been organized to protect London and the south-east of England from attack by aircraft based on French territory; but in the changed situation the industrial areas in the Midlands and in the north as far as the Tyne lay within range of bombers operating from north-west Germany. In addition, there was a strong possibility that the Germans might be able to operate from bases in the Low Countries. The effect of this was to add to the already considerable difficulties of fighter defence; and nothing less than an aircraft fighting zone stretching from Portsmouth around London to Middlesbrough would give the necessary protective cover. There was therefore no alternative but to increase the strength of the fighter force. The Chief of the Air Staff was most reluctant to increase the number of fighter squadrons, since this could be done only at the expense of the bomber force; but after careful deliberation and with much misgiving, he finally decided that 28 of the 84 projected squadrons should be allocated to fighter defence.[17] When allowance is made for the 15 squadrons which were intended to perform other duties, it will be seen that there were to be 28 fighter to 41 bomber squadrons, a much higher proportion of fighters to bombers than was laid down in the provisions of 1923.

From the outset, the Air Staff had based their planning on the assumption that only heavy and medium bombers would be suitable for operations in a war with Germany; but when the detailed plans were drawn up the majority of the bomber squadrons were scheduled to be equipped with light bombers.[18] The severe financial restrictions would in any case have influenced the Chief of the Air Staff's decision to equip only 16 of the 41 bomber squadrons with heavy or medium bombers;[19] but even without this particular constraint, there was another one, equally powerful, namely, that there were no suitable heavy or medium bombers available at that time. Of the heavy bombers, the Virginia had long been obsolete, while the Heyford, which was just then coming into service, was already obsolescent. In the medium bomber class, the Sidestrand and its improved version, the Overstrand, both belonged to a previous generation of aeroplanes. In both these classes the prospects lay very much in the future. The heavy bomber being built to specification B3/34, the Whitley, was not due to fly until early 1936, and even the medium bombers, whose specifications were issued in 1932 − B9/32 (Hampden and Wellington) and P27/32 (Battle) − were unlikely to be ready before the end of 1935. And to add to the problems of future planning, all these aircraft contained novel features of design, both in airframes and engines, which were as yet untried.

There were no such problems with the light bomber. In the Hawker Hart the Air Force possessed what was probably the most successful aircraft of this type in squadron service anywhere in the world, and a variant of this aircraft, the Hind, had passed its service trials in May 1934. Neither the Hart nor the Hind possessed the range necessary to operate against Germany from bases in this country, but this was not considered to be a serious handicap in the first phase of the expansion programme; for the assumption on which the planning was based was that the bomber force would be re-equipped with the new medium and heavy bombers during the five years it was estimated that Germany would need to prepare herself to fight a major war. On the other hand, the immediate aims of the first expansion scheme were to provide a deterrent to German aggression and at the same time to create a substantial body of trained aircrew to man an even larger force if the deterrent should fail. The light bombers were particularly well suited to fulfil both these aims. They were cheap and easy to manufacture and, being relatively simple to fly, were ideal for training inexperienced crews on operational types.

Even before the inauguration of the expansion scheme the Air Staff had begun to look for the answers to a number of questions relating to the types of aircraft and equipment that would be needed in a war against Germany.[20] Their task was no easy one in view of the momentous changes which were then taking place in every area of aviation; but it was rendered even more difficult by their own shortcomings, especially in their approach to this kind of investigation. It was all too common for important decisions to be based on judgements relating to First World War operations and on the very limited flying experience of the post-war years, rather than on information derived from scientific research and experiment. At first it seemed as if a new and more rational approach was to be made: a number of specialist committees were formed and their terms of reference were stated with such precision as to suggest that a more searching and objective mode of enquiry was to be pursued. But this was the appearance, not the reality; and this fact is revealed all too clearly in the deliberations of the committee whose investigations were of fundamental importance to the work of strategic planning, the Bombing Committee.

This committee, which was formed in January 1934, met under the chairmanship of the Deputy Chief of the Air Staff and was charged with the task of reviewing the various types of targets likely to be attacked and of making recommendations concerning the future requirements of the striking force in terms of aircraft, equipment and bombs.[21] It was in fact authorized to carry out a most searching enquiry into the problems of bombing, both technical and tactical; and its findings should have pointed the way to the development of the bomber force and its equipment when the new heavy and medium bombers came into service.

Unfortunately, the committee proved themselves to be incapable of visualizing the changes that would be brought about by the new high-speed monoplanes which were already making their appearances both in Europe and in America. Instead, they based their planning largely on the performances of the obsolescent biplanes and on the bomb policy which had been designed for these aircraft; and because of this approach they did not even come within remote distance of formulating a realistic bomb policy.

If proof of this is needed, it can be found in an exchange of views between Sir Robert Brooke-Popham, the Commander-in-Chief of the Air Defence of Great Britain Command, and the Air Ministry, a year after the formation of the Bombing Committee. In a letter dated 31 January 1935, the Commander-in-Chief made the recommendation that the 250 lb bomb should be made the standard missile for the bomber force and that all types of high explosive bombs below that weight should be discarded. He also recommended that provision should be made for aircraft to carry bombs up to 2,000 lb in weight, for he believed that there would be a requirement for heavy bombs for attacks against targets such as battleships in harbour and bridges.[22]

The Air Ministry reply, which was approved by the chairman of the Bombing Committee,[23] rejected both of these recommendations. The response to the first one was based on the view that

> the result of air action is, to some extent, dependent upon the number of bombs dropped rather than on their size. Furthermore, the chances of hitting a given target are greatly increased by dropping four distributed bombs instead of two ... It is thought that the majority of factories, for instance, would be affected to a greater extent by four 120 lb bombs than by two 250 lb bombs.

The case for the heavy bombs was dismissed with the statement that any attempt to accommodate 1,000 lb and 1,500 lb bombs in the new medium and heavy bombers 'would be most detrimental to performance and would unduly complicate the task of the designers'.[24]

In his reply, Sir Robert Brooke-Popham pointed out that there was no evidence at all to show that the average factory would suffer more damage from a larger number of small bombs than from a smaller number of large ones. In fact, he thought that such evidence as did exist pointed to the opposite conclusion: for example, the attacks carried out by the Independent Force against targets in Germany showed that the greatest damage had been caused by large bombs. The Air Ministry commission which had inspected bomb damage in the Rhineland area soon after the war were unanimously agreed that 'no really effective material damage to typical German factories or ordinary buildings in towns could be expected using bombs smaller than the then existing 230 lb type'. Nor could he accept the statement that the large bombs would cause serious problems for the designers of the new aircraft. He himself had consulted the designers involved in this work and they had assured him that they would have no difficulty in modifying the designs of the new aircraft to enable them to carry the large bombs.[25]

The final word in this dispute is to be found in the minutes of a sub-committee of the Bombing Committee which was set up early in 1935 to make recommendations concerning the types of bombs that would be needed 'to produce the required effect on every type of target which the Air Force might be required to attack'. When the sub-committee met for the first time in May 1935, they were asked to decide whether or not there was a need for the heavy type of bomb. In view of the importance which this decision would have in shaping future bomb policy, the members of the sub-committee might reasonably have been expected at least to examine the evidence relating to the damage caused by bombs of various sizes during the First World War; or better still, they might have called urgently for bombing trials to be undertaken so that they could base their judgement on results which had been scientifically evaluated. In fact, they did neither of these things. Instead, they discussed the question in a somewhat cursory fashion, and, apparently finding no reason to reverse the decision taken in 1932, they re-affirmed the ruling that no bombs over 500 lb should be produced.[26]

While the Air Staff generally seemed unaware of the problems which the new high-speed bombers would create for the striking force, the Air Force staffs responsible for home defence were under no illusions about the magnitude of the threat which the new aircraft would pose for the fighter defences. Sir Robert Brooke-Popham, whose command was also responsible for the fighter element of home defence, viewed the prospects with grave concern. He believed that the new aircraft would not only be able to operate at greater speeds than previous types – he estimated that around 200 m.p.h. would soon be normal – but would also be able to use the new scientific aids to navigation which were then in widespread use in Germany to carry out more attacks in darkness and in poor visibility. He had already commented on the high standards of all-weather flying achieved by the Germans and had in 1934 quoted as an example the fact that the Lufthansa night service between Cologne and Croydon had failed to operate on only four occasions during the previous twelve months. Nor did the prospects of warding off daylight attacks seem much better. The cruising speed of the bomber was still increasing, while the rate of climb of the fighter seemed incapable of any substantial improvement. The fighter squadrons were even then almost drawn back to the areas they were intended to protect; and any further increase in the bomber's speed would render this type of defence impossible. The commander of the Fighting Area, Air Vice-Marshal P.B. Joubert, stated the problem in specific terms: he thought that if the enemy bombers were to operate at more than 200 m.p.h. and over 10,000 feet and were able to cross the coast without prior warning of their approach, it would be impossible to intercept them from the ground before they reached London or the Midlands.[27]

These facts and the interpretation placed upon them were sufficient to convince the Air Ministry that there was an urgent need to take a fresh look at the whole question of home defence. Towards the end of 1934 Mr H.E. Wimperis, Director of Scientific Research at the Air Ministry, secured the approval of the Air Minister, Lord Londonderry, to form a small committee of scientists whose fields of work and experience would enable them to carry out, as the name of the committee indicated, a scientific survey of air defence. The head of the committee was Mr H.T. Tizard, who had made an important contribution to experimental work in the flying service in the First World War and who was currently chairman of the Aeronautical Research Committee; the two other members were Professors A.V. Hill and P.M.S. Blackett.[28] Before the committee held its first meeting, Wimperis consulted Mr R.A. Watson-Watt, the superintendent of the Radio Department of the National Physical Laboratory, on the possibility of producing a beam of electro-magnetic waves of sufficient strength to cause injury both to an aircraft and its crew.[29] There were at that time frequent reports that tests on a beam of this type were being carried out in Germany, and although later accounts of the work of the Tizard Committee imply that Wimperis' concern about a device which was popularly known as the 'death ray' was somewhat absurd, the possible existence of such a device in Germany was taken seriously enough at the time. Several months later, at a meeting of the Tizard Committee, Wimperis told the members that 'the Air Council was anxious that the possible development of a destructive beam should not be forgotten' but that 'if at any time the outlook regarding a destructive beam appeared promising, further funds and staff would be provided'.[30]

Watson-Watt did not believe that the destructive beam was a feasible proposition, since the vast amount of power it would need could not be produced with the technical resources then available; but he suggested, as an alternative, that the approach of aircraft might be determined by the use of radio waves. He set down his ideas in a brief note entitled 'Detection and Location of Aircraft by Radio Method', and this was discussed by the Tizard Committee at their first meeting on 28 January 1935.[31] The method he advocated was based on the technique evolved by Dr E. V. (later Sir Edward) Appleton during a series of experiments carried out in the previous decade. Dr Appleton's work in the field of radio was of outstanding importance; for it provided answers to many questions which had long puzzled scientists and pointed the way to new fields of discovery. Since the beginning of the century, radio waves had been transmitted great distances round the world, but no one could offer certain proof to explain why these waves, which were known to travel in straight lines from the point of transmission, should be able to follow the curvature of the earth. The most widely accepted explanation was that contained in the theory propounded, independently, by Oliver Heaviside in Britain and A. E. Kennelly in the United States, in 1902. They suggested that the upper atmosphere of the earth contains an electrified region which will reflect radio waves, so that when the waves reach the electrified region they are reflected back to earth, and then from earth skywards to the region again, and so on over considerable distances. But this was no more than a theory, and such it remained until 1924, when Appleton devised an experiment which not only proved the existence of the electrified region, later called the ionosphere, but also measured its height above the earth. And so for the first time ever radio waves were used to measure the distance of a reflecting surface from the point of transmission. In the following year, two American scientists, Doctors Gregory Breit and Merle A. Tuve, invented the pulse-method, i.e. the transmission of short bursts of radio waves, to measure distances, and this technique was subsequently adapted and improved by Appleton in his further investigations into the nature of the ionosphere.[32]

It was, however, the engineers of the British Post Office who first drew attention to the fact that aircraft could be detected by the reflection of radio waves. During a series of experiments in short-wave communication in December 1931, they repeatedly experienced 'interference' on their receivers when aircraft were flying in the vicinity. They recorded these incidents in their report of June 1932, and it was the recollection of this report by A. F. Wilkins, a member of the Radio Department staff, which caused the matter to be brought to the notice of Watson-Watt. As has been shown, the latter suggested to the Tizard Committee the possibility of using radio waves to give warning of the approach of aircraft; and within a few weeks he had given a practical demonstration which showed the idea to be a feasible one. And so the first step was taken to open up a new field of technology which was eventually to be known as radar.[33]

From that time onwards the Government gave unstinted support to the building of the early warning system, and it is not to detract from the achievements of Watson-Watt and his staff of scientists and engineers to emphasize that without that support the chain of radar stations would probably not have been functioning in time to give warning of the German air attacks in the summer of 1940.[34] Indeed, the measure of that support may be seen as typical of the response of Government to the needs of air defence during the remaining years of peace. Official defence policy was still, apparently, founded on the counter-offensive strategy, yet at the same time the Government gave the highest priority to those instruments of defence whose sole function was to ward off air attacks on this country. Even as approval was given for work on the early warning system to begin, plans were already in being to produce a new high-speed monoplane fighter with a heavy armament. And when this aircraft, the Hurricane, came into squadron service, to be followed some time later by an even more successful fighter, the Spitfire, the policy was carried to its logical conclusion, and precedence was given to the production of fighter over bomber aircraft.

The benefits which the bomber force was eventually to derive from the development of radar lay very much in the future but they were to be of inestimable value. The construction of the early warning system was of course given first priority, but the knowledge and experience gained in this work suggested many new possibilities for the use of radar. Among the most important of these, which were proposed in the period immediately before the war and in the early part of the war, were aids to navigation and bombing, and the instruments which were produced from these ideas were to have a decisive effect on the conduct of bombing operations in the second half of the war.

Meanwhile, the Air Ministry estimates of German air expansion had been rising steadily. A forecast made at the end of 1933 assumed that Germany would possess no military aircraft at all before the second half of 1935, and only some 200 for several years after that;[35] but within a few months these figures were shown to have seriously under-estimated the planned German expansion. Information received during the first half of 1934 indicated that the Germans were working on an expansion programme which was to be completed in several stages, the first one of which was intended to produce 504 first-line aircraft by 1 October 1935. The Air Staff used this figure as the basis for a revised forecast and concluded that the best the Germans could achieve would be to double the 504 aircraft by 1939 and perhaps treble that number by 1942.[36]

It is one of the singular ironies of the inter-war period that Winston Churchill, who as a minister in the 1920s had been a fierce and unbending advocate of retrenchment in defence expenditure, should as a back-bencher in the 1930s have become an equally consistent advocate of re-armament. Early in 1934, he began his campaign, both inside Parliament and in the country, to impress upon the Government the seriousness of the threat which German air expansion posed for this country. In a speech in the House of Commons on 7 February 1934, he painted a lurid picture of the damage which might be inflicted on London in an air war, talking of 'the crash of bombs exploding ... and cataracts of masonry and fire and smoke'. In later speeches he produced detailed, though not always accurate, statistics to support his claim that Air Ministry predictions of the expansion of the German Air Force were seriously in error. He frequently repeated his claim that the Government was grossly under-estimating both the scale and pace of German rearmament, and he predicted that Germany would soon reach air parity with Britain.

The first jolt to the Government's confident belief that Britain was still very much stronger than Germany in the air came from a casual remark made by Hitler to Sir John Simon, the Foreign Secretary, in March 1935. The British minister had gone to Berlin to explore the possibility of reaching agreement on the limitation of air arms, and during the course of the meeting between the two men Hitler had boasted that the German Air Force (whose existence had been officially admitted only two weeks before) had already reached equality in numbers with Britain's metropolitan air force and would soon attain parity with the French metropolitan and African air forces. It was discovered that the Germans estimated the total strength of Britain's air force to be about 850 aircraft – an accurate enough figure – and that of the French air forces to be about 2,000 aircraft. If this claim was to be believed, then Britain's expansion scheme which was intended to provide a force of 960 home-based aircraft by April 1939 was manifestly inadequate.[37]

The Cabinet were seriously disturbed by Hitler's statement and at once called for a new plan to increase the strength of the home-based force. A further expansion, however, was the last thing the Air Staff wanted. Even the modest targets set by Scheme A were proving difficult to attain. The British aircraft industry did not possess the productive capacity to meet the demands being made upon it, and the training facilities in the Air Force were too limited to increase the output of trained aircrews without a lowering of standards.[38] In any case, the Air Staff thought that Hitler's claim was greatly exaggerated; that is if it was intended to mean that the German Air Force had already matched the strength of the home-based force in fully trained and equipped first-line squadrons. They estimated that Germany's current phase of expansion, far from aiming at a target of 2,000 aircraft, was more likely designed to produce about 1,500 first-line aircraft by 1 April 1937. Nevertheless, Lord Londonderry, the Secretary of State for Air, sounded a note of caution for the future. 'We are at present', he wrote, 'and for the next three years, at least, far ahead of the German Air Force in efficiency. The position as to reserves, however, is less satisfactory and there is reason to believe that the organisation of the aircraft industry for war purposes in Germany is already in advance of that in this country'.[39]

As was to be expected, the new plan (Scheme B) which Sir Edward Ellington submitted to the Cabinet was intended to provide the best possible defence for the least possible expansion. The plan was based on the premise that numerical parity should be sought only in bomber aircraft, while different criteria should be applied in deciding the requirements in other types of aircraft. For example, the provision of fighter aircraft should depend upon the size of area to be defended and the probable scale and intensity of attack. Or again, the number of aircraft required for coastal duties should be determined by the length of coastline to be patrolled. The Cabinet would not however accept these proposals, and conscious of the growing pressure both in Parliament and in the country for a large-scale expansion of the Air Force, they appointed a ministerial sub-committee under the chairmanship of Sir Philip Cunliffe-Lister to advise them on what action should be taken to implement the Government's declared policy of maintaining parity with the strongest air force within striking distance of the United Kingdom.[40]

The Air Parity Sub-Committee interpreted the term 'air parity' in a very different way from the Air Staff and ruled that Britain must seek to achieve numerical equality with the total first-line strength of the German Air Force. In order to determine the next stage of expansion, Hitler's boast to have about 850 first-line aircraft, the current strength of Britain's metropolitan air force, must be accepted at face value; and in addition, it must be assumed that this number was to be increased to 1,500 by 1 April 1937. On the basis of these recommendations, the Air Staff prepared a new expansion plan (Scheme C) which aimed at producing 123 squadrons of 1,512 aircraft by 1 April 1937, and this submission was approved by the Cabinet in May 1935. From the point of view of the established Air Staff doctrine, the new scheme was more orthodox than Scheme A, in that it restored the balance between bomber and fighter aircraft. There were to be 68 bomber squadrons with 816 aircraft as against 35 fighter squadrons with 420 aircraft.[41]

Even after the introduction of the new expansion scheme, Winston Churchill still continued to insist that Germany was drawing ahead of Britain in air strength at an ever-increasing rate. In a private letter sent in August 1935 to the new Secretary of State for Air, Sir Philip Cunliffe-Lister, he maintained that the German 'lead in the air is growing hourly greater';[42] and in a paper submitted to the Air Ministry in the same month he argued that even if we reached our target of 1,500 first-line aircraft by 1 April 1937 we still would not have attained parity, since the German first-line strength would have reached 2,000 aircraft by that date.[43] The Air Staff note prepared in reply to Churchill's paper still gave the estimated German first-line strength as 1,500 by 1 April 1937;[44] but the Chief of the Air Staff had already accepted the possibility that a further scheme to increase the strength of the metropolitan air force to some 2,000 aircraft might soon be necessary.[45]

However, the new expansion scheme could do nothing to improve the striking power of the bomber force. The only medium bomber then in service, the Boulton Paul Overstrand, was not modern enough to put into mass production, and the light bombers could not operate against Germany except from continental bases; and since none of the new aircraft would be available in any numbers before 1937, the Air Staff had no alternative but to equip a substantial number of squadrons with the light bombers which were still not obsolete. This meant that until the arrival of the new types – the Fairey P 27/32 (Battle), the Armstrong Whitworth B 3/34 (Whitley), and the two B 9/32 designs from Vickers and Handley Page (Wellington and Hampden respectively) – the medium and heavy bomber squadrons would have to be equipped with aircraft that were no more than stop-gaps. Scheme C was in fact merely an expedient to accelerate Britain's air expansion as Scheme A had been to launch it: it certainly did not provide for a bomber force capable of operating effectively against Germany.

During this period, the German expansion programme was following a somewhat similar course. In 1935 the bomber force was in the main equipped with aircraft of inadequate performance, but plans were already in being to re-arm it with aircraft which would transform its operational capability. It will be evident that the speed at which this re-arming could be carried out would be a crucial factor in determining the length of time that would be required to prepare the German Air Force for war. The British Air Staff estimated that the re-arming would be completed in three years and were convinced that at the end of that time the German bomber force would be equipped with high-speed aircraft capable of bombing many parts of Britain direct from bases in Germany.[46]

A frequent criticism levelled against the British Air Staff is that they were entirely mistaken in their estimate of the function which German air power was intended to perform in a major war of the future. It is often asserted that the German Air Force was designed and equipped primarily to give tactical support to the land forces in a succession of short and decisive campaigns and that it was quite unfitted to undertake a long-term offensive against this country at long range. However, the considerable evidence we now possess relating to German air rearmament from 1935 to the outbreak of war does not reveal anything of the clear-cut line of development one would expect if, as is suggested, the air force was being prepared for one specific function.

It will be remembered that General von Seeckt, the Chief of the Army Command in the period immediately after the First World War, had made plans to ensure the eventual revival of German air power. He based his thinking on the concept of an independent strategic air force and this concept was to dominate German air policy for many years to come. Up to 1933 this concept was expressed in a general preference for using air power to make direct attacks against an enemy's war-making capacity; but after the advent to power of the Nazi party, attention was focussed on the specific requirements of the force that would be needed in the war against the ultimate enemy in Hitler's plan of conquest, the Soviet Union.

This then was the main influence which determined the policy of the first German Chief of the Air Staff, General Walther Wever. Wever was one of the small group of outstandingly able officers whom von Seeckt had brought together in the early 1920s as a kind of air staff at the Defence Ministry. Among the other members of this group were Felmy, Sperrle, Kesselring and Stumpff, and all of these were destined to attain the highest ranks in the German Air Force.[47]

Wever was an ardent supporter of Hitler and his plans for a new Germany, and he saw it as his primary duty to plan for the type of air force that would be needed for the coming war with the Soviet Union. He envisaged a bomber force equipped with large four-engined aircraft which would be capable of striking at targets deep in Soviet territory. A specification for the projected aircraft, which was known officially as the Uralbomber, was drawn up by the Air Ministry, and the firms of Junkers and Dornier were invited to produce designs. By the early part of 1936 the prospects for the new aircraft were decidedly encouraging. The two manufacturers had produced satisfactory prototypes, the Ju 89 and the Do 19, and in spite of some problems caused by the inadequate power of the engines, there was every reason to believe that the aircraft would be entering squadron service within two years.[48]

At this point the German Air Force suffered a setback from which, it might be argued, it never recovered. On 3 June 1936 Wever was killed when the aircraft he was piloting crashed on take off; and his death marked the beginning of a period of dissension and intrigue at the highest levels of the Air Force which seriously retarded the operational development of the service and which came to an end only with the defeat of Germany in 1945. During his tenure of office Wever had established excellent relations with the Air Staff and with the various operational units; but more significantly he was able to advance his plans without antagonizing either of his ambitious and ruthless superiors, Goering and Milch, and in the light of subsequent events this was no mean achievement. In view of the diverse backgrounds and personalities of the men who directed the German Air Force, the period of relative harmony which existed under Wever's leadership was perhaps unnatural; but whatever the truth of this assertion, no comparable period of steady, unhindered progress is recorded in the subsequent history of Goering's Luftwaffe.

After Wever's death there was a steady decline in interest in the four-engined bomber, but even as late as the spring of 1937 the Ju 89 and the Do 19 were still listed as aircraft being developed for full-scale production. Soon afterwards, however, Goering gave instructions for work on the four-engined aircraft to be halted. The most obvious reason for this change in direction was that the greater amount of material required for the larger aircraft would have slowed down the numerical expansion of the Air Force, and this was a situation that Goering was not prepared to accept. At the same time there was a growing preference among the Air Staff for the shorter range tactical support aircraft. The change in emphasis from a mainly strategic to a mainly tactical policy occurred slowly at first, but after the success of the German air tactical units in the civil war in Spain it received a strong impetus.[49]

Nevertheless, there was still considerable support within the German Air Force for the four-engined aircraft, and an attempt was made to rehabilitate the heavy bomber programme. In 1938 the Heinkel company was authorized to produce a design for a four-engined bomber. The aircraft manufactured to this specification, the He 177, was beset by many technical problems, but its eventual failure was brought about, not so much by any inherent weakness in the design of the aircraft, as by the lack of interest in the project among the air leaders, who were now preoccupied with the concept of tactical support, and in particular with dive-bombing.[50]

The British Air Staff interpreted the situation in Germany as being one in which the Air Force was concentrating its efforts on building up the greatest number of twin-engined bombers in the shortest possible time, while still retaining the option to switch the emphasis to the four-engined type at any time. This impression was strengthened not only because of information received about the revival of interest in the strategic bomber, but also because Germany had, during this period, produced two efficient four-engined transport aircraft, the Focke-Wulf 200 (Condor) and the Ju 90, both of which, it was believed, could be modified in design to produce a military type with the minimum of effort and delay. As has been noted, the British Air Staff had long been convinced that transport aircraft could with ease be converted for use as bombers.

It is somewhat fallacious to argue, as is sometimes done, that since the Germans possessed no heavy long-range aircraft they were in no position to carry out effective strategic bombing of this country. It is true that the concept of strategic warfare as conceived by Wever in his plans for a war with the Soviet Union had been modified in the German Air Force since the Uralbomber project had been dropped; but that is not to say that the use of medium bombers in the strategic role, that is, to attack the vital centres of an enemy in preparation for the final assault by the German army, in a campaign in the West, would be any the less effective than the use of heavy bombers over the greater distances involved in a war in the East. It cannot reasonably be maintained that the German strategic offensive against Britain in 1940 and 1941 failed mainly because the attacking force was equipped with the wrong type of aircraft, though this may be accounted a relevant factor. There is little doubt that the massive German attacks against this country in the summer of 1940 failed largely because the German Air Staff, like their counterparts in Britain, seriously underestimated the ascendancy which the new multi-gun fighter had attained over the bomber in daylight operations. The poorly armed Heinkels and Dorniers, even with defending fighters in close attendance, were no less vulnerable to fighter attack than the better armed but unescorted Wellingtons had been in the early months of the war.

Nor can it be maintained that the night attacks on British cities which lasted from October 1940 to May 1941 were ineffective, if effectiveness is to be judged by the scale of injury which was inflicted on the major centres of population throughout the country. It is true that these night raids did not succeed in bringing Britain to her knees, as Goering had intended that they should, but the failure to achieve this aim can hardly be attributed to the shortcomings of the aircraft employed, though again this factor may have played its part. The inadequacy of the preparations for an offensive on such a scale and the lack of a consistent strategic policy were far greater weaknesses; but the crucial factor in this failure was Hitler's less than enthusiastic support for the campaign. Although he countenanced the attempt to remove the last area of resistance in Western Europe, he did not set great store on the outcome of the campaign, believing that Britain could be dealt with at leisure when other more pressing problems had been eliminated. And so, when the night operations against Britain began to intrude on his preparations for the assault against the Soviet Union, he ordered them to be brought to an end.

In May 1935, Lord Weir, who had been the Air Minister at the end of the First World War, accepted an invitation from the Air Ministry to advise on the many industrial problems arising from the expansion programme. Soon after taking up his duties, Lord Weir put a number of questions to various members of the Air Staff, and the papers which he received in answer to these questions indicated the trend of Air Staff thought on a number of topics, ranging from the types of aircraft and equipment required for the bomber force to the operational tactics to be employed in a war with Germany.[51]

All the papers submitted to Lord Weir showed that there was a growing concern among the Air Staff about the formidable threat which the new multi-gun fighter would pose for the day bomber. They believed that the bombers 'must be expected to be engaged by fighters, perhaps more often than not, in the course of their missions' and that they would be able to survive in combat only if they were provided with a more powerful armament. It was not merely a question of increasing the number of conventionally mounted guns, since this would not necessarily lead to a worthwhile increase in effective fire-power. The manually operated free-firing guns with which most aircraft were then equipped were extremely difficult to handle in the slipstream of a high-speed aircraft. The only practical answer was to enclose the guns in power-operated turrets. This type of armament had been tried experimentally with the Boulton Paul Overstrand and had brought about a dramatic improvement in the power and accuracy of the bomber's fire. Unfortunately, the solving of one problem led to the creation of others. These turrets were so heavy and bulky that they could be fitted only to the medium and heavy bombers, and even then they could not be accommodated without causing some difficulties for the designers.[52]

This firm requirement for a powerful armament in the bomber of the future seemed to rule out the light bomber for use in a war against Germany; but Lord Weir had already posed the question as to whether it would be possible to produce a light bomber of sufficient speed to enable it to operate without defensive armament. It was truly unfortunate that the forerunner of one of the most outstanding light bombers ever produced should have made its appearance at the very time that Air Staff opinion was (rightly) turning away from this type of aircraft. The De Havilland Comet Racer, the DH 88, from which the Mosquito of the Second World War was directly developed, first attracted attention by winning the MacRobertson Air Race from England to Australia in 1934. The Comet had a large load-carrying capacity for its size and power and was faster than all but the most modern fighter in service with the Air Force; and in view of Lord Weir's question about the feasibility of the unarmed bomber it was inevitable that the impressive performance of this aircraft should evoke comment from the Air Staff.

The Air Staff did in fact admit that the Comet was a remarkable aircraft; but they believed that its great success should be attributed, not to anything inherently superior in the concept of the aircraft, but to the fact that it had progressed from design to production in such a short space of time that the manufacturers had been able to incorporate in it all the technical improvements made up to 1933. They pointed out that in contrast to this swift progress the aircraft which came into service in the Air Force in 1934 were built to 1929 specifications − a situation made inevitable by the severe financial restrictions − and were therefore much less up to date. The Air Staff were convinced that the lead which the Comet had established over contemporary aircraft would be lost as soon as the new fighters came into service. 'The lesson to be learned from the Comet', they concluded, 'is not that a bomber can be made, by stripping it of its defence, so much faster that it needs no defence, but that the watch kept upon technical progress must be so close and alert and the procedure for producing fresh design so rapid that an enemy cannot steal a march upon us in that way.'[53]

The outstanding wartime success of the Mosquito may suggest that the Air Staff were mistaken in their judgement not to develop a light bomber of this type; but when it is remembered that strategic planning at that time was concerned primarily with daylight operations, this decision was clearly the most rational one to make. In 1935 the only clear indication of future developments in military aviation was that the next generation of fighters would be greatly superior to the bombers in speed, fire-power and manoeuvrability; and in the light of this certain knowledge, the Air Staff were fully justified in refusing to contemplate the production of an aircraft which would have to match the performance of the short-range interceptor at least in speed and ceiling, and at the same time carry a useful bombload. There seemed to be only one practicable answer to this problem of defence, and that was to equip the bombers with a sufficiently powerful armament so that they could, by flying in tight formations, meet the fighters on equal terms, in much the same way as the day bombers had done in the First World War.

The decision to make the bomber self-defending was a pointer to the answer to Lord Weir's query as to the feasibility of using fighter aircraft to escort the bomber formations. Indeed, the Air Staff were no more convinced of the usefulness of escort fighters than they had been in 1923 when the tactics for the bomber force were discussed at some length, and they advanced the same arguments to support their view. They stated that single-seat fighters armed with fixed forward firing guns could easily be drawn away from the bomber formation by enemy fighters; and that if that should happen, they would have great difficulty in regaining station after combat, since the heavy load of fuel they would have to carry would reduce their speed to little above that of the bombers. It was felt that two-seat fighters might well be able to maintain station in the face of enemy attack, but even if that were possible, they would still not be able to give more effective protection than the bombers could provide for themselves.

Towards the end of 1935, when a fairly clear picture of the needs of the bomber force in terms of aircraft and equipment was beginning to emerge, Sir Edward Ellington determined to resolve his own doubts about the need for a light bomber in the striking force. 'It seems to me doubtful', he wrote, 'whether in reality the Light Bomber, with its short range and small load, has any value in a European war against such a country as Germany'. He called for advice on this matter from various members of the Air Staff, and, presumably to satisfy himself that the views expressed were based on sound reasoning, he asked them to support their conclusions with detailed information relating to the principal differences — cost, performance, bombload and so on — between the light and medium bomber.[54]

In response to this enquiry, the Operational Research Branch expressed a strong conviction that there was no place for the light bomber in a war of the future in which the bomber must expect to be engaged by hostile aircraft on the flights both to and from the target. At that time the light bomber was intended to defend itself 'by a combination of ... evasion by speed and ability in formation to put up an approximately equal volume of fire to that of the contemporary two-gun fighters'; but neither of these tactics would afford any certain protection in the future. It was true that the most modern light bomber could attain speeds approaching 300 m.p.h., yet at the same time the latest fighters were capable of speeds in excess of 300 m.p.h. and were armed with eight machine guns; so that even with its improved performance the light bomber would have no better chance of evading interception, and if it were intercepted would not be able to 'beat off or survive an attack by eight gun single-seat fighters of the modern era'. Indeed, it was felt that the only way to ensure the survival of the light bomber would be to transform it 'into something resembling the medium bomber class, which fits well with our ever increasing requirements of load and range'.[55]

The Deputy Chief of the Air Staff, Air Vice-Marshal C. L. Courtney, expressed very much the same view, stating that there was 'no justification for keeping the light bomber in its present form'. He pointed out that the main characteristics of the light bomber which had attracted the Air Ministry in the past — its cheapness to manufacture and operate, for example – had been achieved at the expense of range and bombload, the two most important considerations in the current situation. Even so, it was not merely a question of increasing the endurance and carrying capacity of the present type of light bomber: the crucial problem was to find room for all the equipment that a long-range bomber would have to carry. It was impossible, for instance, to install the necessary armaments and bomb aiming equipment in an aircraft the size of the light bomber. Nor did he see any way of overcoming the problems caused by the lack of space. 'There has always been', he wrote,

> great difficulty in fitting into the small fuselage all the various items of equipment required, and even if they could be fitted in, they constitute too large a proportion of the total weight. For instance, we cannot afford to put an automatic pilot into a light bomber and the fitting of wireless equipment or camera, the navigational equipment, ammunition for the rear gun etc. have always been a source of much difficulty.[56]

The longest and most detailed appreciation was submitted by the Deputy Director of Plans, Group Captain A.T. Harris, who added further weight to the case against the light bomber. He believed that in view of the importance which the Germans attached to the long-range bomber we should concentrate our efforts on producing the type of aircraft which would give the best performance both in range and bombload. There was no doubt that the medium bomber was incomparably superior to the light bomber in both these respects; yet even within the medium bomber class the twin-engined aircraft was preferable to one with a single engine, for it was only with two engines that the high degree of reliability needed for all-weather operations both by day and night could be achieved. Group Captain Harris also reinforced the argument that it would be impossible to stow away in the light bomber all the equipment necessary for long-range operations.[57]

Sir Edward Ellington was left in no doubt as to the Air Staff's views on the light bomber, and all that remained for him to do was to record his decision to work for 'the gradual elimination of the present light bomber for European warfare'.[58]

In the second half of 1935 the already dangerous situation in Europe took a turn for the worse. In October of that year, Italy attacked the African state of Abyssinia, a backward country but, like Italy, a member of the League of Nations; and although Britain and France severely censured Italy for this act of aggression they received little support from other members of the League. Britain then took the lead in imposing limited economic sanctions upon Italy, but when these measures failed to stop Italy from continuing the war, she recoiled from applying what was then considered to be the ultimate sanction, that of oil, fearing that such an action would lead to war with Italy. The limited sanctions did in fact cause Italy considerable economic difficulties, but they did not prevent her from winning the war in Africa. Britain on the other hand paid a high price for her intervention, for the long-standing friendship between Britain and Italy was brought to an end and Italy joined Germany and Japan on the list of potential enemies.

One important effect of this crisis was to focus attention on the fact that of the three potential enemies only Germany was within air striking distance of Britain; and this point was underlined in a report which had recently been passed to the Government. In 1934 the Joint Planning Committee of the three staffs had been charged with the task of defining the role which each of the services would play in the defence of Britain. The committee spent two years preparing their final report, but in August 1935 they produced an interim report which dealt exclusively with the possible courses of action open to Germany. They also considered the element of danger which each course of action would pose for this country; and their investigations pointed to the conclusion that the most dangerous situation would arise if Germany should attempt a 'knock-out blow' from the air. They thought that Germany might seek to achieve this either by seizing the Low Countries and building up an offensive at short range or by launching an immediate attack from bases in Germany. Their own view was that Germany would probably favour the first course of action.[59] Once again the threat from the air was judged to be the greatest potential danger to this country; and this assessment, coming as it did from a well-informed official source, had the effect of increasing the fears already felt by many members of the Government that air attacks on our major centres, of which London and the ports would be the principal targets, might well inflict a crippling blow on Britain at the very outset of the war.

CHAPTER FIVE

RE-ARMING THE BOMBER FORCE
1936−7

The intelligence received from Germany during the course of 1935 seemed to confirm the Government's worst fears. The various estimates of German air expansion all pointed unmistakably to the rapidly growing power of the German Air Force. And equally disquieting were the indications of the pace at which the German aircraft industry was developing and expanding. It was now obvious that a re-assessment of Britain's air defence needs had become a matter of urgency. This was carried out by the Ministerial Committee on Defence Policy and Requirements (previously called the Ministerial Committee on Disarmament) and the recommendations submitted by this committee to the Cabinet in February 1936 led directly to a further expansion of the home-based force.

The new expansion programme, which was designated Scheme F (Schemes D and E had been drawn up but not proceeded with) was the most significant of all the pre-war expansion schemes, since it marked the beginning of Britain's preparations to create a bomber force which would be a credible weapon of war.[1] It also marked a change in the character and purpose of the bomber force. The Ministerial Committee were convinced that in the event of war the Germans would despatch highly mobile forces at great speed into the Low Countries in order to establish air bases there before the British Expeditionary Force could reach the continent. The Committee agreed that such an attempt must be prevented at all costs, and concluded that the recent advances in the range and bombload of aircraft would endow the bomber force with the necessary power to achieve this. They therefore submitted recommendations which were intended to transform the striking force into an offensive weapon capable of intervening rapidly and decisively on the continent, instead of being merely an instrument of defence intended to stave off defeat in the air over Britain. In a memorandum prepared for the Committee of Imperial Defence, the Chancellor of the Exchequer, Neville Chamberlain, was at pains to explain that the policy designed to convert 'the Air Force from a defensive organ into a weapon of aggression with unprecedented powers of destruction' had been formulated by the members of the Committee themselves and had not been suggested in any plan submitted to them by the service staffs.[2]

The most important feature of Scheme F was the provision to re-equip the light bomber squadrons with the new medium bombers. The light aircraft such as the Harts, Hinds and Wallaces were to be replaced by the medium Battles, Blenheims and Hampdens, so that with the disappearance of the light bombers the number of medium bomber squadrons would be raised from 18 to 48. The proposed number of squadrons in the bomber force was to remain, as under Scheme C, at 68; but the total number of aircraft was to be increased from 816 to 990 by raising the initial establishment of over half the medium squadrons from 12 to 18 aircraft. Thus, in place of the Scheme C force of light, medium and heavy bombers in the ratio of 3:2:2 there was to be created a force of medium and heavy bombers in the ratio of 5:2 in squadrons and 3:1 in aircraft. The new force was intended to be ready for war by the spring of 1939, and for that reason Scheme F aimed at providing the 225 per cent reserves — 75 per cent for immediate allocation to the squadrons and 150 per cent war reserve — which were considered essential to sustain an air offensive in a major war.

It must be emphasized that no practicable scheme of rearmament could have been produced before Scheme F because hitherto the designs of the new medium and heavy bombers had been largely speculative. As late as the summer of 1935 Lord Weir could still point to the necessary risks of relying upon 'the advanced, and to some extent, untried designs of the Medium and Heavy bombers'.[3] By February 1936, however, the prospects for the future were significantly clearer: the prototypes of all the new bombers had already been completed or were near to completion, and although none of them had yet been tested in the air, there was sufficient evidence to justify reasonable confidence in their success.

The initiation of the new expansion programme was followed by a major reorganization of the command structure in the Air Force; and the most significant change to be made was the replacement of the Air Defence of Great Britain Command, with its bomber and fighter components, by two independent commands, Bomber Command and Fighter Command, which were placed directly under the control of the Air Council. Since its establishment in 1925 the Air Defence of Great Britain Command had been essentially a bomber command with a fighter force attached to it. The Commander-in-Chief, who was directly responsible to the Air Council, was in fact the commander of the bomber element of the force and he was expected to devote most of his energies to the direction and development of the counter-offensive force.

During the first period of expansion this was a feasible arrangement, since it was planned to form three bomber groups as against a single fighter group. While France was considered to be the only potential enemy and the chances of war seemed remote, a single Fighting Area was all that was required to direct the fighter squadrons which formed a protective cover stretching from Salisbury Plain to the Wash. But when Germany replaced France as the potential enemy a wider area was exposed to attack, and the fighter screen was extended from the Wash to Middlesbrough. The increased fighter force which this involved would be spread over a much wider area and could no longer be controlled effectively by one headquarters. It was therefore proposed to establish three fighter groups; and this was in addition to the expansion of the bomber force which was eventually to be reorganized in six groups.[4]

It was now recognized that the task of directing an organization as large as the Air Defence of Great Britain Command was to become would be too heavy a burden for one officer to carry. There was also the fear that the growing complexity of fighter defence would divert the Commander-in-Chief's attention from his primary function of developing the bomber force. It was therefore to be expected that the Air Council would agree unanimously that some decentralization of command was essential. It was accepted that this could be done in one of two ways. In the first, the Commander-in-Chief would retain overall responsibility for the Command, while two officers subordinate to him were appointed to command the bomber and fighter forces. The alternative to this would be to create two independent commands, each under the direct control of the Air Council. Opinion within the Air Council was evenly divided as to which would be the better course of action, but after considerable debate it was decided to form two separate commands, Bomber and Fighter. The Commander-in-Chief of the Air Defence of Great Britain Command, Air Marshal Sir John Steel, became, by a natural transition, the first head of Bomber Command, while Air Marshal Sir Hugh Dowding, the Air Member for Research and Development since 1930, became the first Commander-in-Chief of Fighter Command.

In the long term, the new command structure created a barrier which prevented the most effective use of Britain's air power. It caused the division between the offensive and defensive elements of the Air Force to become even more marked, and it inhibited the interchange of information and experience between the two commands. As a result, there was little co-ordination between Bomber and Fighter Commands, each one concentrating on its own specialist role; and exercises in which both forces were involved were rarely undertaken. It may, however, be argued that this arrangement allowed a greater concentration of effort on the new defence system than would have been possible if Fighter Command had remained one part of a larger command in which the development of the offensive would have been given the highest priority. As it was, Sir Hugh Dowding was able to direct his attention solely towards the perfecting of a system of fighter defence which, as was becoming increasingly apparent, would have to bear the brunt of enemy air attacks, at least in the early part of the war. And it was the defence system constructed by him which defeated Goering's Luftwaffe in the summer of 1940, and in so doing stemmed the tide of German advance in the west.

It has been shown that Britain's re-armament plans were based on the assumption that her armed forces would not be called upon to fight a major war before 1939; but no sooner had these plans been approved than a further deterioration in the world situation threatened to undermine the basis on which that assumption was made. In the main, these new dangers may be traced, directly or indirectly, to the unsuccessful intervention of the League of Nations in the Italo-Abyssinian war. Britain had failed to get the necessary support from the League in her efforts to impose economic sanctions on Italy, and her action produced no other effect than to drive the Italian dictator, Mussolini, into seeking closer ties with his fellow dictator in Germany. But perhaps the most serious consequence of the League's failure to take effective action against Italy was the encouragement it gave to the militant regimes in Germany and Japan, which could now be assured that the League did not possess the will to resist even the most blatant aggression.

Hitler was quick to take advantage of the deep preoccupation of the European nations with the Abyssinian crisis. On 7 March 1936, having denounced the Locarno Treaty on the ground that it had been abrogated by the alliance which France and the Soviet Union had contracted in 1935, he ordered German troops to re-occupy the zone of the Rhineland which had been demilitarized under the Treaty of Versailles. And with that incredible audacity which was the mark of Hitler's 'diplomacy', he accompanied this flagrant breach of the Treaty by the offer of a 25-year non-aggression pact with France, Belgium and Holland, with Britain and Italy as guarantors. In addition, he offered to sponsor a Western European Air Pact and to sign non-aggression treaties with his immediate neighbours to the east and south. The British Government interpreted this offer as a move by Hitler to secure his position in the west in preparation for an attack on the Soviet Union, France's new ally. Nevertheless, Britain sent a note to Germany asking for clarification of these proposals, but no reply was ever received.

When it became evident that neither Britain nor France was prepared to take action to force Germany to withdraw her troops from the Rhineland, Leopold, King of the Belgians, asked that his country be relieved of its obligations under the Locarno Treaty. The demilitarization of the Rhineland had been a vital element in the security of Belgium, and the King obviously felt that his country had more to gain by reverting to a status of neutrality than by relying upon such aid as Britain and France could provide. In the circumstances, Britain and France had little choice but to accede to this request. The change in Belgium's status had an immediate effect on Britain's defence plans. Henceforward, no advance arrangements could be made for the defence of Belgium. Military assistance could be sent only if Germany actually invaded Belgium, and by the time British forces arrived on the continent it would probably be too late. This restriction applied equally to the Air Force. No air bases would be available on Belgian territory before the outbreak of war, and this fact served to emphasize the importance of the type of bomber which could reach targets in Germany direct from bases in Britain.

As has been stated, Britain's quarrel with Italy seriously damaged relations between the two countries and Mussolini began to draw closer to Hitler. On the outbreak of the Spanish Civil War in 1936, the two dictators worked together to send arms and men to support General Franco's rebellion against the Republican Government, and in the following year they expressed their common aims in the foundation of the Rome–Berlin Axis. Meanwhile, in November 1936, Japan and Germany, the aggressive powers of east and west, forged a link between themselves by signing the Anti-Comintern Pact, an agreement which was directed against the Soviet Union with whom France, to secure herself against Germany, had signed a treaty of mutual assistance in 1935. Once again, the worsening of the world situation had eroded the foundations on which Britain's rearmament calculations were based.

During the course of 1936 Winston Churchill intensified his campaign against the Government's air rearmament policy. In particular, he rejected the figures relating to German air expansion which the Government used as a basis for assessing the defence needs of the country. He was convinced that the Air Staff's estimates of 1,500 first-line aircraft by 1 April 1937, rising to a total of 2,000 by the beginning of 1939, were wide of the mark. In July 1936, he led a deputation of Conservative members of both Houses of Parliament to the Prime Minister, Stanley Baldwin, to express concern at the slow growth of our air defences in view of the rapid expansion of the German Air Force. He told the Prime Minister that the French Government had informed him in confidence that they estimated the German air strength to be 1,236 first-line aircraft at the beginning of May 1936. On the basis of this figure, he estimated that the present German strength would be 1,556, with a possible total of 2,000 being reached by the end of 1936. 'The Air Staff', he concluded, 'thought the French estimate too high. Personally I think it is too low. The number of service machines constructed in Germany and the number of pilots trained leads me to the conclusion that they could already put into action simultaneously nearer 2,000 than 1,500 aeroplanes. Moreover, there is no reason to assume that they mean to stop at 2,000.'

Churchill then questioned whether the Government had given sufficient thought to the problems concerned with the defence of the civil population which 'might have to endure an ordeal in our great cities and vital feeding ports such as no community has ever been subjected to before'. He was particularly concerned about the vulnerability of 'London and its seven or eight million inhabitants' to air attack, believing that the greatest danger might well be caused by the use of incendiary devices such as the thermite bomb. 'Nearly two years ago', he stated,

> I explained in the House of Commons the danger of an attack by thermite bombs. These small bombs, little bigger than an orange, had ... been manufactured by millions in Germany. A single medium aeroplane can scatter 500. One must expect in a small raid literally tens of thousands of these bombs which burn through from storey to storey .... One must expect that a proportion of heavy bombs would be dropped at the same time, and that water, light, gas, telephone systems etc would be seriously damaged .... Nothing like it has ever been seen in world history. I ventured to warn the House of Commons two years ago that there would be a vast exodus of the population of London into the surrounding country. This would present to the Government problems of public order, of sanitation and food supply which would dominate their attention, and probably involve the use of all their disciplined forces.[5]

The Air Staff were in general agreement with the views which Churchill expressed to the Prime Minister, but they could not accept his figures for the likely growth of the German Air Force during the next two and a half years. They did, however, agree with his view that the Germans were in a strong enough position to accelerate their expansion programme whenever they wished. Indeed, within a few months they began to suspect that the Germans were planning to push their expansion to the utmost. Their information suggested that the German air strength at the beginning of 1939 would probably be nearer 2,500 than 2,000 first-line aircraft, and that of these the bomber strength would be 1,700.[6] It was therefore clear that, if these figures were accurate, the current Air Force expansion scheme would not provide a force comparable in numbers to that of the German Air Force in 1939. Even if Scheme F was completed according to schedule, the Metropolitan

Air Force would then comprise only 1,736 first-line aircraft, of which 1,022 would be bombers; and of the striking force less than half would be capable of attacking targets in Germany direct from bases in Britain.[7]

There was now an urgent need to increase the first-line strength of the home-based force by 1939, but in view of the Government's ruling that defence commitments must not be allowed to interfere with normal trade the likelihood of attaining the necessary increase seemed remote in the extreme. The crux of the problem was that the British aircraft industry had already reached saturation point with orders for new aircraft. Scheme C had placed a heavy burden on the industry and this was further increased with the introduction of Scheme F. It is true that Lord Weir had done much to improve the output of aeroplanes and aero-engines and was then organizing a scheme to introduce other sectors of industry into aircraft production;[8] but a great deal more needed to be done if a significant increase in production was to be achieved. It was necessary, for example, to introduce overtime and shift working as a first priority, but such measures would not only have been costly to operate but would also have involved the recruitment of large numbers of skilled men for an industry which the Government regarded as nonproductive so far as the country's 'business' was concerned.[9] At the same time, however, the Government were committed to the policy of attaining numerical parity with the German Air Force, and in consequence the Air Staff were driven to suggest various expedients to achieve this aim. An obvious method, and one which was used as the basis for Scheme G, was to reduce the scale of reserves, but as Sir Edward Ellington rightly observed, no genuine expansion could be achieved 'unless the output of aircraft and engines ... can be improved. I fear the reverse is likely to be the case.'[10]

In fact, Air Staff policy was now largely determined by the output of aircraft and aeronautical equipment, and this is clearly reflected in a number of meetings which were held at the Air Ministry in December 1936 and January 1937. During these meetings the most consistent support was given to a long-term policy which aimed to create a bomber force which would make good its lack of numerical superiority by being equipped with aircraft greatly superior in range and bombload. This proposal, however, offered no easy or straightforward alternative to the policy of building a numerically stronger force of lighter aircraft, for much more was involved than the mere problem of hauling greater bombloads over longer distances. The long-range aircraft would need a larger crew to man it and would have to carry more equipment to enable the crew to locate and bomb their targets; and all of this would add to the weight of the aircraft. Not only weight, but space also presented a difficult problem. It was no easy matter to find room in the fuselage for a mass of equipment, and at the same time provide reasonably spacious accommodation for the crew to prevent excessive fatigue on the long flights.

Among this equipment, the defensive armament would be a vital item; for with its greater range the bomber would be able to penetrate deeper into hostile territory, so increasing the length of time when it would be exposed to fighter attack. It was now recognized that the fire-power of the modern high speed fighter could be neutralized only by arming the bombers with machine guns mounted in power-operated turrets. At least two, and probably three, turrets would be needed, and the bulk and weight of these turrets would be important factors in determining the size and power of the new bombers. All the evidence pointed to the need for a large and heavy type of aircraft, and with this concept in mind the Air Staff prepared specifications for a four-engined heavy bomber (B12/36) and a twin-engined heavy-medium bomber (P13/36). From these specifications were eventually produced all the heavy bombers of the Second World War: the Stirling, Halifax, Manchester and Lancaster.[11]

It will be remembered that in 1934 the Chiefs of Staff had instructed the Joint Planning Committee — a committee of three officers, one from each service — to make a detailed study of the situation which might arise in the event of a war with Germany in 1939 and to define the part to be played by each service in the defence of Britain. In August 1935 the Committee issued an interim report, which dealt solely with the possible courses of action open to Germany, and in October 1936 produced its final report.[12] Even before the Committee began its work, the three services were generally agreed that if Germany were to launch all-out air attacks against our ports, communications and industrial centres, and if the scale and weight of such attacks could not be substantially reduced within three or four weeks, the war might well be lost. It was also agreed that the most likely method of defeating such an onslaught would be to launch a bombing counter-offensive, directed mainly against the German Air Force and the industries which supported it. It was therefore to be expected that the danger of a 'knock-out blow' from the air and the means by which it might be countered were the most important themes in the Committee's report.

The Committee believed that in 1939 Germany would almost certainly be better prepared for war than either Britain or France, and would therefore 'endeavour to exploit her preparedness by a rapid victory — within a few months'. There seemed to be two possible courses of action by which she might seek to achieve this. She might attempt to gain a decisive victory over France by striking with powerful land and air forces through the Low Countries, thus creating a favourable situation for an attack on Britain. Or she might launch an immediate air offensive against Britain, with the object of crippling that country before her war preparations were completed. The Committee were inclined to think that the Germans, keenly aware of Britain's vulnerability to air attack and fearful of the great power which Britain could develop as the war progressed, would be tempted to follow the second course.

The Committee left nothing to the imagination in their description of the situation which they believed would arise 'if Germany were to concentrate her air striking force against us, and adopt unrestricted air attack as a method of war'. Basing their assumptions on data compiled by the Air Ministry, they estimated that in the opening phase of the attack 400 tons of bombs could be dropped every 24 hours for a limited period of perhaps 30 to 40 days. If attacks on this scale were directed against ports and communications, with the aim of disrupting the receipt and distribution of food, every port in the United Kingdom might well be seriously affected within two weeks. However, the Committee thought that the danger might be still greater if the attacks were intended to break the morale of the civilian population by causing death and destruction in the great urban centres.

> Our civilian population has never been exposed to the horrors of war and the Germans may believe that if our people, and particularly our women and children, were subjected to these horrors in the most intensive forms that can be achieved through air attack, the majority would insist that surrender was preferable to continuation of the attacks.

An onslaught of this type, in which London might suffer 20,000 casualties during the first 24 hours, would cause devastation and chaos on a massive scale.

> Within a week attacks of this sort could have forced the partial evacuation of half-a-dozen of the centres of most dense population in England, forcing many millions of people to abandon their homes, caused casualties in the order of 150,000, completely disorganised telephone and telegraph communications throughout the country, and to a varying degree dislocated railway, postal, and electrical services, and the distribution of food. A very high standard of organisation by local authorities and great fortitude on the part of the whole people would be essential if a degree of order was to be maintained and loyal support given to the government.

The Committee agreed that if the war should open with an all-out air offensive against Britain neither the Navy nor the Army could bring immediate pressure to bear on Germany. Only the Air Force, or more precisely the bomber force, could exert a decisive influence on events during the vital opening phase of the war. It was, however, one thing to state a broad strategic aim, namely, to neutralize the German attacks quickly and effectively, but another to devise a plan to carry it out. It was clear that the counter-offensive would have to be directed against targets that were critical to the enemy war effort and at the same time vulnerable to air attack; but when the Committee turned their attention to this question they found it was easier to describe such targets in general terms than to name specific examples. They were able to discover only three operational schemes which seemed to offer even a remote chance of success, and of these only one was given serious consideration. The first scheme was intended to break the morale of the German people 'by methods similar to those we foresee the Germans using against us'. The second one had as its aim to 'discover and attack some target, the security of which was regarded by Germany as vital to her survival during the limited period within which she hoped to gain a decision over us'. The third was a plan to attack the bases, communications and maintenance organization of the German air striking force.

The Committee at once ruled out the first two schemes. So far as the first one was concerned, they felt that 'any attempt to demoralise the German people before German air attacks could demoralise our people would operate under severe handicap'. They accepted that Britain was in general more vulnerable to air attack than Germany, but it was the fact that London presented the Germans with such an easy and important objective that was decisive in ruling out this course of action. The second scheme seemed even less promising, since the Committee had been unable to discover any such vital target in Germany. The third scheme appeared to offer the best chance of success, but it was by no means an easy option. It was acknowledged that 'the German air striking force and its maintenance organisation is not a very satisfactory target for air attack, and there is a possibility that, notwithstanding a considerable bombing effort, we may not succeed in reducing the scale of German air attack to manageable proportions'. Nevertheless, the Committee thought that if Britain were forced by events to direct the counter-offensive against the German air striking force, there would be at least one advantage in pursuing this course of action in that 'it would result in a higher wastage in the German air striking force than in our own, so long as Germany adhered to the policy of attacking our vulnerable points'.

On the other hand, Germany might open hostilities with an attack against Belgium and France. In the event of such an attack, the employment of the bomber force would be determined by the course of events in the subsequent campaign. If an air attack against the morale of the French people should pose the most serious threat, the bomber force would be directed against the German air striking force; but if the enemy land offensive should constitute the greatest danger the force would be launched against 'the rear organisation and lines of communication' of the advancing German armies.

These then were the possible courses of action open to the bomber force in the first phase of the war. They were defensive in concept and were intended to contain the onslaught of an enemy which would possess the initiative and which would almost certainly have a more powerful striking force. As soon as the initial German offensive had been reduced to 'bearable proportions', the bomber force would then be called upon to carry the war into Germany itself. Its task would be to attack and destroy those targets which were the sources of the enemy's war potential.

The Chiefs of Staff found little that was unacceptable in the recommendations made by the Joint Planning Committee, and after due consideration prepared a paper entitled 'Planning for a War with Germany' which outlined the strategy upon which the three services were required to draw up their detailed operational plans. This document was of great significance to the Air Force, for it acknowledged the validity of certain assumptions which had long been basic to Air Staff thought. It recognized that an attack from the air represented the most serious threat to Britain and that the bomber force would play a major part in repelling such an attack; and it accepted the claim that in the second phase of the war the striking force would make a substantial contribution to final victory.

The year 1937 may be seen as a crucial one in the transformation of the bomber force into a credible weapon of war. By the end of that year all but one of the 68 squadrons of Expansion Scheme F were already formed or were in the process of formation, and the new types of aircraft, the Whitleys, Blenheims and Battles, were beginning to make their appearance in the squadrons. On the other hand, Bomber Command was thrown into turmoil by the expansion, which was taking place too quickly and on too large a scale for the very limited resources of the Air Force. In particular, the training facilities in the service were wholly inadequate to sustain the burden placed upon them by the constant formation of new squadrons. The most serious result was an acute shortage of trained aircrews and, as was inevitable in the circumstances, the flying personnel to form the nuclei of the new units had to be drawn from among the most experienced crews in the existing squadrons, a practice which resulted in a constant dilution of the skill and experience of the force as a whole. To make matters worse, there were at that time no operational training units and so the task of training recently qualified personnel up to operational standard fell upon the squadrons which were already required to undertake a good deal of elementary training.[13] The burden of this training became so heavy that the squadrons had little opportunity of improving their standard of efficiency in such important skills as navigation, bombing and air gunnery.

During the course of the year the situation deteriorated perceptibly as the force began to re-equip with the new monoplane bombers. These aircraft were fundamentally new in design and represented a revolution in flying and operational techniques which required considerable adjustment on the part of every member of the crew. The conversion of the crews to these aircraft involved a tremendous amount of re-training, and this did not exclude even the most experienced crews, the majority of whom had previously flown only in biplanes.

The situation which existed in Bomber Command at the end of 1937 was frankly admitted in the command's annual report for that year.

> During the last few years all effort has unavoidably been concentrated on the administrative problems involved in our process of expanding the Force to an extent that is really beyond its capacity; and the inevitable result has been the attenuation of efficiency in every department. Moreover, the expansion happens to have coincided with a remarkable development in the science of aviation. Sudden and sensational progress has been made within the last few years in the performance of aircraft and in the means of navigating them both in the air and from the ground. These developments have introduced operational and navigational problems hitherto unknown in the Service.[14]

The re-arming of the bomber force had in itself caused immense problems of organization and training, but these were aggravated by a severe shortage of all kinds of equipment. For example, the majority of the new aircraft were delivered to the squadrons without such basic items of equipment as gun turrets, bombsights and automatic pilots; and it was the lack of this type of equipment, coupled with a serious deficiency of much ground equipment, which prompted Sir John Steel to express his profound misgivings.

'I am concerned', he wrote to the Air Ministry, 'at the delay in the provision of the organisation and equipment which are necessary, both on the ground and in the air, before operational training and long distance flying by night and day in conditions of bad visibility can be carried to a satisfactory stage of development.'

He gave a long list of deficiencies, and one of the most serious of these was the type of direction-finding wireless equipment which was intended to provide the basic navigational aid for the bomber force.

'At present', he stated, 'the available Air Force D/F organisation is limited to two groups of M.F. D/F [medium frequency direction-finding] stations covering between them the whole country, but serving all commands and heavily overloaded' and 'no bombers are yet fitted with D/F loops, which would make them partially independent of D/F ground stations'.[15]

Sir John Steel was still grappling with these problems when he handed over his command to Air Chief Marshal Sir Edgar Ludlow-Hewitt in September 1937. The new Commander-in-Chief, later described by Sir Arthur Harris as being 'far and away the most brilliant officer I have ever met in any of the three services',[16] brought immense knowledge and experience to bear on his difficult task of preparing the bomber force for war readiness within two years. He quickly took stock of the situation, and in a letter forwarded to the Air Ministry with the Bomber Command annual report he left the Air Staff in no doubt as to how serious he judged the position to be.

> If war were to break out with any first class European power in the immediate future the prospects would be grave indeed and so long as there is any danger of war within the next twelve months or so the state of unpreparedness of this Command can only be regarded with the greatest anxiety.

In the report itself he emphasized the importance of an all-weather capability and pointed to the shortage of essential equipment as being the most serious handicap in training the force for all-weather operations.

> In any North European theatre of war bad weather conditions involving cloud, fog, snow, sleet and heavy rain are prevalent. On the other hand it has long been recognised that decisive air action will ultimately depend upon the power of the Air Force to maintain sustained attack ... It follows therefore that an air force can only expect to have a decisive effect in war if it can maintain its operations in all weathers by day and night. A fair weather air force is relatively useless and is certainly not worth the vast expenditure being poured out upon the air arm of this country. And yet today our Bomber Force is, judged from a war standard, practically useless and cannot take advantage of its new and expensive aircraft.
>
> In recent years Civil Aviation has made remarkable progress in providing for the navigation of aircraft through every kind of weather, and today the airline pilots of all the leading European and American airlines are capable of and accustomed to fly their aircraft for long periods and for great distances through thick

clouds, fog, snow and other adverse conditions. But these pilots depend upon navigational aids and homing devices, combined with an efficient and adequate D/F, meteorological, and control organisation on the ground, which are at present far from being available to Royal Air Force pilots.[17]

Indeed, Bomber Command lacked many of the facilities that were essential for all-weather flying. Only half the stations in the command possessed a meteorological section and not one was equipped with a 'blind landing' system such as Lorenz, to enable aircraft to land safely in bad weather. The provision for night flying, even in good weather conditions, was equally poor, there being a general shortage of such basic items of equipment as beacons, floodlights and electric landing Ts. The position as regards air equipment was even less satisfactory, since many of these deficiencies were caused less by a shortage of equipment already being manufactured than by the lack of equipment whose need had not been foreseen. For example, no provision had been made for a 'homing' direction-finding system which would enable the pilot or navigator to obtain accurate wireless bearings quickly and easily. Again, although the new aircraft were expected to fly at greater altitudes and in all weathers, there was no equipment in service for combating the effects of icing and precipitation: that is, for preventing ice from forming on the wings and in the instrument panel, and for keeping windscreens clear of ice, snow and rain.

As has been stated, the majority of the bomber squadrons were prevented by the pressures of expansion from carrying out more than a small fraction of their normal practice in navigation, bombing and gunnery. Although the virtual suspension of normal operational training occurred at the very time when even more intensive flying should have been undertaken to enable the crews to master the techniques of the new aircraft, this would not have produced so serious an effect if Bomber Command had possessed an experimental unit similar to the type which had already been established in Fighter Command and in Coastal Command. A unit such as this, unencumbered with the many duties which bore so heavily upon the ordinary squadrons, would have been able to concentrate on the development of bombing methods and techniques. As it was, the Commander-in-Chief's recommendation that such a unit should be formed in Bomber Command was not acted upon, with the result that the operational techniques of the bomber force showed virtually no improvement during the critical period up to the outbreak of war.

In general, the operational techniques employed by the bomber force in 1937 differed little from those that were in use at the end of the First

World War. In some cases, this was because there was little scope for change, but in others it was because the Air Staff were slow to appreciate the need to adopt new techniques, even when the experience of the war itself had indicated clearly the need for change. An example of the latter case, and one which has already been mentioned, was that of navigation. All the evidence provided both by German and British strategic operations showed the need to devise more effective methods of navigation. In Britain, the Navy had pointed the way by introducing new navigational techniques and equipment in their own squadrons, but when the two air services were amalgamated in 1918 this was soon forgotten. After the war, the Air Force, which was dominated by the thought and traditions of the military air service, reverted to the ideas held during the days of the Flying Corps, when the pilot looked over the side of his cockpit in order to establish his position with the aid of a map.

In 1937 the pilot was the only member of the crew who received any training in navigation, and so, in addition to flying the aircraft, he was expected to find his way to the target by map-reading. The observer, who was later to take over the duties of navigator, was not at that time even a full-time member of the crew, but a ground tradesman who carried out his normal duties when he was not required to fly. With this kind of approach it is not surprising to find that the requirements of navigation had been largely ignored in the design of the new aircraft. Air Commodore A. T. Harris, the commander of No. 4 Bomber Group, wrote of the 'derisory navigational provision of the Whitley, the Wellesley and the Battle',[18] and attributed this to the fact that there was no department at the Air Ministry responsible for navigational requirements. In fact, almost all the new bombers had to be modified in some way to improve the facilities for navigation. In the Hampden, for example, there was no room at all in the narrow fuselage to accommodate the navigator, and so it was necessary to remove the front gun turret from the nose of the aircraft and replace it with a navigator's compartment.[19]

At this time, too, tentative efforts were being made to discover what aids would be needed to enable the crews to navigate to their distant targets. For many years direction-finding wireless had been regarded as a useful auxiliary to the basic method of position-finding by direct observation of the ground; but when, owing to the greater operating speeds and heights of the new aircraft, it was accepted that map-reading would be a less reliable method of fixing an aircraft's position, greater importance was attached to D/F wireless as a navigational aid. The decision to place more reliance on this aid was based on nothing more than the assumption that it would prove to be effective over the long distances that the bombers were expected to operate; but in fact there was very little in the way of knowledge and experience to justify such an assumption. Owing to the lack of facilities in the Air Force, there was limited scope for using D/F wireless, and practically nothing was known of its accuracy under various conditions.

The only system operating in the Service at that time was one in which the work was done almost entirely by the ground station. The aircraft seeking aid transmitted its callsign, followed by a continuous signal of sufficient length to enable the ground station to measure the angle from which the signal was received. If the ground station worked as a single unit, it informed the aircraft of its bearing from the station. If it worked as the main station in a group of three stations, each of which took a bearing on the aircraft, it plotted the three bearings to obtain a 'fix' and notified the aircraft of its position in latitude and longitude. The aircraft's request for aid and the information given by the station were transmitted in morse code, and, depending upon whether the information required was a bearing or a position, the procedure took between two and five minutes to complete. Whenever several aircraft required aid at the same time, it was inevitable that there would be delays in providing the information; and there was also the danger that with the aircraft all working on the same frequency the information might be given to the wrong aircraft. The most obvious objection to the use of this system in wartime was that an aircraft would betray its position to the enemy by transmitting a signal. This objection could not of course be sustained in the case of aircraft which were lost or in distress while on operations; but there would still be the unacceptable (and dangerous) delays in providing information when several aircraft were seeking aid at the same time.

The alternative to this system was to equip the aircraft with a direction-finding loop aerial which would enable the wireless operator to take bearings on transmitters of known position. This would make the aircraft wholly independent of the ground stations. It was intended that the loop aerial should be a standard piece of equipment in the new aircraft, but owing to the general shortage of these aerials in 1937 none were fitted to the aircraft that were delivered to the bomber force during that year; and so the squadrons had no opportunity of testing them in the air until the following year. And even when the new equipment was received on the squadrons, the pressure of expansion prevented systematic tests from being carried out, and so almost nothing was discovered about the limitations of D/F wireless. There was little appreciation of the extent to which bearings diminished in accuracy as the distance between the aircraft and the transmitter increased; nor was there sufficient understanding of the deterioration which occurred in the accuracy of bearings taken after the hours of daylight. It is true that certain specialist officers at the Air Ministry gave warnings against placing too much reliance upon D/F wireless,[20] but these made no impression on the bomber groups, where it was believed that the existing errors in the measurement of bearings would be largely eliminated when technically more advanced equipment was provided.

Even the cursory examination which Bomber Command gave to the requirements of navigation served to underline the fact that night operations would present their own special problems. It was recognized that map-reading would prove to be an even more difficult task over unfamiliar and blacked-out terrain and that 'night effect' would diminish the accuracy of wireless bearings. There was clearly a need for a dependable secondary aid, and this need, it was felt, could best be fulfilled by astro-navigation. Since the end of the First World War this method of navigation, by which position lines are obtained by observations of various celestial bodies, was practised successfully by many of the world's leading airlines, and had been the basic navigational aid used in several pioneer flights during that period.

The instrument used to make these observations was a sextant designed specially for use in the air. It performed the same function as the traditional instrument, the marine sextant, in that it measured the angular distance between the horizontal and the celestial body being observed; but whereas the marine sextant used the sea horizon as a datum the air sextant used an artificial horizon obtained by means of a bubble clinometer incorporated in the instrument. This meant that in contrast to the marine sextant, which could be used only when the sea horizon was visible, the air or 'bubble' sextant could be used over land and sea, in all conditions of weather, and by night as well as by day. The versatility of the 'bubble' sextant was not, however, matched by its accuracy when used in flight; for the erratic manner in which the piston-engined aircraft moved through the air, even when it was being flown on the automatic pilot, caused the bubble to give false indications and induced considerable errors in the sextant readings. The sextant errors increased with the speed of the aircraft, and for that reason the type of high speed aircraft which was then coming into service with the bomber force was a most unsuitable platform for making astronomical observations.

It may be asked why the airline crews and the pioneer flyers were so successful with an instrument of such dubious accuracy. The answer is to be found partly in the slower speeds of the aircraft in which they flew and partly in the fact that they were navigators of high calibre who acquired by constant practice great skill in the use of this difficult instrument. It would therefore have been quite unrealistic to expect the average Air Force navigator, who had received only the minimum of training in this skill, to reach anything like their standard of proficiency. In fact, there were from the outset indications that he would have some difficulty in reaching even a basic level of competence.

Nevertheless, astro-navigation was introduced into the bomber force without any trials being made to determine how effective it was likely to be when used by the average squadron navigator. Without doubt, it found favour at Bomber Command because it was a self-contained aid, that is, it required no participation by an agent outside the aircraft. The navigator, it was reasoned, would require only a sextant, the relevant astronomical tables, and an accurate watch to be able to fix the position of his aircraft whenever the sky above him was clear enough for observation. Arrangements were quickly put in hand to provide the necessary training and equipment. A three weeks' course in astro-navigation for bomber pilots was organized at the School of Navigation, instructions were issued for the production of special astronomical tables which would reduce to a minimum the work required to obtain an astronomical position line, and orders were placed for essential equipment, including sextants and astro-hatches for the new aircraft.[21] Yet in spite of such large expectations, this investment in effort and material was not destined to yield the expected return. When astro-navigation was attempted on war operations the bubble sextant was found to give results of wildly fluctuating accuracy, and even the simplified procedure for obtaining the two or three position lines required to establish the aircraft's position proved to be a laborious task in the difficult conditions in which the bomber navigator had to work. In this way a second untried navigational aid was introduced into Bomber Command, and, as was the case with direction-finding wireless, the air staffs both at command and group levels were painfully slow to acknowledge its limitations even when practical experience had revealed them all too clearly.

But if the Air Staff acted with despatch to provide the new navigational aids, they did not display the same urgency in their efforts to frame a bombing policy for the new force. By July 1937, the Bombing Committee, which it will be recalled came into being in 1934, had held 15 meetings, but had still not come to grips with the problems of re-arming the bomber force. The committee had based their investigations on the performances of the already obsolescent biplanes and on the equipment and policies relating to them; and in any case, any recommendations that were made by the committee were, in the absence of facilities for carrying out practical tests, founded purely on untried theories. An example to illustrate both these points is to be found in the selection of bombs which the committee recommended for the bomber force. When approval for this range of bombs was obtained in September 1935 the bomber force was composed entirely of biplanes and the Air Staff ruling which prohibited the consideration of bombs over 500 lb was still in force. These bombs first became available in the middle of 1937 and by that time the aircraft for which they had been designed were already being phased out of service. This meant that virtually nothing was known about the effectiveness of the bombs as high explosive weapons, since no practical tests had been carried out on them, and even less was known about the characteristics and performances of the new bombers from which they would be dropped.

In justice to the committee, it must be stated that they realized the weakness of their position and on three separate occasions pressed for the establishment of the bomber development unit where systematic experiments to test both bombs and aircraft could be made.[22] Unfortunately, their urgent appeals made no impression on the Air Ministry, and it was only when, in the following year, the Air Staff themselves became involved in the detailed work on the Bomber Command war plans that the seriousness of this deficiency was appreciated. Not unnaturally, it was a member of the Directorate of Plans, Group Captain J.C. Slessor, who first pointed to this weakness. 'We appear', he wrote in October 1938, 'to be neglecting practical research and experiments bearing on the relative vulnerability to air bombardment of various kinds of targets and on the types of bombs and tactics, which will bring about the destruction with the least expenditure of effort of each type of target.'[23]

In the absence of an experimental unit there was no other source from which information could be gained about the degree of bombing accuracy that might be expected in wartime. The squadrons carried out their practice bombing in conditions that were so different from those that would be experienced in wartime that the results obtained were in no way indicative of the accuracy that might be achieved on war operations. The flights were carried out mainly in daylight and in good weather conditions, and the bombs were dropped from altitudes that would have been dangerously low in wartime against defended targets. Moreover, the crews did their bombing in areas that were well known to them, and so their ability to locate their targets while flying over unfamiliar terrain was never put to the test.

It is not therefore surprising to find that the deliberations of the Bombing Committee reveal how tentative and unsure were the ideas on which the Air Force tactics were based. Yet, at the same time, the *Manual of Air Tactics*, which was first produced by the Air Ministry in 1937, described explicitly how the various bombing methods were to be carried out. The manual stated that while the primary function of the bomber force was to attack land targets from high level in daylight, the squadrons should also be trained to carry out low level attacks and high and low level dive attacks. Each method of attack was described in some detail and the class of target for which each one was most appropriate was specified;[24] but, as was inevitable, the tactics described in the manual were the product of untested theories, since there was no empirical evidence to show the practicability of any of the bombing methods to which the manual gave approval.

It was intended to revise the manual annually 'in the light of experience and with the help of criticisms and suggestions which we hope to receive from the Service generally',[25] but it is not easy to imagine how such experience was to be gained. It did not long escape the notice of the officers concerned with planning at the Air Ministry that the statistics contained in the manual indicated a much higher degree of bombing accuracy than those produced by Bomber Command, and that was at a time when the Air Staff were convinced that the Bomber Command figures were unduly optimistic.

It will be remembered that early in 1935 a small committee of distinguished scientists, under the chairmanship of Mr. H. T. Tizard, had been appointed to investigate the possibilities of improving methods of air defence. This committee worked with a speed and effectiveness rare among official bodies of this type, and within two years of its formation had been instrumental in laying down the foundations of the early warning system which was to play a vital part in the winning of the Battle of Britain. Such immediate and impressive results encouraged the Air Ministry to hope that similar methods of investigation might be employed to solve the problems of the offensive. Accordingly, a second committee was appointed, and Tizard accepted the invitation to be its chairman, while continuing to serve on the defence committee. The new body was known as the Committee for the Scientific Survey of Air Offence and was instructed 'to consider how far recent advances in scientific and technical knowledge can be used to strengthen present methods of offence in the Royal Air Force'.[26]

Early in January 1937, each member of the committee was sent a copy of a paper entitled 'Notes on the Present Position of Air Armament Offence' which was intended to supply the essential background information for the committee's investigations.[27] The paper originated in the directorate at the Air Ministry concerned with armaments and dealt mainly with guns, bombs and bombsighting; and from this it is clear that the Air Staff thought of the major problems of strategic bombing as being concerned chiefly with armaments. It should be noted that there was no reference at all to the important areas of navigation and navigational aids, and this persistent 'blind spot' in Air Staff thought caused Tizard to observe, as late as November 1938, that 'relatively too much work has been put into what you do when you find the target and too little on the actual finding of the target'.[28]

Indeed, the paper could have been a summary of the findings of the Bombing Committee, since it reflected all the doubts and uncertainties expressed by that committee. It was recognized that the revolution in aircraft design would cause fundamental changes to be made in operational techniques and equipment, but because of the speed at which this revolution had occurred it had not yet been possible to establish in specific terms what kinds of adjustments would have to be made. The technique of bombsighting was cited as an example. 'At present the significance of the forthcoming high speeds, and the greater bombing heights, can only be guessed at. An important effect of increased air speed is that sighting will commence, and release will occur, further from the target.' Likewise, there was no less uncertainty as to how far the course-setting bombsight would decrease in accuracy at altitudes greater than 12,000 feet, since no practical bombing tests had been carried out above that height. But if bombsighting became more difficult with the increase in operating heights and speeds so would target identification, and recent experience pointed to this conclusion. For example, an investigation of the bombing results obtained during the 1935 Air Defence of Great Britain exercises had shown 'that the poor bombing results obtained were due almost certainly to difficulties in identification of targets, and not to actual bombsighting', and this seemed to be inevitable when the exercises, such as the one quoted, were carried out 'under conditions more nearly approaching those of war than those usually obtained in peace time'.

It seems that at first there was some support for the aims of the new committee, but as the expansion programmes imposed increasing pressure upon the overworked departments of the Air Ministry and upon an overstretched Bomber Command the work of the committee came to be viewed as irrelevant to the fundamental task of rearmament. The success which Tizard achieved with his first assignment was not to be repeated with the second one. It must, however, be admitted that the work of the Defence Committee was the easier one; for the main problems of defence − the location, interception and destruction of enemy bombers − had long since been established, and the simulation of war conditions was comparatively easy to achieve in the peace-time training of the fighter units. In contrast, the major problems concerned with long-range bombing operations had not even been identified, and for various reasons the provision of realistic training for the bomber crews was still not possible. There were, however, other factors which may be held to account for the failure of the Air Offence Committee, and many years later Professor P.M.S. Blackett, who was himself a member of both committees, suggested what they might be.

Possibly, Tizard was too heavily involved in air defence problems easily to switch his interest: possibly the failure was partly due to the not very sympathetic response by those in the Air Force then concerned with bombing policy. Whatever the cause, I think it would be fair to hold that until the war was well advanced, Bomber Command was less scientifically minded than Fighter, Coastal or Anti-Aircraft Command.[29]

Unfortunately, the Offence Committee found Bomber Command to be a remote organization much preoccupied with its own internal problems and was unable to make contact with those formations which most needed its help. Tizard himself was keenly aware that the committee had failed to fulfil its appointed task, and after almost two years of less than satisfactory progress he voiced his frustration to Sir Wilfrid Freeman, the Air Member for Development and Production. 'But the fact is', he wrote, 'that no one seems very anxious to get our advice on these subjects, or to follow it, if offered. We have had no meeting for a long time and there seems to be no anxiety on the part of the Air Ministry that we should meet.'[30]

Meanwhile, Britain had reached the point where its defence needs were outrunning its capacity to satisfy them. The heavy burden which rearmament was imposing on the industrial, manpower and financial resources of the country was such that by the middle of 1937 it had become imperative to make a comprehensive review of the situation and to decide how the available resources could be used to the best advantage. This in effect meant weighing the needs of one service against those of another and deciding an order of priorities. The Government had for some time accepted the need to integrate the planning for Britain's defence needs and had, early in 1936, created a new ministerial post for the Co-ordination of Defence. The first minister to hold this post was Sir Thomas Inskip, and it is sad to reflect that he is remembered less for his considerable achievements in office than for the unjust attacks made on him in a book called *Guilty Men* which was written in 1940 by a trio of journalists of curiously assorted political views, and which is now chiefly remembered for the virulence of its attack on those in power who tried and failed to avert a general war and for the distorted views it presents of motives and events.[31]

The new minister applied much hard thinking and common sense to his task and this is nowhere seen more clearly than in his reasoned opposition to the Air Staff's policy of the offensive. His intervention in the Air Force rearmament programme occurred soon after the Chancellor of the Exchequer had, in July 1937, called upon the three services to make comprehensive reviews of their requirements and to

force, and this is precisely what he proposed. Indeed, he went one stage further in his plan to reduce the cost of the bomber force, and suggested that 'we might substitute a larger proportion of light and medium bombers for our very expensive heavy bombers'. He believed that these types of bombers could be used effectively against Germany from bases on the continent and might even be converted into fighters to supplement our air defences at home. 'The point I want to put to you, therefore,' he concluded, 'is as to whether you can devise a revised programme based on the conception that at the outset of a war our first task is to repulse a knock-out blow within the first few weeks, trusting thereafter to defeat the enemy by a process of exhaustion, resulting from our command at sea, in the later stages.'[36]

It is not difficult to imagine how fiercely the Air Ministry reacted to these proposals, but their objections made little impression on the Cabinet, who were determined to secure the obvious financial and industrial advantages of replacing expensive bombers by less costly fighters, especially since the prospects of achieving an effective close defence system were so much improved. And so, in spite of strong Foreign Office support for the Air Staff's plans, the Cabinet accepted Sir Thomas Inskip's recommendations, and Scheme J was rejected.[37] An alternative programme of expansion was decided by negotiations between Inskip and the Air Ministry, and in deference to the strong representation of the Air Staff it was agreed that the all-heavy bomber programme should be retained in return for a later completion date. The Air Staff then prepared a new expansion programme, designated Scheme K and scheduled for completion by 31 March 1941, which reflected the change in emphasis from bombers to fighters. Under its provisions the fighter force was to be retained at the Scheme J figure, with provision for full reserves, while the first-line bomber strength was to be reduced from 1,442 to 1,360 aircraft, in 77 instead of 90 squadrons, and the scale of reserves was to be cut from a figure estimated to provide for 16 weeks' war wastage to one estimated to provide for a period of no more than nine weeks.[38]

The Air Staff were greatly depressed to find themselves compelled to accept a policy which was the very negation of their long-held strategic doctrine. The bomber force was to be relegated to a place of secondary importance in the defence of Britain, and the aim of parity, even in the limited concept of striking power, was now officially abandoned. The position as seen by the Air Staff was that the German bomber force would 'probably attain a first-line strength of 1,350 by the summer of 1938, while this strength will not be attained by our Air Striking Force with complete personnel and reserves until 1941, by which date the Germans may well have reached a first-line strength considerably greater'.[39]

And the Chief of the Air Staff, Sir Cyril Newall, struck an even more sombre note regarding the consequences of the new expansion scheme when he attended an Air Staff meeting on 18 January 1938.

> There would be an Air Force, well housed and well equipped, of a first-line of 1,350 aircraft; not ready for war, with 9 weeks reserve behind it, a small training capacity and a war potential which, though considerable, would not be in full production for many months after the outbreak of war. It appeared probable that there would be a period when the Air Force would come to a standstill owing to lack of reserves and the potential would consequently be useless (since the war would have been lost), if it were not destroyed.[40]

CHAPTER SIX

PREPARATIONS FOR WAR 1938-9

It will be remembered that in February 1937 the Chiefs of Staff had prepared a paper outlining the strategy to be pursued in the event of a war with Germany in 1939. The recommendations contained in this paper were approved by a ministerial committee under the chairmanship of the Prime Minister, Stanley Baldwin, and in May 1937 the Committee of Imperial Defence called upon the three services to prepare detailed operational plans based on that strategy. And so for the first time since the doctrine of the offensive was formulated in the summer of 1923 the Air Ministry were faced with the task of translating their strategic ideas into operational plans which could be carried out by the bomber squadrons. If the assurance with which these ideas were proclaimed had been a measure of the nature of the task, it should have presented few problems; but in fact it proved to be a most difficult one and pointed all too clearly to the wide gulf which existed between strategic theory and operational reality.

The directive from the Committee of Imperial Defence was despatched to the Air Ministry in the middle of May 1937,[1] but it was not until the second week in August that work on the plans was begun.[2] The reason for this delay was that all the preliminary work had to be done by the already overworked departments of the Air Ministry. It was intended that the second phase of the planning should be done at Bomber Command, but since the command was stretched to the limits by the expansion programme, Sir John Steel, the Commander-in-Chief, insisted that he could not undertake the work unless he was provided with extra staff.[3] This argument was accepted, and it was finally agreed that the Air Ministry should draw up a list of plans corresponding to the requirements of the directive and that a small planning staff should be set up at Bomber Command to prepare a tactical appreciation of each plan as it was required.

Work on the plans continued to make slow progress and it was not until 1 October 1937 that the Air Ministry finally gave their approval to a document which listed thirteen operational plans. These were known as the Western Air Plans, and each plan was designated by the initials W. A., followed by a number ranging from 1 to 13.[4] The plans covered a wide range of air operations, and for that reason it was considered neither possible nor desirable to begin work on more than a small number of them. The Air Ministry therefore decided to concentrate on the three most important plans involving the bomber force. These were:

W. A. 1   Plans for the attack on the German Air Striking Force and its maintenance organization, and targets in the German aircraft industry.

W. A. 4   Plans for the attack on German military rail, canal and road communications (a) during the period of the concentration of the armies; (b) to delay a German invasion of the Low Countries and France.

W. A. 5   Plans for the attack on German manufacturing resources (a) in the Ruhr; (b) outside the Ruhr; (c) in the inland waterways between the Ruhr and Baltic and North Sea ports.

On 13 December 1937 intelligence summaries of the three plans were forwarded to Bomber Command and the Commander-in-Chief was instructed to give them first priority.[5]

This is perhaps the appropriate point to consider briefly the sources from which the Air Ministry obtained its intelligence information. In 1936 the Committee of Imperial Defence had sanctioned a general reorganization of the intelligence system, and this included the establishment of the Air Targets Intelligence Committee to deal specifically with objectives which were most suitable for air attack. The new committee naturally gave first priority to the investigation of targets in Germany, and by the summer of 1937 had produced a number of reports covering groups of German industrial and military targets.[6]

Thus, the Air Ministry had in its possession a good deal of information relating to German industry and the German armed forces; but, as was to be expected, the intelligence it possessed on the German armed forces, and in particular on the air striking force, was neither as comprehensive nor as reliable as was desirable. Unfortunately, it did not seem likely that much worthwhile intelligence relating to the air striking force would be obtained in peacetime; for the Germans had a large number of airfields from which they could operate and would almost certainly make no firm decisions about their war dispositions until hostilities were imminent. Intelligence would therefore have to be obtained by systematic reconnaissance after the outbreak of war; but at that time the Air Force possessed neither the aircraft nor the organization to carry out this type of operation and had made no plans to provide for them in the current expansion scheme.

The small planning staff which had been established at Bomber Command quickly ran into difficulties. Group Captain F. P. Don, the officer who directed the staff, soon discovered that certain information which was essential to his work was not available to him. For example, he had no information on the probable strength and composition of Bomber Command in 1939; nor did he possess a reliable estimate of the likely German air strength at that date.[7] He wrote urgently to the Air Ministry explaining the difficulty of his position, but was told that the information was not immediately available to send to him.

Meanwhile, the new Commander-in-Chief of Bomber Command, Sir Edgar Ludlow-Hewitt, having studied the three plans, suggested that there should be a geographical redistribution of his squadrons; and while these proposals were being considered by the Air Ministry there was a further delay in the work of Group Captain Don's staff. The Commander-in-Chief noted that the plans called for attacks against targets over a wide area of north-western Germany and in the Ruhr and Rhineland; and since there was a distinct possibility that Belgium and Holland would remain neutral, thus forming a barrier around which our bombers would have to operate, he emphasized that the consideration of aircraft range would be a crucial one. From these observations he reasoned that the long-range aircraft should be based in the north of England, the medium-range aircraft in the East Midlands and the short-range aircraft (the Battles and Blenheims) in East Anglia and Kent. There then followed lengthy negotiations between Bomber Command and the Air Ministry concerning the proposals, but in the outcome the Commander-in-Chief was able to achieve his most important objectives.[8]

Of the three plans which were sent to Bomber Command for appraisal, W. A. 4 was the one least favoured by the Air Staff who judged, correctly, that it would meet with no better reception at Bomber Command. The chief objection of both was that it might cause a large part of the bomber force to be drawn into army co-operation duties; and this was strengthened by the conviction (shared by the Army) that a German invasion of France and the Low Countries could not be effectively hindered by air attacks on communications and storage depots.[9]

When the plan was studied at Bomber Command Group Captain Don and his staff could do little more than make an intelligent guess as to whether it would be a feasible task for the bomber force to undertake; for they were no better placed than previous staff committees to judge the efficacy of the various bombing tactics required by the plan. The bombing data essential to this kind of investigation were still not

available — the Bomber Command experimental unit was as remote
a prospect as ever — and so the planners were compelled to base their
appreciation on assumptions which might or might not be true. The
limitations of this method of work were clearly indicated in that part
of the report which dealt with attacks on railway lines.

> Throughout this report we have assumed that a double line railway
> track is a fair bombing target, day and night, i.e. that both lines
> can be definitely breached or seriously obstructed without
> unreasonable expenditure of effort, bearing in mind that several
> routes must be attacked simultaneously and that attack must be
> sustained. This is a large assumption, and unless data are already
> available, experiment is necessary to ascertain the effort required
> to breach a line, since effort must be the basis of any calculation
> of the air forces required to interrupt a number of routes. Such
> experiment will naturally include consideration of the weight and
> type of bomb to be used as well as the different methods of
> attack.[10]

It is somewhat ironical that they should have had cause to complain
about this particular shortcoming, because arrangements had already
been made to carry out a series of trials which would have provided
that information. Unfortunately, these trials, which were scheduled to
take place at the Royal Engineers Railway Training Centre at Longmoor,
were so long delayed that Group Captain Don was not able to use the
results obtained from them to prepare his report.[11] It is worthy of note
that when these trials were eventually completed and the preliminary
results obtained, this was one of the rare examples where technical
information derived from practical experiments was made available for
future planning.

It would have seemed obvious to give the most careful attention to
W. A. 1, since this was the only plan which the Joint Planning Committee
thought at all likely to reduce the intensity of a German air attack on
Britain. On the other hand, the committee had recommended this course
of action, not because they had much faith in it, but because they could
find no practicable alternative. Indeed, in this respect they were in full
agreement with the Air Staff who had for long held the view that attacks
on aerodromes and ground installations would be a costly and ineffective
method of dealing with an enemy air force.[12] An Air Ministry planning
conference, held on 1 October 1937, showed how strongly the view was
still held.

> Discussion showed that the extent to which the German air striking
> force could be successfully attacked was a matter of doubt.

Attempting to attack the enemy's aerodromes, landing grounds, and first-line aircraft would be difficult, certainly without considerable previous reconnaissance. It was known that the Germans did not mean to operate from their peace stations and the whereabouts of their war stations was at present unknown. Similarly the whereabouts of aircraft reserves could not at the moment be ascertained. Attack on airframe, and more particularly, aero-engine factories might therefore be more effective than on the air striking force itself, though little immediate effect might be obtained.[13]

In the Bomber Command appreciation of this plan the Commander-in-Chief underlined the operational difficulties of attacking the German air striking force from bases in this country, especially if Belgium and Holland remained neutral. In this situation, the bombers would first have to complete a 200-mile flight over the North Sea before they could penetrate enemy territory along the short German coastline between the borders of Holland and Denmark. The long distances involved in these operations would restrict the Battles and the Blenheims almost entirely to attacks on aerodromes which were now regarded as being the least promising of the various suggested targets; for recent experiments on Salisbury Plain had demonstrated how difficult it would be to destroy well dispersed and camouflaged aircraft by high level bombing. Aircraft factories would certainly be easier targets for daylight operations, but the majority of these lay beyond the range of the Battles and Blenheims. These targets would have to be attacked at night by the slower Whitleys and Harrows, though it was appreciated that the chances of identifying a particular factory during the hours of darkness were by no means good.

In any case, the Commander-in-Chief did not believe that the Battles and Blenheims would be able to survive in daylight against the new German fighters unless they themselves were protected by long-range fighters. He urged the Air Staff to reverse their traditional policy and provide fighter escorts for the bombers; and warned them that if they were not prepared to make this concession they must face the fact that the day bombers would have to carry an even more powerful armament than was planned for the Hampdens and Wellingtons if they were to operate without prohibitive losses.

This review of the situation convinced the Commander-in-Chief that it would be impossible to launch an effective attack against the German air striking force from bases in Britain. Success could be expected only if a large part of the bomber force were based in France; and even if advance arrangements were made for such a transfer of air strength, there would still be some delay before the squadrons could begin

General Walther Wever

Erhard Milch

Junkers Ju 52 1932

Focke-Wulf FW 200 (Condor) 1938

full-scale operations from their new stations. Thus, there would be no chance of achieving an immediate reduction in the weight of the German air attack against Britain. In other words, he had ceased to regard Bomber Command as an immediate counter to an attempted knock-out blow from the air, and he made this abundantly clear when he concluded that Britain would find her strongest defence in a combination of the North Sea and the most powerful fighter and anti-aircraft defences.[14]

Of the initial group of plans to be considered, W.A.5 was the only one which cast the bomber force in an independent role. This was a plan of attack against German industrial and transportation targets and was intended to be put into operation in the second phase of the war, after defeat had been warded off by the fighters and anti-aircraft defences in the opening phase. The Air Staff were encouraged by their study of the plan to believe that there was a good chance of finding a group of objectives, relatively small in number and vulnerable to attack, whose destruction would seriously impair Germany's war-making capacity. The Joint Planning Committee had failed in their search for such a vital group of targets, but the Air Staff thought that the intelligence which had been gathered during the last year had greatly increased the possibility of discovering targets 'the destruction of which would not only tend (though probably not immediately) to cause a reduction of the German air offensive, but would at the same time have an adverse effect on the German war effort and German economic life generally'.[15]

Sir Edgar Ludlow-Hewitt agreed with this view and indeed believed that he had found such a group of objectives in the Ruhr. From the list of possible targets contained in the plan, he selected 45 power plants, comprising 26 coke-producing plants and 19 electricity generating stations, whose destruction he believed would be a feasible operation of war. He thought that 'the output of these coking plants and electricity generating stations can be reduced below the critical minimum in about a month by 300 aircraft ... or in half that time by 600 aircraft', estimating that even if 75 per cent of the attacks were comparative failures this effect could be achieved with 3,000 sorties and the loss of 176 aircraft. This assessment led him to conclude that provided the aircraft were based sufficiently close to their targets to enable them to maintain a sustained bombardment 'it ought to be possible to paralyse the industry of the Ruhr'.[16]

The Air Staff thought that this appreciation was altogether too optimistic. They could not accept the assumption that the destruction of these plants would be sufficient to cripple the industry of the Ruhr; nor did they believe that targets such as these would be easy to hit and destroy. Nevertheless, they agreed that power plants were important and vulnerable targets and accorded them a high priority on the list of possible objectives.[17] The Air Targets Intelligence Committee did not, however, share this enthusiasm for power targets. They thought that the 3,000 sorties which the Commander-in-Chief had estimated would be required to destroy the 45 power plants could more profitably be directed against the Möhne and Sorpe dams, for they believed that the destruction of these dams would cause serious disruption to the industry of the Ruhr. They also regarded the canal system linking the Ruhr with northern Germany as being especially vulnerable, and believed that well directed attacks against such sensitive points as locks and aqueducts would result in the dislocation of a considerable part of German industry.[18]

The study of the three plans had shown that there was little hope of using the bomber force as a counter-offensive weapon against the German armed forces in the opening phase of a war: on the other hand, the study of W.A.5 had again brought to the fore the idea of the independent bomber force as the eventual war-winning weapon. It was envisaged that within a relatively few months of the outbreak of war the bombing would so disrupt the enemy's war industries and communications that it would bring his armed forces to a standstill and soften them up for their eventual defeat. It was also appreciated that if the bomber force was to develop the necessary strength to deliver such a blow it should not be committed to a large scale offensive too soon after the beginning of hostilities but should be conserved until it was sufficiently powerful to strike with real effect against the enemy.[19]

Sir Edgar Ludlow-Hewitt was very conscious of the weakness of the bomber force, and clearly appreciated the danger of operating it beyond its natural capacity. In March 1938 he demonstrated this point convincingly when he produced for the Air Ministry three graphs showing the probable losses in aircraft and aircrews in a determined attack on Germany if war should come in 1939. Using the terms 'maximum', 'intensive' and 'sustained' to indicate the degree of operational effort involved, he estimated that if the force operated at 'maximum' effort for the first five days, 'intensive' effort for the following seven days and thereafter at 'sustained' effort, all the medium bomber squadrons would be eliminated by the end of three and a half weeks and all the heavy bomber squadrons after seven and a half weeks, while 'literally hundreds of fresh crews will be required in the first weeks of war'.[20]

Inevitably, the study of the first Western Air Plans again raised crucial questions about the bombing tactics to be used in a war with Germany, and, as ever, there were no rational answers to them. It is true that the Air Force had assembled a comprehensive body of tactical doctrine in the *Manual of Air Tactics*, but, as has been seen, this was based wholly on untested theories; and even when the second edition of the manual was issued in January 1938 the bombing tactics described in it were no better founded either on practical experiment or scientific investigation than those in the original edition.[21] The situation might have been better if the Offence Committee under Tizard had been able to get a clear indication of the problems which needed investigation, but since there was no body delegated to act as a link between the Air Force and the committee, as there was in the case of the Defence Committee, the Offence Committee was forced to work without proper guidance from the service and so was unable to make any real progress.

It was not until March 1939 that action was taken to remedy this omission, when a new sub-committee of the Bombing Committee was formed to deal with bombing policy. The sub-committee was instructed

> to consider from the tactical standpoint the policy which is to be adopted in regard to different methods of bombing, taking into consideration the characteristics of modern aircraft; the end in view is the guidance of research into, and the technical development of, the most suitable aircraft and apparatus for the satisfactory execution of the bombing methods decided upon.[22]

These terms of reference clearly indicate that the ideas on bombing techniques and equipment were not as well founded as was suggested in the *Manual of Air Tactics*, and this impression is strongly reinforced by the minutes of the first meeting of the sub-committee and by the Air Staff paper on bombing policy which was used as its agenda.

The Air Staff paper began with the assumption that the various types of objectives to be attacked could be divided into two main categories, namely, 'precise targets' and 'target groups'. Of these two the target group was by far the easier proposition. It would be an area of considerable size, such as an area of docks, an industrial town or a military concentration area, and would contain many objectives which it would be desirable for the bombers to destroy. The great advantage of this type of target was that no great degree of bombing accuracy was required in order to obtain worthwhile hits. A precise target, on the other hand, would be as small as a ship, a bridge or a power station and direct hits would have to be scored to put it out of action. Targets as small as these were extremely difficult to hit, but since they included some of the most sensitive elements in the enemy's war machine, they were objectives of the first importance. It was therefore considered essential that the bomber force should seek to attain a standard of efficiency which would enable it to make successful attacks against precise targets.

This at once raised the question as to whether the squadrons were likely to reach such a degree of accuracy with their normal high level bombing techniques. The opinion expressed in the paper was far from encouraging. It was believed that 'high level bombing, after many years of development, has failed as an effective and economical means of destroying the precise target and as such should be discarded by the Air Striking Force' which 'should therefore be trained and equipped in high level bombing to attack the target group only, with incidental simplification and saving in tactics, training and equipment'. In support of this contention, it was pointed out that the bombing results obtained during recent exercises were far below the standard of accuracy required to hit a precise target. Results had shown that an average day bombing error of 150 yards or less would be difficult to achieve, and in the 1935 exercises it had been 508 yards. Night bombing had naturally proved to be much less accurate, and in the 1937 Combined Exercises the results had been appallingly bad. During these exercises 47 sorties were carried out by aircraft which flashed a light (known as a sashalite) at the instant of time when the bombs would have been released to hit a specified target, and of these only one aircraft had signalled the dropping point with sufficient accuracy for the result to be plotted on the ground. And even that one, it was calculated, would have fallen 1890 yards wide of the mark.

Evidence such as this convinced the Air Staff that there was little hope of achieving the necessary improvement in bombing accuracy in the foreseeable future. In making this judgement they took full account of the considerable progress that was being made in the design of aircraft and equipment, but felt that any increase in efficiency brought about by such technical advances would be largely offset by the higher speeds of the new aircraft and by the fact that the greater accuracy of anti-aircraft fire would necessitate a shortening of the bombing run. They therefore concluded that although some squadrons should continue to be trained to attack precise targets from high altitude this method of attack would be too costly in time and effort to be employed generally by the bomber force on war operations.[23]

The Bombing Policy sub-committee were most reluctant to accept the pessimistic conclusions recorded in the Air Staff paper, and this was not because they disputed the facts that were presented, but because they were far from satisfied that enough was being done to enable the bomber squadrons to improve their operational performance. They responded by challenging many of these conclusions, expressing their dissent most strongly on those relating to night bombing and daylight precision bombing.

The difficulties of operating during the hours of darkness had been underlined by the bombing results obtained during the 1937 Combined

Exercises. These results were contained in a report produced by No.3 Bomber Group,[24] and Sir Edgar Ludlow-Hewitt (who was the senior Bomber Command representative at the first meeting of the Bombing Policy sub-committee) had himself forwarded this report, together with his own observations, to the Air Ministry. 'We must recognise', he wrote, 'that precision bombing at night especially with highspeed aircraft against unilluminated targets, i.e. in war conditions, remains a matter of very great difficulty. This is not the first time this lesson has been clearly demonstrated: exactly the same thing was shown in the A.D.G.B. exercises of July 1935, and again in the Winter Exercise 1936.'[25] The point that he made in his letter was not that there was no possibility of hitting a precise target at night, but that there was little chance of success with the current bombing methods. He suggested to the sub-committee that flares should be used to illuminate the targets; and there was in fact a good deal of evidence to show that bombing accuracy could be greatly improved by their use. Indeed, the need to experiment with the design and use of flares was expressed on many occasions during the inter-war period, but these were never followed up.

On the question of day precision bombing, the sub-committee were forced to admit that this type of bombing carried out at high level presented many difficulties, but pointed out that this was very different from saying that there was no alternative to the current method of high level individual bombing. They thought that other methods might be used successfully against the precise target, but emphasized that since none of them had been thoroughly tested there was no way of determining their feasibility in war. They could not accept the Air Staff's view that pattern bombing, a method by which a number of aircraft flying in formation dropped their bombs on a pre-arranged signal from the leader, would be no more effective than individual bombing, because, as they pointed out, the desultory experiments in this method of bombing had been terminated before any valid conclusions could be drawn. They recorded that interest in this type of bombing seemed to have lapsed completely, noting that the committee which was formed specifically to consider the potential of pattern bombing had not yet held its first meeting.

The sub-committee also pointed out that shortcomings in training and organization were responsible for many weaknesses in the bomber force. They were agreed that the most serious errors which occurred during the recent exercises were caused, not by faulty bomb aiming, but by incorrect target identification and by the setting of incorrect winds on the bombsights. Sir Edgar Ludlow-Hewitt believed that these failures were in large measure caused by the unrealistic training methods used in Bomber Command. He cited as an example the fact that the bombing exercises were carried out in conditions which in no way resembled those which would be experienced in wartime. He thought that frequent exercises should be organized to give practice 'in locating unfamiliar targets in various parts of the country', but added that if the crews were to get the maximum benefit from these practice flights it was essential that more careful attention should be given to the details of planning. He recommended that the crews should be given an adequate briefing before take-off – he advocated the establishment on every station of a full-time intelligence officer to perform this function among his other duties – and that the results of each bombing run should be checked either by camera obscura or by the exposure of a photographic plate.

The only bombing method which the sub-committee thought was at all likely to succeed against the precise target was that carried out from low level, provided the distance of penetration into enemy territory was not too great. The most attractive feature of this method of attack was that only a small amount of crew training was required to produce acceptable bombing results. In 1937, for example, when no service aircraft was fitted with a low level sight, the average error for a trained crew bombing from between 200 and 300 feet was 50 yards. On the other hand, the disadvantages of bombing from a low altitude were patently obvious. The difficulties of navigating to the target area and of actually identifying the target would be greatly increased, and the bombers would be much more vulnerable to anti-aircraft defences.

Sir Edgar Ludlow-Hewitt attached great importance to the nuisance value of the bomber and thought that it should be exploited to the full. He suggested to the sub-committee that provision should be made for aircraft to be used for what he described as harassing bombing. The main purpose of this kind of operation would be to cause the greatest disruption to the routine of everyday life in the enemy country with the smallest expenditure of effort. To achieve this effect the bombers would operate as individual aircraft, at short intervals of time, so that their unpredictable movements would cause frequent air raid warnings to be sounded over a wide area. The type of aircraft he envisaged for this work would be 'a highly streamlined aeroplane of extremely high speed, with limited equipment and carrying comparatively light bombs'. Group Captain Don, who also represented Bomber Command at the meeting, thought that this type of high-speed aircraft could also be used for photographic reconnaissance which he believed 'would be essential at the beginning of the war for the location and study of potential targets'.

During their first meeting the members of the sub-committee had considered some of the most important questions relating to bombing techniques, but they were very conscious of the fact that they could offer only the most tentative answers to these questions; for so long as the

A formation of Hawker Hurricanes

The prototype Vickers Wellington. This aircraft made its first flight in May 1936, shortly after this photograph was taken

practical aspects of bombing continued to be ignored no one could make any reasoned judgements as to which bombing methods were feasible and which were not. They recognized clearly that there was no possibility of being able to formulate a viable tactical policy until the facilities for practical experiments were made available; and this led them to state that 'there was a crying need for a Bombing Development Establishment' and to record that on three separate occasions the Bombing Committee had recommended that such an experimental unit should be formed, but without result.[26]

On 12 March 1938 German troops marched into Austria, and this was the first of a series of events which led directly to the outbreak of the Second World War. Once again Britain's defence plans and preparations were overtaken by events, and the Government was compelled drastically to revise its attitude towards rearmament and industry. The Cabinet at once authorized the Air Staff to prepare a new expansion scheme and to order up to a total of 12,000 aircraft, this being the number of aircraft it was estimated would be produced during the following two years. Almost immediately afterwards the Cabinet gave approval for double shifts to be worked in the aircraft industry and abandoned its policy of refusing to allow defence needs to interfere with the normal course of trade.[27] The new expansion programme, which was called Scheme L, contained the main provisions of Scheme K, but was to be completed one year earlier, by 31 March 1940. The most significant difference in the new scheme was the raising of the total strength of the home-based fighter force from 532 to 608 aircraft, thus revealing yet another shift towards greater dependence upon a system of close defence.

There were however serious difficulties in the way of fulfilling the requirements of the new expansion scheme. In the first place, it was most unlikely that the aircraft industry would be able to produce the 12,000 aircraft in two years, and second, even if this proved to be possible, the Air Force did not possess the capacity to train the aircrews to fly them, or for that matter, the ground staffs to maintain them. It will be seen that if there was a substantial increase in the requirement for trained aircrews the extra flying instructors would have to be drawn from among the most experienced aircrews on the squadrons, so causing an immediate and serious diminution of the effective first-line strength of the Air Force. The most obvious conclusion to be drawn from these facts is that in spite of the relaxation of financial restrictions the capability of the Air Force to expand during the next few years had little improved; for the limits to expansion now set by industrial output and the training capacity of the service were much the same as when finance was the limiting factor.

Now that the bomber force had been discounted as a weapon of defence in the opening phase of the war, the Air Staff increasingly turned their attention to the composition of the force that would come into its own in the second phase of the war. This led them to look beyond the force that was then coming into being and to build up a picture of the characteristics of the heavy bombers that were to be the spearhead of the force after 1941.

A study of the Western Air Plans had indicated that the bombing would be most effective if it were directed against German industry and communications, and an examination of the main types of objectives in both these categories suggested that few of them could be seriously damaged by bombs smaller than 250 lbs and that many of them would require bombs of at least 1000 lbs. When these assumptions were related to the great distances involved in reaching many of the major targets, the importance of increasing both the range and the bombload of the aircraft of the future was further emphasized. These considerations are most clearly reflected in the minutes of the Bombing Committee. During 1938 this committee authorized the development of a 1000 lb bomb and agreed that the bomber should have a minimum radius of action of 750 miles, with a range of at least 2000 miles. It was also firmly established that for the average length of flight involved in bombing targets in Germany — the greater part of which would be either over the sea or over hostile territory — it was essential to have two engines to achieve the necessary performance and reliability, and that in some cases it might be desirable to have four.[28]

It had long been accepted that the bomber must be capable of fighting its way both to and from the target. Not even the most modern bomber could be expected to depend upon its speed and powers of evasion to avoid combat, for the contemporary fighter was immensely superior to the bomber in speed, rate of climb and manoeuvrability. The bomber's main chance seemed to lie in the possession of a heavy defensive armament, consisting of machine guns enclosed in power-operated turrets. There was however a high price to be paid for this defence. The turrets, guns and ammunition added considerably to the weight of the aircraft and claimed a large part of the limited space in the fuselage. There was also the need to protect the crew and vital parts of the aircraft from the heavy fire of the modern fighter, but again weight was the problem. Experiments were already being carried out with bullet-proof glass, armour plating and self-sealing fuel tanks, and although the results were far from unsatisfactory, the protective device often represented an increase in weight that was quite unacceptable. For example, a new type of fuel tank, which was developed in 1938, sealed itself satisfactorily but weighed twice as much as the ordinary tank.[29]

Perhaps the most effective means of protecting the bomber was to improve its operational performance, and especially its cruising speed and operational ceiling, and this consideration provided a strong case for increasing the number as well as the power of the engines. The greater an aircraft's cruising speed the less time it would need to remain over enemy territory to complete a given mission, and the higher it was able to operate the less effective the enemy anti-aircraft defences would be against it. There were however special problems to be faced in flying at the high altitudes (something over 20,000 feet) envisaged by the Air Staff. At this level the air contains too little oxygen to permit a man to carry out normal activities, so that the aircrews would have to be supplied with oxygen to enable them to perform their duties efficiently. But the most serious problems to be overcome were those caused by the low temperatures which are experienced at high altitudes. Heated flying suits would be essential for the aircrews and an efficient heating system would be needed to prevent guns, instruments and wings, among other things, from being affected by ice. For example, the new Browning gun froze at 10 degrees centigrade, a temperature which would frequently be experienced at about 15,000 feet.[30] Finally, a more obvious factor to be taken into account would be the extra fuel the aircraft would consume in climbing to a high level; for the greater the altitude to be reached, the greater the weight of fuel the aircraft would have to carry to retain its normal range.

It was now generally agreed that the three 'heavy' bombers then coming into service were too small to provide sufficient space for the growing mass of equipment and for adequate accommodation for the aircrews whose members would be required to perform specialist functions. There was a limit to what could be fitted into the relatively small amount of space available in the Whitleys, Hampdens and Wellingtons, and already that limit had been reached. In any case, the range, speed and bombload of these aircraft were already considered to be inadequate to bear the weight of a full-scale attack against Germany. It may be said that the limitations of these aircraft were seen plainly enough, but at this stage there was no clear conception of what the new bombers would be like. What was certain however was that they would be larger, heavier and more powerful than any aircraft previously contemplated.[31]

After the annexation of Austria in March 1938, Hitler turned his attention to Czechoslovakia whose position was seriously weakened by the coup in Austria. He deliberately created tension between Germany and Czechoslovakia by interfering in the quarrel between the Czech government and certain elements among the Sudeten Germans, a considerable German-speaking minority living within the borders of

Czechoslovakia. He exploited this quarrel, first, to claim special autonomous rights for this German minority and, later, to demand the cession to Germany of those areas of Czechoslovakia where Germans were in a majority. When it became apparent that he was prepared to go to war to achieve his aims, Britain and France intervened in the dispute and brought pressure to bear on Czechoslovakia to yield to Hitler's demands. On three occasions in September 1938 the British Prime Minister, Neville Chamberlain, flew to Germany to meet Hitler, and on the third occasion, on 29 September at Munich, a settlement was made which permitted Germany to occupy the Sudeten German territory. The agreement reached at Munich has often been condemned as the betrayal of a small state to satisfy the unjust demands of a ruthless dictator, and in the light of subsequent events this may appear to be a reasonable conclusion. But if the benefit of hindsight is set aside and a judgement is based solely on the mood of public opinion in Britain up to the time of the Munich agreement, this will indicate how unlikely it was that *any* British Government would have gone to war to preserve a Czechoslovak state which contained three and a quarter million Germans as well as other large dissident minorities, any more than any British Government would have been prepared to use force to maintain the demilitarization of the Rhineland and the separation of Austria from Germany.

This sudden and unexpected turn of events in Europe suggested to Britain's military leaders that the main assumptions on which their war plans were based were no longer valid. There was now a distinct possibility that war would break out before 1939, and that if it did, it might well be caused by a German attack on Czechoslovakia. If this should happen, it would lead to a very different situation from that envisaged by the Chiefs of Staff. If war were to begin in central Europe, the Germans would obviously concentrate their land and air forces in that area and would probably remain on the defensive in the west, at least in the early part of the war. Thus, the land and air attacks on France and the Low Countries or the air assault against Britain would probably be postponed; and if that should happen, the military and political leaders alike were agreed that it would be sheer folly for Britain to be the first to begin an unrestricted bombing campaign against an enemy who was greatly superior in the air. The most prudent course of action would be to restrict the bombing to purely military objectives; and this at once raised the question as to what kinds of target these were, where they were situated, and which, if any, of the air plans included them.

The first step was to obtain a ruling as to what constituted a legitimate target for air bombardment in a restricted phase, and when this was done early in September the Air Staff issued provisional instructions for the guidance of the Commander-in-Chief of Bomber Command.[32] These instructions were based on the three principles which the Prime Minister had enunciated in the House of Commons on 21 June 1938, and were as follows:

> It is against international law to bomb civilians as such and to make deliberate attacks upon civilian population.
>
> Targets which are aimed at from the air must be legitimate military objectives and must be capable of identification.
>
> Reasonable care must be taken in attacking these military objectives so that by carelessness a civilian population in the neighbourhood is not bombed.[33]

The Air Staff emphasized that these principles were to be strictly observed, and advised that if the Czech crisis should lead to war the most suitable plans to adopt would be those concerned with the German armed services, that is, W. A. 1 and W. A. 4, since these contained a large number of targets which were by the strictest definition military objectives. Yet even within these narrow limits, it was intended that the greatest care should be taken to ensure that no target selected for attack should involve the slightest risk of causing civilian casualties. On no acount must Germany be given the opportunity of pointing to Britain as being the first to begin unrestricted air attacks, in order to justify retaliatory raids against this country.

Of the three Western Air Plans which had been selected for appraisal by Bomber Command, W. A. 5 – the plan to attack German industry in the Ruhr and elsewhere – was ruled out completely by these restrictions, while considerable parts of W. A. 1 and W. A. 4 would no longer qualify for consideration. A large number of targets in the German aircraft industry, for example, were situated in populated areas and must therefore be excluded from the list of possible objectives. The immediate effect of these restrictions was to induce Bomber Command to seek other ways of employing the striking force during a period of restricted operations. Many plans and ideas were considered, including contributions both from the Navy and the Army, but strangely, the plan which commanded the widest support was one which was wholly non-offensive in character. It was a plan to drop propaganda leaflets over Germany and was suggested by Sir Edgar Ludlow-Hewitt himself, who stated in his outline of the plan that 'skilfully dropped propaganda distributed by aircraft may prove a more potent weapon than bombs'. It is hard to judge how far the Commander-in-Chief really believed that the morale of the German people could be undermined by propaganda; but it is certain that the plan commended itself to him for two other reasons, both equally cogent, namely, that it unquestionably fell into the restricted category and that it could be put into operation with the minimum of risk to the bomber squadrons.[34]

The more the Commander-in-Chief studied the other plans the more he was convinced that it was beyond the resources of his command to attempt a bombing campaign on any scale. He was so conscious of the inability of the bomber force to strike with any effect against Germany that he constantly urged the necessity of avoiding any action which might bring down reprisals against this country. Indeed, he went so far as to suggest that we should refuse to be drawn into making retaliatory raids even if attacks were made against our naval and air bases. Only if the Germans made an all-out attack upon London should we take retaliatory action and launch an offensive against the Ruhr; but if the Germans refrained from making such an attack, the bomber force should not be committed to any operations which might seriously weaken it.

At the height of the Czech crisis the Commander-in-Chief learned for the first time that the Air Staff were thinking of setting aside ('rolling up') 50 per cent of his first-line strength for use as reserves immediately on mobilization. This served to reinforce his conviction that it was 'not possible to devise an effective air bombardment role for our bombers immediately on the outbreak of hostilities'. He thought that the best use he could make of the night bombers would be for the dropping of leaflets over German territory, while the medium bombers could most usefully be employed in support of the land operations of the French Army and in co-operation with the French Air Force. He also strongly recommended that immediate steps should be taken to convert a number of Blenheims for use as fighters during the initial period before the bombing offensive began.[35]

And in the same defensive vein, he was prepared to sanction the evacuation of the squadrons from their operational bases in order to preserve the striking force from injury. He thought that if war should come the Germans might well launch an overwhelming attack against the exposed bomber aerodromes in East Anglia and Yorkshire. He reasoned that if Bomber Command were correct in their assumption that in a counter-offensive against the German Air Force they would 'be able to compel the Germans to evacuate and retire from aerodromes within 50 or 60 miles or more of their north-west coast' there was no reason 'to suppose that the Germans would not be similarly able to compel us to evacuate our most exposed aerodromes, those up to say 30 or 40 miles from the coast'. He proposed that during any future period of strained relations with Germany the bomber aircraft should be moved from their exposed stations to the comparative safety of airfields further to the west, and he at once put in train the necessary preparations, which were well advanced at the outbreak of war.[36]

It may appear that the Commander-in-Chief took an unduly pessimistic view of the situation, but this is not so, for the deficiencies in Bomber Command were really as serious as he judged them to be. In fact, the situation in the Air Force as a whole at the time of the Czech crisis was described by the Air Minister, Sir Kingsley Wood, as being 'positively tragic', since there were 'no real reserves, whether fighters or bombers'.[37] To translate such impressions into actual figures can easily be done by examining the records of the Mobilisable Committee, a body whose task it was to estimate the number of squadrons which could be assembled for action during a given period.

At a meeting held on 15 September 1938, the committee reviewed the prospects for the six-month period from 1 October 1938 to 31 March 1939 and concluded that at the beginning of this period it would be possible to mobilize 42 bomber squadrons.[38] Of these, 32 would be medium bombers – 13 Battle, 16 Blenheim, 3 Wellesley – and ten heavy bombers – 5 Whitley and 5 Harrow; but behind these squadrons there were virtually no reserves, either of aircraft or men, so that in the event of war there would have been no alternative but to 'roll up' some of the squadrons to provide reserves for a smaller first-line strength. The Air Staff had not yet made a firm decision as to what fraction of the force would have to be set aside for reserves, but if the figure of 50 per cent which had been mentioned to the Commander-in-Chief is applied in this case the Mobilisable Committee's 42 squadrons would be reduced to something like half that number. From this it will be evident that the bomber force was numerically too weak to have been effective in a major war; and in any case it was composed mainly of aircraft which lacked the range, bombload and armament required for successful attacks upon Germany.

The review of Britain's air defences which followed immediately after the Czech crisis emphasized the importance of giving first priority to Fighter Command, now recognised throughout the service as being our first line of defence against a 'knock-out blow'. Even Sir Edgar Ludlow-Hewitt had admitted that Britain's best hope of safety lay in the strongest possible system of 'close defence'. A number of Air Staff meetings in October produced a new expansion programme, Scheme M, which received Cabinet approval on 17 November. Scheme M gave the highest priority to the rearming of Fighter Command which was now fully confident that the Hurricanes and Spitfires then coming into service in small numbers would be capable of dealing with any of the new enemy bombers. The number of aircraft to be provided by 31 March 1940 remained approximately the same as under Scheme L, but beyond that date there was to be a second stage of expansion, to be completed by 31 March 1942. During the second stage of expansion the strength of

Fighter Command was to be increased to a total of 800 aircraft in fifty squadrons, with full reserves both of aircraft and personnel, while the number of aircraft in Bomber Command was merely to be restored to the level authorized in Scheme L, that is 1360 aircraft. As a temporary measure, introduced at the beginning of the new scheme, a number of Blenheim squadrons were converted into fighters and transferred from the bomber force to Fighter Command.

Fighter Command was also to be given first priority in the allocation of trained pilots, both regular and reserve, and again this hit hardest at Bomber Command where there was already a shortage of trained pilots. Immediate steps were however taken to alleviate the effects produced on the bomber squadrons. Commissioned pilots who were on the point of completing short service engagements were invited to extend their service, and non-commissioned pilots due to revert to their basic trades were encouraged to remain on flying duties. Efforts were also made to increase the number of trained flying personnel in the service as a whole. A new scheme for recruiting a greater number of pilots in Britain was launched, and more trained pilots were sought from the Dominions.[39] At the same time, the output of the existing flying training schools was to be increased, though without shortening the courses or reducing standards, and three new training schools were to be opened early in May 1939. Beyond that, plans for a further six schools were likely to be approved in the near future.[40]

In spite of this setback, there was some consolation for the Air Staff in that Scheme M was designed to carry forward the 'all-heavy' bomber policy. It was anticipated that when the end of the second stage of the scheme had been reached, on 31 March 1942, the majority of the 85 projected squadrons would be equipped with aircraft built to 1936 specifications. It is true that some of the squadrons would still be operating with the Whitleys, Hampdens and Wellingtons, but these types would in due course disappear as the Battles and Blenheims would have disappeared before them. When all the squadrons were eventually equipped with the four-engined Stirlings and Halifaxes and the twin-engined Manchesters, Bomber Command would possess a strong first-line force backed by adequate reserves of aircraft and trained aircrews. Such a powerful force, it was believed in 1938, would be capable of striking with real effect at the very outset of the war and might so change the balance of air power that it would be Germany and not Britain that would be threatened with defeat from the air.[41]

On 15 March 1939, German troops occupied Czechoslovakia and this act of aggression marked a complete change in Britain's relations with Germany. Whereas previously British opinion had in general been prepared to countenance a revision of the Versailles Treaty in Germany's favour, now it was unanimous in condemning the annexation of Czechoslovakia. In fact, Neville Chamberlain accurately traced the movement of public opinion regarding the actions of the Nazi government in a speech he made in Birmingham on 17 March 1939.

> Germany, under the present regime, has sprung a series of unpleasant surprises upon the world. The Rhineland, the Austrian Anschluss, the severance of Sudetenland – all these things shocked and affronted public opinion throughout the world. Yet, however much we might take exception to the methods which were adopted in each of those cases, there was something to be said, whether on account of racial affinity or of just claims too long resisted – there was something to be said for the necessity of a change in the existing situation.
>
> But the events which have taken place this week in complete disregard of the principles laid down by the German Government itself seem to fall into a different category, and they must cause us all to be asking ourselves: 'Is this the end of an old adventure, or is it the beginning of a new?'
>
> 'Is this the last attack upon a small State, or is it to be followed by others? Is this, in fact, a step in the direction of an attempt to dominate the world by force?'[42]

A few days later, on 23 March, Germany annexed Memel, a German city incorporated into Lithuania under the Versailles Treaty, and this action was seen as a direct threat against Poland. Indeed, it was widely believed that Poland would be Hitler's next victim and the aggressive attitude of Germany following the recovery of Memel suggested that a German attack on Poland would not long be delayed. There were hurried consultations between the British and Polish governments, and, with the approval of the French government, the Prime Minister announced in the House of Commons on 31 March that 'in the event of any action which clearly threatened Polish independence, and which the Polish Government accordingly considered it vital to resist with their national forces, His Majesty's Government would feel themselves bound at once to lend the Polish Government all support in their power. They have given the Polish Government an assurance to this effect. I may add that the French Government have authorised me to make it plain that they stand in the same position in this matter as do His Majesty's Government.'[43] The guarantee to Poland has often been criticised on the ground that neither Britain nor France were in a position to give direct military support to Poland if she were attacked by Germany. There is some substance in this criticism, but, on the other hand, it must be remembered that there was widespread support for the Prime Minister's view that no time should be lost in making clear to Hitler that a German attack on Poland would mean war with Britain and France.

Not unnaturally, the Chiefs of Staff were less than happy about the guarantee, since they could see no way in which Britain and France could bring direct support to Poland by sea, on land or in the air in the event of a German invasion. Indeed, they were somewhat embarrassed by their inability to offer a positive plan, and this led them to suggest that it might be necessary to change our bombing policy and direct our air attacks from the outset against important war targets in Germany. They thought that in the event of a German attack on Poland we should have great difficulty in finding a justification for our present restricted bombing policy, but the Committee of Imperial Defence was not prepared to change its policy.[44]

Scheme M was destined to run for less than a year before Europe was faced with the crisis which led to war. During that time the worst deficiencies of Bomber Command had been repaired, but much remained to be done to fashion it into an effective weapon of war. At the outbreak of hostilities all the squadrons had been re-equipped with modern aircraft, but few of these were really suitable for long-range operations. The medium bombers which comprised almost half the force were not capable of reaching targets in Germany from their home bases, and of the three heavy bombers in service only the Wellington was an aircraft of adequate performance. Nor was this weakness in striking power in any way compensated for by the numerical strength of the force. At the beginning of September 1939 there were a nominal 55 squadrons in the command, but because of the almost total lack of reserves it was necessary to 'roll-up' 22 squadrons on mobilization. The first-line strength of the force was therefore reduced to 33 squadrons, but since ten of these were equipped with Battles and six with Blenheims there were only 17 squadrons that were capable of playing an effective part in a strategic offensive.[45]

The formidable task which faced Sir Edgar Ludlow-Hewitt when he became Commander-in-Chief was rendered even more difficult by the failure of the Air Ministry to grasp the magnitude of the problems which beset the command. For reasons that are difficult to establish, the Air Staff had convinced themselves that the preparation of the bomber force for war was proceeding steadily (if somewhat slowly) and when the Commander-in-Chief constantly expressed his concern about the serious inadequacies of the force they refused to accept his judgement.

In his annual report of 1938, forwarded to the Air Ministry in March 1939, the Commander-in-Chief identified the basic weakness of the command by referring to a statement he had made in the previous year's report, namely, that the bomber force was expanding 'to an extent

Handley Page Hampden

Armstrong Whitworth Whitley

Neville Chamberlain on his return to Heston on 30 September 1938 after signing the Munich Agreement with Hitler. Note that the Prime Minister made his flight, not in a British aircraft of the national airline, Imperial Airways, but in an American aircraft, a Lockheed Model 14, of British Airways, an independent company that is really beyond its natural capacity.' It was in fact the over-expansion of the force, involving new and virtually untried aircraft, which had created the most difficult problems. Of these, the training of new aircrews was one of the most serious, as was stated in the report.

> The further twelve months' experience which has been acquired by all ranks since my last report was submitted has to a considerable degree been discounted by the fact that almost the entire effort of the Command has been devoted to the elementary training of new drafts of inexperienced personnel, and to mastering the maintenance and elementary operation of new equipment.[46]

This situation had arisen mainly because the Air Staff were slow to realize that the highly specialized training needed for the new aircrews could not be adequately provided on the squadrons. For most of the inter-war period the pilot was the only full-time member of aircrew and was the only one to receive a formal course of instruction before being posted to a squadron. His training also included an element of navigation since he was expected to navigate as well as to fly the aircraft. In aircraft which carried two pilots it was usual for the second pilot to carry out the navigational duties. The other aircrew members — the gunners and wireless operators — were recruited from ground tradesmen and received the whole of their flying training on the squadrons.

The initial break with this system was made when the new aircrew category of observer was introduced and the first Air Observers School was opened on 1 January 1936. The early entries at the school were taught only armament subjects, for it was intended that the observers should receive the navigational element of their training on the squadrons. Soon after, special provision was made to give formal training in navigation to those observers who were to fly in the types of aircraft which could carry only one pilot (Battle, Blenheim, Hampden); and finally, at the end of 1937, a full-time navigation course was provided for all air observers. It was not however until the severe shortage of trained aircrews had directed attention to the obvious wastefulness of employing trained pilots on navigational duties that the decision was taken, in May 1939, to make the observer fully responsible for the navigation of the aircraft.[47]

Strangely, the provisions for training air gunners remained almost non-existent until the very eve of the war, for if the new multi-gunned fighters were to prove as formidable as was predicted the safety of the bombers might well depend upon the accuracy with which the gunners could direct their fire. The Commander-in-Chief pointed to this deficiency in a letter written to the Air Ministry in May 1939.

No proper provision has yet been made for the adequate training of air gunners, and I fear that the standard of efficiency of air gunners and their ability to resist hostile attack remains extremely low. At present, in addition to the complete absence of any comprehensive school of instruction for air gunners, there is also a lack of recognised standard procedure, and the training of air gunners is left mainly to such knowledge, energy and initiative as can be found at units where there is an extreme shortage of qualified or efficient instructors.[48]

It must not however be imagined that any members of the aircrew received an adequate training before joining their squadrons. Even the pilots and observers fared indifferently. They were taught no more than the basic skills of their flying duties at the training schools and required a considerable amount of additional training to reach operational standard. And so, during the vital period of re-organization, from October 1938 to August 1939, the squadrons were little more than training units, as the Commander-in-Chief made clear in his annual report.

The results of this are illustrated by the lack of progress made in the programme of investigation of operational problems which was sent to the groups for action last March ... all units have been pre-occupied with elementary training and the crews have not as a whole attained a standard of operational efficiency in which these problems could be usefully explored.[49]

In these circumstances the need for a special unit to investigate the problems of bomber tactics and equipment acquired an even greater urgency. Again the Commander-in-Chief pressed for the formation of a Bombing Development Unit, emphasizing that 'without such a centre we should go to war in ignorance of the best answer to many questions vitally concerning the bombing offensive – questions, the answers to which, if not found in peacetime, can only be gained at great cost under the rigorous conditions of actual war.'[50]

Another problem which caused great concern to the Commander-in-Chief was the low serviceability rate in the bomber force. This was caused mainly by the lack of an adequate maintenance organization, but other important factors were the poor design and low reliability of much of the air equipment and the fact that modifications of one kind or another had to be carried out on all the new aircraft. The situation was in fact most serious, for the very limited operational effort of which Sir Edgar Ludlow-Hewitt believed his force was capable was based on the expectation of 75 per cent serviceability, whereas the command had achieved only 50 per cent serviceability during the period covered by his report.[51]

The Commander-in-Chief again stated the urgent need for an efficient intelligence organization. The intelligence officers for which he had asked had just been established on the bomber stations, but the command still possessed no detailed information relating to potential targets. Nor had any consideration been given to the provision of suitable aircraft for reconnaissance in wartime.

> So long ... as we have to depend only upon the heavy bombing missions to obtain our information and photographs we cannot expect the best results, which will only be obtainable when we have aircraft suited for special reconnaissance missions, which would normally be combined with harassing bombing. It is therefore to the speed bomber that I look to provide this important requirement in the future.[52]

The Commander-in-Chief also reaffirmed his belief in the need to develop long-range fighters,[53] but his arguments still failed to convince the Air Staff, who insisted that the use of escort fighters offered no solution to the problem of defending the bomber formations.[54]

Soon after submitting his Annual Report for 1938, Sir Edgar Ludlow-Hewitt represented his views in even stronger terms in a letter sent to the Air Ministry on 25 May 1939.[55] In it he repeated his warning that the operational efficiency of Bomber Command was still a long way below the standard that would be required of it in war, but again his warning was ignored. For there was still a deeply rooted conviction among the Air Staff that in the last analysis the efficacy of a bombing campaign would depend upon the morale of the squadrons and the aggressive spirit of the individual crews. The 1937 Bomber Command Annual Report had evoked the following comment from the Deputy Director of Operations: 'I am rather perturbed at the somewhat defeatist attitude which seems to pervade the report';[56] and the Commander-in-Chief's letter of 25 May 1939 elicited a similar reaction from the Chief of the Air Staff who noted on the file: '... he does, in my opinion, take a somewhat more pessimistic view than is justified as regards the progress which is being made in raising the standard of efficiency of the Bomber Command.'[57] Unfortunately, the experience of war all too quickly justified the Commander-in-Chief's fears.

CHAPTER SEVEN

BOMBING POLICY AND PLANS
OCTOBER 1938 TO SEPTEMBER 1939

As has been seen, the events which led to the Czech crisis had suggested that if war should break out Germany's initial offensive would probably be launched in the east. It was reasoned that if this should prove to be the case, there was every possibility that Britain would escape an onslaught from the air, provided that Bomber Command was committed to no offensive action that might provoke the Germans to retaliate. In such circumstances, it was deemed prudent to confine the activities of the bomber force to purely military objectives, at least in the opening phase of the war. In other words, the policy of restricted bombing was adopted simply because it was expedient to do so. There was no question of rejecting unrestricted bombing because it was felt that it contravened the laws of war. There were in fact no internationally agreed laws relating to air warfare; and in any case, official opinion in Britain inclined to the view that even if such laws were made they would be too artificial to survive the stresses of modern war. The belief that 'bombing, even if prohibited, could always be resorted to as an act of reprisal against some real or imagined breach of the laws of war'[1] was still strongly held. The fact that after the Munich Agreement first priority was given to the restricted plans was simply an acknowledgement of the grave weakness of Bomber Command. Planning for the unrestricted operations was of course continued, for this weakness was considered to be no more than a temporary ill and one which would gradually be overcome as the squadrons were re-equipped with the larger and more powerful aircraft.

The narrow margin by which war had been avoided in the Czech crisis served as a forceful reminder to the Air Staff of the inadequacy of their preparations for war; and as soon as it was clear that a respite had been gained by the Munich Agreement there followed a period of feverish activity at the Air Ministry to make good the obvious deficiencies in operational planning. It would have seemed logical to delegate more of this work to Bomber Command where the information essential to the planning could most easily be obtained; but in fact the Air Staff moved in the opposite direction and decided to take upon themselves even more of the responsibility for basic planning. This meant that the Air Ministry assumed responsibility for producing an operational appreciation for each of the approved plans, while Bomber Command was required to do nothing more than prepare operational orders and instructions.[2] The Commander-in-Chief opposed this change from the beginning, chiefly because he had no say in determining the practicability of the plans which were submitted to him; and when he attended a planning conference at the Air Ministry on 30 November he insisted that 'what he wanted from the Air Ministry was a memorandum rather than a plan. If he could have a reasoned statement showing the best targets to go for and their order of importance, he would then decide which of these it was possible to attack and the best method of execution.'[3]

The Air Staff soon found that their planning work was held up by the lack of technical information. And this could hardly have been otherwise, for owing to the fundamental changes which were being brought about by the rearming of the bomber force, much of this information was only just becoming available in an ordered form to the staff at Bomber Command. The Deputy Director of Plans, Group Captain J.C. Slessor, explained his difficulties to the Assistant Chief of the Air Staff, Air Vice-Marshal W.S. Douglas, in a minute dated 4 November. 'The staff officers engaged in the work', he wrote,

> are confronted at the outset by the need for certain assumptions regarding such matters as accuracy of bombing, types of attack, types and number of hitting bombs to destroy various kinds of target etc. Without such assumptions it is quite impossible to draw up war plans, as the planners can assess neither the vulnerability of targets to air attack nor the number of aircraft which should be earmarked on each target.

Group Captain Slessor proposed that a special committee should be set up to advise the planning staff,[4] but Air Vice-Marshal Douglas was not in favour of this approach. He ruled that every effort should first be made to obtain the information within the Air Ministry, and if that did not produce the desired result, the matter should then be referred to a committee specially convened for the purpose.[5] Predictably, the Air Ministry could not provide the required information, and so the ad hoc committee, of which the Commander-in-Chief was the senior Bomber Command representative, was called to meet at the Air Ministry on 30 November.[6]

The record of this meeting is in effect a brief but comprehensive survey of the war potential of the bomber force as described by the Commander-in-Chief less than a year before the outbreak of war. In it he expressed a greater degree of optimism regarding the future prospects of the force than is to be found in any other assessment he made either before or after this meeting. It is as if he were describing the force as he would have wished it to be, rather than as it actually was. Or it may be that he was looking further ahead to some unspecified time beyond the force then in being. Whatever the reason, the picture he painted did not remotely correspond to the force that went to war in 1939.

He thought that the force would be developed mainly for daylight operations, and predicted that even when all the aircraft types were capable of both day and night operations 75 per cent of the attacks would be made by day. He assumed that the precise target would be a feasible proposition, and, basing his argument on suspiciously low figures for daylight bombing errors (300 yards from high level, 75 yards from low level and 200 yards from a bombing run made in a shallow dive), he predicted that the regular mode of attack against precise targets would be from low level in daylight. And he was equally optimistic in his assessments of success for attacks carried out at long range. He fully appreciated that the chances of success would diminish in proportion to the increase in distances the aircraft were required to penetrate into enemy territory, yet he anticipated good results for distances up to 200 miles. Assuming three degrees of penetration, representing distances of 80, 150 and 200 miles, he estimated that for each of the three distances the percentage of the attacking force that would succeed in bombing the target would be 80, 50 and 40 respectively. For the aircraft despatched to attack area targets at night, he thought that an overall 75 per cent would find and bomb the target.

All too soon, however, events were to show how far the bomber force fell short of such expectations. Within four months of the outbreak of war, daylight operations were suspended after heavy losses had been sustained in raids against Germany where no penetration at all of enemy territory was involved; and when, early in 1940, the bomber force was compelled to turn to night raids against Germany, only a small fraction of the attacking force could find their targets in the dark.

Among the plans which clearly fulfilled the requirements of the Government's restricted bombing policy, those designed to attack the German Navy and its bases seemed to offer the most obvious advantages. They were genuinely offensive in character, yet they involved the smallest risk to civilian life and property and could be carried out with the minimum of penetration into enemy territory. When the Admiralty were asked to specify the targets whose destruction would most benefit the naval conduct of the war, they were emphatic in giving the highest priority to the German naval forces at Wilhelmshaven and Kiel; and in descending order they nominated the Kiel Canal locks at Brunsbüttel and Kiel and then the naval bases at Kiel, Wilhelmshaven, Cuxhaven and Bremerhaven.[7]

As soon as this information was received at the Air Ministry on 16 September, Bomber Command was asked to prepare a tactical appreciation of the Western Air Plan (W.A.7a) which dealt specifically with an attack on the German naval units at Wilhelmshaven. After carrying out a detailed examination of the plan, the Bomber Command staff were forced to conclude that the two elements vital to the success of such an attack – surprise and concentration – would be impossible to achieve with the force then in being. The element of surprise could best be attained by making the attack soon after dawn, but if this were to be attempted, the greater part of the flight would have to be made during the hours of darkness when accurate navigation would be a matter of the greatest difficulty. After making a flight of such long duration over the sea, the bombers would be obliged to make a landfall in order to check their position, and in so doing would forewarn the Germans of the attack. Nor was there any better chance of achieving concentration. The crews were not trained to fly in formation at night so there was no possibility of the attacking aircraft being able to make their way to the target as a single force.

The Air Staff did not dispute these arguments, but mistakenly assumed that the plan would be more acceptable to Bomber Command if the attack did not involve a long flight in the dark. In fact, the Commander-in-Chief was equally opposed to the idea of a daylight attack on this target. He was convinced that if the Whitleys were despatched across the North Sea in daylight the only predictable result would be the heavy losses they would sustain. The Air Staff then turned to the proposition that air attacks might force the German fleet to put to sea where it could be engaged by the Navy, but this idea was received with no greater enthusiasm by the Commander-in-Chief. He did not believe that the enemy fleet would be driven out to fight by such action, and this opinion was shared by the Commander-in-Chief of the Home Fleet.

In spite of these gloomy predictions, the Air Staff insisted, in a letter of 28 March 1939, that Bomber Command should maintain their aim to inflict as much damage as possible on the German fleet and to sink at least one German battleship. In his reply, the Commander-in-Chief made clear that he could not accept the assumption – implicit in the Air Staff letter – that his squadrons would be capable of hitting the enemy warships. Indeed, he pointed out that owing to their very limited

BSAP-M

training against naval targets it was most unlikely that they would be able to do so. But the most compelling argument in this debate was contained in a naval staff paper of 1 April 1939 which expressed the strongest doubts as to whether any kind of warship could be destroyed in an attack using the 500 lb bomb – the largest bomb then available in the Air Force.[8]

The plan to attack the Kiel Canal lock gates at Brunsbüttel and Kiel produced an even more pessimistic report from Bomber Command. The Commander-in-Chief thought it most unlikely that his aircraft would be able to cause significant damage to the lock gates by high altitude bombing until much larger bombs were available. The most effective method of attack would, he believed, be at low level with torpedoes, but at that time the Air Force possessed no torpedo-carrying aircraft capable of reaching either target. He was therefore forced to conclude that the destruction of these lock gates would not be a feasible operation until suitable torpedo-carrying aircraft were available, or alternatively, the squadrons were armed with bombs of much greater destructive power. The Air Staff not only accepted this appraisal but also discovered evidence which appeared to support it. A minute of 8 October 1938 from the department concerned with air tactics drew attention to the poor results which had been achieved against the Zeebrugge lock gates during the First World War. It stated that 48 tons of bombs had been dropped on these lock gates, which were only half the size of those on the Kiel Canal, yet the resulting damage had only temporarily put them out of action.[9]

At this point work on the plan was suspended, and nothing further was done until June 1939 when the Air Staff asked the Commander-in-Chief to investigate the tactical aspects of an attack on the lock gates using 1000 lb bombs. Since, however, no bomb of this size had yet been produced, the Bomber Command Staff were most unwilling to attempt an assessment of its probable effectiveness, pointing out that it would be 'impossible to make definite recommendations until further particulars are available regarding the ballistics and technical behaviour of the 1000 lb bomb'. The most they were prepared to say was that an attack with the 1000 lb bomb would probably be a feasible operation.[10]

During the early exchange of views between the Air Ministry and Bomber Command, consideration had been given to the possibility of blocking the Kiel Canal by sinking a ship actually in transit. It was agreed that such an attack would be a most difficult operation to carry out successfully, but when the plan was finally rejected it was for quite a different reason. The Commander-in-Chief had first raised the question as to 'whether it would be wise to attempt attacks on ships in the Kiel Canal thereby risking sinking a neutral merchant vessel'; but it was not merely the risk of bombing neutral ships that was a matter for concern, for the restricted policy also prohibited the bombing of enemy merchant ships.[11]

The lowest in priority of the three groups of naval targets — the one directed against the German naval bases — was the least favoured both at the Air Ministry and at Bomber Command. This was chiefly because of the fear that any misdirected bombs might fall on the civilian quarters of these ports, and so provide the Germans with a reason or an excuse for beginning unrestricted bombing against Britain. All the ports included in the list, with the single exception of Kiel, lay within range even of the medium bombers, but the Commander-in-Chief selected only Wilhelmshaven for attack, on the ground that the restricted bombing policy was least likely to be contravened against that target. The Bomber Command appreciation therefore recommended that the bombing of shore installations should in the first instance be confined to Wilhelms-haven alone.[12]

It would be absurd to imagine that Sir Edgar Ludlow-Hewitt had the slightest confidence in his command's ability to carry out any of the naval plans successfully; and it is a measure of his awareness of the serious limitations of the bomber force that it was he who initiated work on the least offensive of all the restricted plans, the dropping of propaganda material over Germany.[13] He first suggested the possibility of using the bomber force for this purpose in a letter to the Deputy Chief of the Air Staff, Air Vice-Marshal R.E.C. Peirse, on 14 September 1938.

> I wonder whether any steps are being taken for the production of suitable leaflets for dropping in hostile territory in the event of war. In my opinion, it may well prove that skilfully dropped propaganda, distributed by aircraft, may prove a more potent weapon than bombs.

Air Vice-Marshal Peirse had no knowledge of what, if anything, was being done in this matter and was compelled to seek information from the Committee of Imperial Defence. On 21 September he was informed that 'a certain amount of thought has been devoted to this but not as much as we could wish for and there are at present no plans in detail'. Two days later, however, he received a second note, and in it he was assured that action had already been started.

> This matter has been launched as a question of the utmost urgency. The individual responsible is Sir Hughe Knatchbull Hugessen ... The Foreign Office are preparing a draft in conjunction with an appropriate propaganda expert and are arranging for its proper

translation. The Stationery Office have been put in touch with Hugessen to make the necessary arrangements for rapid printing.

From that moment onwards the project quickly gained momentum, and before the end of September 1938 several government departments were involved in the work and experiments with various sized packages of leaflets had been carried out at the Air Force station at Mildenhall.

The Air Staff supported the plan but thought that it was 'desirable to utter a note of warning that this use of aircraft must be strictly limited and confined to the essential minimum and that it may be necessary to resist pressure from some quarters to overdo this form of activity'. The plan did in fact generate a wave of enthusiasm which was out of all proportion to its value as an operation of war; and there was a real danger that such enthusiasm would cause an exaggerated importance to be accorded to a plan which owed its existence almost entirely to the difficulties of finding any other practicable scheme which would conform to the policy of restricted bombing and at the same time fulfil the need to conserve the force. It is true that there were advantages to be gained by putting the plan into operation at the outset of hostilities. The leaflets were cheap and easy to produce and could be dropped at night, with negligible risk to the bombers. This would enable the aircrews to gain invaluable operational experience, while the Air Staff would be provided with first-rate evidence for assessing the efficiency of both crews and aircraft.

On the other hand, there was a grave risk that if the operations were planned on too ambitious a scale — Berlin had already been suggested as a possible target — the losses in first-line aircraft might be no less severe than those that would be experienced on the smaller scale raids against the restricted targets. Indeed, the Commander-in-Chief soon began to think along these lines, and in a letter to the Deputy Chief of the Air Staff of 28 September he expressed strong doubts as to the wisdom of risking his aircraft on this type of work and suggested the possibility of using balloons for distributing leaflets, as had been done in the First World War. Air Vice-Marshal Peirse agreed that an exaggerated importance was being given to the propaganda plan, and his pencilled note in the margin of this letter made this clear. 'I do not think it permissible', he wrote, 'to send Whitleys to Berlin for the business of dropping leaflets whilst our bomber resources are so limited'. Nevertheless, arrangements for the production of suitable material continued to move forward at a brisk pace, and on 12 May 1939 the Commander-in-Chief was informed that eight million leaflets, the number intended to be dropped on the first day of war, would be delivered to the headquarters of the bomber groups during the next few days.

These then were the only plans which could be put into operation so long as the restricted bombing rule was in force. But there was no way of knowing how long the restriction would last in wartime: it might be for a short or for a considerable period of time, or it might not come into force at all. If the Germans refrained from unrestricted air action it would be politic for Britain to do the same. If, on the other hand, they opened the war with unrestricted bombing against Britain, it would be incumbent upon Bomber Command to reply in kind with whatever force it could muster; and for this reason it was essential for the Air Staff to keep the unrestricted plans under constant review and to make whatever revisions seemed necessary from time to time.

It will be remembered that the unrestricted plan most favoured both by Bomber Command and the Air Ministry was the one directed against the industry of the Ruhr. The Air Targets Intelligence report of 8 September 1938 had described the Ruhr as the 'greatest and most centralised industrial area in the world', containing more than half the industrial population of Germany and producing 75 per cent of the country's steel, 60 per cent of its heavy engineering and by far the greater part of its basic chemicals. Moreover, the report had rated its importance to Germany to be such that 'if it were paralysed the German economic system could not function, and Germany ... would become impotent to wage a war on a large scale in less than three months'.[14]

As has been shown, Sir Edgar Ludlow-Hewitt was much impressed with the plan and thought that provided a sustained bombardment could be maintained it would be possible to cripple the industry of this vital area. From the list of suggested objectives he chose a group of 45 targets – 26 coking plants and 19 electricity generating stations – whose destruction he estimated would achieve this effect.

> I have made an approximate calculation of the number of sorties which would be necessary in order to cover the 45 targets ... including an allowance of 75 per cent of the attacks being comparative failures; the figure I get is something over 3,000 sorties which would represent a wastage of 176 aircraft ... As an indication of the task involved, it is possible that given good weather, the output of these coking plants and electricity generating stations can be reduced below the critical minimum in about a month by 300 aircraft working at 'sustained effort' or in half that time by 600 aircraft.[15]

The Air Staff could not accept this assessment, considering that it was altogether too optimistic. They did not believe that these targets would be as vulnerable to attack as the Bomber Command appreciation suggested, nor did they accept the Commander-in-Chief's view that the

45 objectives he had selected constituted a vital target group. They thought a different approach should be made and called upon the Plans Department of the Air Ministry to prepare a plan of broader scope for the attack on the German war industry.

This plan, which was forwarded to the Chief of the Air Staff on 3 February 1939, was written by the Director of Plans, Air Commodore J. C. Slessor. In it he stated that although 'we have located no key industrial group, the destruction of which would dislocate the whole of German War Industry ... there is a key service, Power, which is mainly electricity, the dislocation of which would bring about a very important reduction of all German War Industry'. He believed that there were two possible ways in which this effect might be achieved. The first one, which was considered the more desirable, would entail the destruction in the first six weeks of the war of 64 electricity generating stations and ten gas coking plants. The drawback to this course of action was that it would involve considerable operational difficulties; for the 74 targets were scattered over the whole of Germany, and the majority of them would have to be attacked from low level.

The alternative to this was to aim for the dislocation of the Ruhr industry; for it was believed that if this could be achieved it would cause severe damage to the rest of the German war industry. Forty-eight power targets in this area were selected for attack and, of these, 33 were considered large enough to be bombed from high level. Of the two courses of action, the second one was selected as being the one more likely to succeed; and the overriding consideration which determined this choice was that if the route over the Low Countries should be denied to the bomber force, the targets in the Ruhr would not call for deep penetration into German territory. And even if the second course of action were decided upon, it would still be possible to bomb some of the targets nominated in the first one, whenever circumstances permitted.[16]

When the Air Staff plan was sent to Bomber Command for comment on 31 January 1939, the Commander-in-Chief was already having second thoughts about the idea of attacking the Ruhr. As was so often the case, the closer he examined the details of a plan the less confident he felt that his squadrons were capable of carrying it out. It was now apparent that the neutrality of the Low Countries would be maintained until some time after the outbreak of war, so that he could not plan on the assumption of being able to fly over these countries to reach the targets in Germany. This meant that the Blenheims would not be able to reach the Ruhr from bases in England unless they could refuel in France. And to make a difficult situation even worse, the Commander-in-Chief had now decided that he could no longer regard the poorly armed Battle as an effective day bomber. He was convinced that it would not be able to survive against the latest German fighter, the Messerschmitt 109, and for that reason did not intend to use it in the early attacks on the Ruhr, as the Air Ministry plan required. He was also critical of the quality of the staff work which was bestowed upon the plan. He stressed the need for better information concerning the targets and pointed to the fact that some assumptions regarding the destructive power of various bomb-loads were incorrect.[17]

The Air Staff reply to these comments, dated 27 March 1939, promised to look into the matter of providing better target intelligence, and stated that it was generally believed that the restriction on flying over the Low Countries would not last long after the outbreak of war, so that the Blenheims could then be used directly against the Ruhr. On the question of the Battles, it was thought that they would, of necessity, have to be committed to the initial attack, since they represented nearly half the command's medium bomber strength.[18]

It is somewhat surprising to discover that no plan for an attack on oil — a commodity that would be vital in a future war — was prepared until shortly before the outbreak of hostilities. It was not until 1 July 1939 that the first draft of the Air Ministry appreciation was sent to Bomber Command, to be followed by a revised version at the end of the month. The appreciation was based on the correct assumption 'that the maintenance of adequate supplies of oil is one of the weakest links in Germany's war potential'. It was no secret that Germany was heavily dependent upon imported oil or that the industry established by the Nazi government to produce synthetic oil from coal (though technically very successful) had failed to supply more than a fraction of the country's normal consumption. The appreciation estimated that if Germany's supply of foreign oil could be cut off and if air action could destroy a part of her oil stocks, her position within a year would be serious. The three sources of Germany's oil supply were stated to be imported crude oil, domestic oil and synthetic oil produced from coal by the Berius method of hydrogenation and by the Fischer-Tropsch process. It was believed that oil storage sites, refineries and (in the case of synthetic oil) processing plants would be the most suitable targets, and a list containing 32 of the most important objectives was included in the appreciation. Of these targets, 23 lay within reach of the western frontier; and it was recommended that if political considerations allowed the attacks to begin within the first four weeks of the war the above-ground stocks of imported oil should be attacked first, to be followed by the hydrogenation plants, the domestic refineries and the Fischer-Tropsch plants, in that order.[19]

The oil plan was the last of the independent plans to be drafted in peacetime, and when, a few weeks later, Europe was plunged into war, the Air Staff were still no nearer to formulating a bombing policy than they had been at the time of the Czech crisis. They had studied the operational requirements of a wide range of both restricted and unrestricted plans, but they had no confidence in the ability of the bomber force to execute any of the plans, save for the non-offensive propaganda plan. Whatever differences of opinion the Air Ministry and Bomber Command might have had as to the war readiness of the force, both were agreed that it was an instrument of very limited striking power. The squadrons were still suffering from the over-rapid expansion of the force, and this was most clearly reflected in the lack of valid flying experience among the aircrews and in the serious shortage of all kinds of ground and air equipment.

During the last few months of peace, the Air Staff increasingly turned their attention to the task of finding a role for the bomber force in the event that the Germans should open the war with a land campaign in the West. The German annexation of Czechoslovakia in March 1939 had convinced the Government that a full exchange of views between the British and French armed services should no longer be delayed, and on 5 April the air staff talks opened with a meeting in London between Commandant Bailly of the French Air Force and Air Commodore Slessor, Director of Plans at the Air Ministry.[20]

As soon as the Air Staff had had time to consider the ideas put forward by the French, the Director of Plans informed Sir Edgar Ludlow-Hewitt of the substance of his discussions with Commandant Bailly and of the Air Staff's reaction to them.[21] 'The French Delegation', he wrote,

> showed a preoccupation, amounting almost to an obsession, with the probability of the German initial course of action consisting of a major land and air offensive against the Low Countries and France. The French fear that German armies might achieve surprise in a sudden attack on Southern Holland and Belgium and might, by a rapid advance through those countries, be able to outflank the Maginot Line. They therefore attach great importance to action calculated to interfere with and delay the German Army in its advance.

If such a situation should arise, he told the Commander-in-Chief, the allied bombing forces would be concentrated to prevent the German advance and 'the role of your Command might for a time be to operate with your whole mobilisable striking force in collaboration with the French Army and Air Force in the land battle'.

During the meeting Commandant Bailly suggested three ways in which air bombing could be used to delay the advance of the German Army.

These were: to attack enemy columns moving along the roads; to attack rail and road communications in the zone of operations; and to attack the German Air Force, in order to reduce the weight of air attack upon the French Army.

The discussion opened with an exchange of views on the influence that German air power might be expected to exert on the outcome of the campaign. Commandant Bailly thought that it was essential that the British and French air striking forces should be prepared to take a course of action that would neutralize the power of the German bomber force. He stated that this could best be achieved by attacking the aerodrome surfaces of the German bomber stations, estimating that if 20 tons of bombs were dropped on each aerodrome this would cause operations to be suspended for a considerable time. The Director of Plans was very familiar with the difficulties associated with this type of attack and he pointed out to the Commandant that since there was no way of discovering which of the many available aerodromes the Germans intended to use in war it was most unlikely that 'the plan ... would be *wholly* successful even for a short period, and that our inter-ference with enemy air operations would thus be only temporary and partial'.

Nor did he give any greater support to the suggestion that an attack should be made on that part of the German aircraft industry which was engaged in manufacturing the Junkers 88, 'a high performance German bomber of which the French were particularly afraid'. He again pointed to the difficulty of knowing which targets to attack. In this case there was the problem of identifying the factories in which the various com-ponents of this aircraft were made. Nevertheless, he promised that full consideration would be given to these ideas and he submitted them to Bomber Command and to the appropriate department of the Air Ministry for comment.

Bomber Command's objections to the idea of an attack on the German Air Force – Commandant Bailly's plan was in essence W.A.1 with a different aim in view – were as strong as ever. In an appreci-ation dated 21 April 1939, the Commander-in-Chief stated that the Netheravon Trials had shown conclusively that the weight of bombs needed to put aerodromes out of action was far beyond anything we could hope to attain; and even when an attack did succeed, it would do no more than cause a 'problematical delay of short duration'. In any case, a campaign of this type 'might entail losses out of proportion to the effect achieved'.[22]

A note from Plans 2 at the Air Ministry intimated that any plan for an attack on the German aircraft industry should include a wider range of targets than that indicated by Commandant Bailly. The note suggested that the provision for an attack on this sector of German industry contained in W.A.1 would serve as well to reduce the scale of the air offensive against France as against Britain; but warned that 'it would not be the best plan if the aim is limited to causing an immediate reduction in the German air operations co-operating with a rapid advance of the German Army through Belgium'.[23]

Less than a week after the initial meeting between the two air staffs, the French sent to the Air Ministry an outline of their plan for large-scale air attacks against rail and road communications (mainly the former) along which the enemy military units were expected to move in order to take up their positions immediately after the outbreak of war. When the Air Staff had studied the plan they realized that once again there were serious differences of opinion between themselves and the French staff. The fundamental difference was that the French believed that the German Army would not have concentrated before the outbreak of hostilities and had therefore based their plan on that assumption, whereas the British considered the assumption to be false. The other areas of disagreement were concerned with the bombing methods to be used and the results they were expected to yield.

The chief aim of the plan was to hinder the movement of enemy formations by means of intensive attacks on rail communications, and this was to be achieved by making repeated breaches in the open stretches of the railway line, as far removed as possible from the rail centres and therefore from the repair depots. The main weight of the attack was to be directed against the area east of the Ruhr in order to sever its rail communications with east and north-eastern Germany. Altogether 18 main and 17 minor lines were selected for attack, and since it was estimated that each line would need to be cut in three places, over 100 cuts would have to be made and maintained.[24]

Shortly before the French plan was sent to the Air Ministry the Air Staff had completed a fresh study of the possibility of attacking communications in the Ruhr. Frequent and well attested reports indicated that the German railways were short of locomotives and rolling stock and that in some districts railway tracks were in a poor state of repair; and this evidence taken together with recent intelligence reports which pointed to the increased likelihood of an initial German attack in the west, suggested the idea of modifying the Ruhr Plan (W.A.5a) in such a way as to bring about the disruption of the Ruhr industry by means of systematic attacks on rail communications. The modified plan, which was designated W.A.5b, was seen to possess the advantage of combining the elements of an independent and an auxiliary offensive, since it would maintain the original aim of dislocating the industry of the Ruhr, while at the same time causing the greatest impediment to a German invasion of the Low Countries. It was thought that the maximum effect would be produced by a large number of small-scale raids spread over a wide area of the railway system. The list of targets for daylight attack included the ten most important railway lines in western Germany, and in addition a number of strategic rail centres were nominated for night attack.[25]

Subsequent meetings between the two air staffs did nothing to eliminate the wide divergences of opinion concerning the railway attack. The Air Staff accepted that a plan of the type proposed by the French was desirable, but insisted that in its present form it was not a feasible proposition with the very limited bomber forces at the disposal of the two allies. They pointed out that the success of the plan would depend upon repeated attacks being made (in all weathers, both by day and night) on a scale that would be impossible to achieve. In any case, the Air Staff did not consider that the type of attack described – against the open track – would be a practicable one, and suggested that it might be better to attack the rail centres listed in the revised Ruhr Plan (W.A.5b).[26]

In spite of this criticism the French continued to believe that the railway plan would achieve the desired results, and on 1 June they submitted to the Air Ministry an assessment of the tactical considerations involved. They claimed that

> the permanent way itself (ballast – sleepers – rails) can be effectively damaged by means of the blast of a medium sized bomb (50 kg). The attack can therefore be carried out at a low altitude, below 1000 metres. In view of the small dispersion, and the possibility of carrying a high number of bombs, optimum results are obtained from the bombing attack.

They thought that if the attacks were made against open stretches of the line there would be little to fear from anti-aircraft defences, but admitted that the operations would involve penetration of enemy territory of up to 150 kilometres, and therefore beyond the range of escort fighters. Then, somewhat surprisingly, they confessed that they did not at that time possess any bombers of sufficiently high performance to carry out these raids, except at night and when there was continuous cloud cover during the day; and this clearly implied that in the present situation the onus of carrying out the attacks would fall mainly on the British squadrons. Nevertheless, the French air staff remained convinced of the vital importance of the plan and insisted on giving it the highest priority until such time as they received positive evidence that the Germans had completed their concentration.[27]

The Air Staff did not reply to this communication until 16 August, but by that time they had gathered more than enough information to confirm their doubts about the plan. Their main contention was that the French estimate of the effort required to breach a railway line was completely at variance with the findings of recent experiments in Britain. These experiments had led to the conclusion that a formation of six medium or three heavy bombers would be needed to cut both lines of a double-track railway, though it was thought that these figures might have to be doubled for war operations. Railway experts believed that such a breach could be located and repaired in a matter of four hours; so that on this reckoning an absolute minimum of 42 raids (the equivalent of 252 medium or 126 heavy bomber sorties) would have to be made each week to keep one line cut. And, indeed, the tremendous expenditure of effort which these calculations suggested would be necessary to cause a disruption in rail communications was borne out by recent evidence of the war in China. It was recorded that Japanese air attacks on the Canton–Kowloon railway had involved 718 sorties in 103 days, in which 1,490 bombs were dropped; yet during the whole of that period the movement of through traffic along the line was suspended for a total of no more than ten days.[28]

The last of the French suggestions for allied air co-operation was intended to check the German advance through the Low Countries by attacking enemy columns on the roads. The initial reaction to the idea at Bomber Command was mildly favourable. The Commander-in-Chief was prepared to admit that 'if large columns of German troops can be found in the open in daylight, air attack may be effective in causing casualties and delays'; but he was not at all sure that the aircraft in his command were suitable for this type of work. He pointed out that recent experiments on Salisbury Plain had shown clearly that fighter aircraft would be more effective against troops in the open than fast modern bombers. He thought that of the day bombers available for use the Battle, a manoeuvrable aircraft which afforded the pilot a good view, was the most suitable type for attacking columns; but he found it 'difficult to envisage an efficient tactical method which could be adopted by such aircraft as the Blenheim, Hampden and Wellington for work of this kind'. He believed that the twin-engined bombers could more profitably be employed against vehicles on the road or in parks and against railway rolling stock, but insisted that only a part of the force should be used in this way. As for the rest of the force, he recommended that it 'should be directed against targets further to the rear, such as train movements, transport parks and depots, and military communications generally. In this connection, Plan W.A.5b seems to be the most effective way of dealing with a German advance on the Dutch frontier'.[29]

When this subject was discussed at a meeting of the British and French army and air staffs at the War Office on 27 April 1939, it was agreed that the French should draw up an operational plan. Nearly a month elapsed before the plan was sent to the Air Ministry and when it arrived it was something less than had been expected. It was in fact simply a list of objectives and these, it was stated, had been

> selected by the French Command along the roads in Belgium and Holland as those on which attack is most liable to hold up the German motorised columns invading the two countries in question. In consequence the selection has lighted principally upon the cross-roads at the entrance or exit of towns and villages, or villages where there is a point at which traffic must become congested as the result of a bridge over a river, etc.[30]

The War Office were less than impressed by the French plan, and in particular by the choice of objectives, believing that there were too many alternative routes which the Germans might use; but it was at Bomber Command that the chief objections were raised. It was felt that roads were difficult targets to damage effectively and would require attacks to be carried out from a dangerously low altitude. There was also the formidable problem of securing information about the movement of enemy troops through a bottleneck and then of being able to get aircraft to the target quickly enough to exploit the situation. But the crux of the matter was that the Commander-in-Chief was reluctant to support a plan which involved his aircraft in low-level attacks over the battle area, and for this reason no further work was done on the plan until the outbreak of war.[31]

During the spring and summer of 1939 events in Europe moved swiftly and inexorably towards war. This last dangerous phase began with a speech by Hitler to the Reichstag on 28 April. In it he demanded the return of Danzig and the granting of an extra-territorial route across the Polish Corridor, while at the same time repudiating the Anglo-German naval treaty and the non-aggression pact with Poland.[32] The pattern of aggression was about to be repeated: the parts played by Henlein and the Sudetenland in Czechoslovakia were now to be filled by Forster and Danzig in Poland. But the situation was different in one vital respect. The Polish people were united in their determination to fight for their independence, and their resolve was strengthened by the guarantee given by Britain and France.

It is true that neither Britain nor France could give direct military aid to Poland if she were attacked, and this fact was clearly recognized by the three countries. Nevertheless, the guarantee stood as an un-equivocal warning to Hitler that any further aggressive action on his part would plunge Europe into war; and it was hoped that this prospect would be sufficient to convince him that he would have to pay too heavy a price to achieve his ambitions.

If, however, Hitler refused to be deterred, Poland stood little chance of surviving a German attack unless the support of the Soviet Union could be secured. The more the British Cabinet considered the possible courses of action open to them the more they were driven to the conclusion that a serious effort should be made to establish a triple alliance between the Soviet Union, Britain and France. Chamberlain was most reluctant to open negotiations with the Soviet Union, not only because he knew that the small nations whose independence he was endeavouring to preserve would be unwilling to accept aid from a country they feared and hated no less than Germany, but also because he distrusted Soviet motives which, he recorded, 'seem to me to have little connection with our ideas of liberty, and to be concerned only with getting every one else by the ears'.[33] Nevertheless, he conceded that it was necessary at least to investigate the possibility of such an alliance, and in June negotiations were begun in conjunction with the French. Later, an Anglo-French military mission was despatched to Moscow, but the negotiations made little headway and there seemed to be no desire on the part of the Soviet government that an agreement should be reached.[34]

Even while these negotiations were still in progress, Hitler made a personal approach to Stalin to seek an understanding with the Soviet leader which would secure his position in the east while he was settling the account with Poland. When he made this move, the date set for the attack on Poland lay only a few weeks ahead, and this would suggest (what other evidence confirms) that he was confident he could secure the agreement whenever he wanted.[35] The subsequent negotiations were carried out at incredible speed, and within a matter of days of the initial move an astonished world was informed, in the early hours of 24 August, that the two apparently implacable enemies had concluded a non-aggression pact.[36]

It has often been asserted that Stalin, having failed to overcome the reluctance of the allied delegation to reach an agreement, had no alternative but to make a pact with Hitler; yet the intervening years have provided no evidence at all to support this view. All the indications suggest that he could have had a pact with Britain and France simply for the asking, but that he did not want one if he could come to terms with Hitler. And the pointers to his preference for Hitler are to be found, first, in the condition which he insisted must first be fulfilled before the pact could be signed and, second, in the price he demanded for the pact itself. So far as the price was concerned, this was to be paid in territory. The Soviet Union was to receive the eastern part of a partitioned Poland and was to be given a free hand to recover certain territories in eastern Europe which she had lost as a result of the First World War.[37] The action which Stalin insisted must be taken before the pact could be ratified was that a trade agreement which had already been drawn up and approved by the two governments should be signed and announced to the world.[38]

This agreement was followed in quick succession by other agreements which aimed at increasing the volume of trade between the two countries. Broadly speaking, the Soviet Union was to receive a wide range of industrial products, including the machine tools which her inefficient industry could not produce, and in return she undertook to supply the raw materials which Germany so desperately needed and without which she could hardly have gone to war in 1939.[39] After the outbreak of war the two countries drew closer together, and the Soviet Union acted on Germany's behalf to purchase on the world's markets raw materials which she herself could not supply.[40] Later, she provided facilities for the Germans to import materials through various Soviet ports and even went so far as to waive charges on all such goods carried on the Soviet railways.[41]

The links between Germany and the Soviet Union which were forged during the last days of peace have been recorded in some detail because of the effects which this unlikely partnership produced on Britain's war plans and preparations. The broad lines of strategic thinking in Britain were founded on the assumption that Germany was economically too weak to sustain a protracted war, and this was especially true so far as the bombing policy was concerned. It must be emphasized that this assumption was based on compelling evidence, and when Air Commodore Slessor, the Director of Plans, stated a few days after the outbreak of war that Germany was 'weak in financial and economic resources' he was expressing an opinion which was widely held by informed observers throughout Europe.[42]

The pact between Germany and the Soviet Union radically changed the situation. Hitler was now able to press on with his aggressive designs in the certain knowledge that he would not fail through the lack of essential war materials. Within months, Germany's economic position was greatly strengthened by Soviet aid and the effect of this was seriously to weaken the impact of the naval blockage upon which Britain placed such great reliance. At the same time, it was of no small consequence that the assessments of Germany's economic weaknesses which formed the basis of important elements of the strategic bombing plans were now no longer valid.[43]

CHAPTER EIGHT

CONCLUSIONS

The immense effort which had been expended in preparing the bomber force for war seemed to have been of no avail. When war finally came, Bomber Command — numerically weak in aircraft and acutely short of every type of air and ground equipment — was in no position to influence the outcome of events in the opening phase of the war. The Air Staff had no illusions about the war-readiness of the force, and it was their firm intention to confine its operational activities to leaflet dropping, reconnaissance missions and small-scale raids against naval targets. This resolve to conserve the force until the initial onslaught of the enemy had been warded off was strengthened by the Government's ruling that no attacks should be made against targets which might put at risk the lives and property of enemy civilians. Whatever criticism may be levelled at the restricted bombing policy, it certainly worked as a shield to protect the bomber force from the heavy casualties it would undoubtedly have suffered if it had been launched upon a campaign of intensive raids in the first phase of the war. And if evidence is needed to support this assertion, it is to be found unequivocally in the experience gained from a number of small-scale raids carried out early in the war against the limited German naval targets which were permitted under the restricted ruling.

Before the end of 1939 Bomber Command had carried out a series of attacks against the German navy; and of these attacks four are of special importance, for they put to the test of battle the ability of the self-defending bomber formation to carry out its mission and survive against the new multi-gun fighters supported by early warning radar and anti-aircraft defences.[1]

The first of these four raids was made on 4 September 1939, when, in bad weather conditions, ten Blenheims and nine Wellingtons attacked German warships in the Heligoland Bight. The Blenheims, making their attacks at low level (500 feet and below), encountered heavy and accurate anti-aircraft fire, and five of them failed to return. Some of the

Wellingtons were engaged by Me 109 fighters and two failed to return. The experience of this raid was difficult to interpret, but it seemed to suggest that whereas the enemy anti-aircraft guns had proved effective the fighters had not.

Prolonged periods of bad weather combined with the difficulties of obtaining reliable and up-to-date information about the movement of enemy ships prevented another raid being attempted until 3 December. On that day, 24 Wellingtons, seeking out enemy ships in the Heligoland area, encountered heavy anti-aircraft fire and were attacked by Me 109 and Me 110 fighters. The bombers had some difficulty in maintaining their formations during the engagement but all returned safely to their bases. The most notable feature of the battle was the tendency of the German fighters to break off their attacks as soon as they came within range of the bombers' guns.

The next encounter took place on 14 December when 12 Wellingtons carried out an armed patrol of the Schillig Roads. Weather conditions in the area were very bad. The bombers came under heavy fire from both naval and flak ships; again enemy single- and twin-engined fighters joined the battle, but on this occasion they pressed home their attacks with more determination. Five Wellingtons failed to return and one crash-landed on arriving at base. Again, it was impossible to determine with any certainty whether the anti-aircraft guns or the fighters had been the more dangerous. The Air Staff inclined to the view that the casualties had been the victims of gunfire, while the fighters had been thwarted in their attacks by the combined fire-power of the bombers flying in formation.

A few days later, on 18 December, the last of these raids took place. On that day, weather conditions, which on previous occasions had confounded both attackers and defenders, were perfect. The sky was cloudless and visibility almost unlimited when 22 Wellingtons, having aimed their bombs from 13,000 feet at enemy warships near Wilhelmshaven, were attacked by enemy fighters which, as on previous occasions, had been warned by radar of the bombers' approach. The fighters pursued the bombers for some 80 miles on the homeward flight and pressed their attacks relentlessly. Only ten of the 22 bombers succeeded in reaching England, and of those, three made forced landings before reaching their bases.

The superiority of the fighter over the bomber in daylight was now proved beyond doubt, and Sir Edgar Ludlow-Hewitt, who had himself stated that the danger and difficulty of daylight operations must be measured by the distance of penetration into enemy territory which they involved, pointed out that none of the raids against the German navy had involved any real penetration of enemy territory.[2] It was now clear that there was not the remotest possibility of attacking inland targets without suffering prohibitive losses. The Commander-in-Chief had therefore no alternative but to call a halt to the daylight operations, and from that moment on he began the conversion of Bomber Command into a force which would operate almost exclusively during the hours of darkness when the German air defences (like our own) were almost non-existent.

Thus, the experience of the first few months of war had shown that the claims made for the bomber force had not been matched by actual performance; and so it is pertinent to ask at this juncture whether, in the light of subsequent events in the Second World War, the Air Staff should not have been able to form a clearer picture both of the nature of strategic bombing and of the aircraft and equipment needed to carry it out. The answer to this may be found by asking two specific questions. First, should it have been possible for them to create a more modern and more efficient bomber force in the time allowed and with the resources which were available? And second, in view of the fact that Bomber Command was designed primarily as a day bomber force, could they reasonably have been expected to anticipate the difficulties inherent in daylight operations?

To take the second question first, the evidence of the Second World War suggests a negative answer. Even a cursory study of the daylight strategic operations carried out by the other major air powers, Germany and the United States, shows that the air staffs of these nations, like the British Air Staff, were beguiled by their own visions of the bomber as an instrument of the offensive uninhibited by the normal constraints of war. In consequence, they seriously overrated the efficacy of strategic bombing and equally seriously underrated the problems involved in carrying it out. Of the three air staffs, the British formed the most accurate assessment of the hazards of daylight operations. They recognized the need to equip the bombers with a powerful defensive armament and were rightly convinced that if the guns were to be fired effectively they must be enclosed in power-operated turrets. Where they erred was in believing that the combined fire-power of the bombers flying in formation would be sufficiently effective to neutralize the fighter's superiority in speed and fire-power. One consequence of the belief in the self-defending bomber formation was that the feasibility of producing a long-range escort fighter was never seriously explored. As has been shown, the vulnerability of the bomber to fighter attack was revealed early in the war, and it was indeed fortunate for Britain that the discovery was made as a result of fairly minor operations and that the losses sustained in them were relatively light.

In contrast, the Germans were to suffer defeat in one of the most crucial battles of the war as the penalty for underestimating the dangers of daylight operations against well-defended targets. By the summer of 1940 they had made themselves masters of most of western Europe and only the Hurricanes and Spitfires of Fighter Command stood between them and victory. When they launched their offensive in the Battle of Britain they appeared to enjoy every possible advantage. They possessed great numerical superiority, and since their bases in France and in the Low Countries lay within short range of their objectives in southern England they were able to use large numbers of conventional fighters to protect the bombers. Yet they failed for the same reason that the British squadrons had failed in their operations across the North Sea: that is, because their bombers, which carried a much less effective armament than the Wellingtons, could not survive against the multi-gun fighter. Without doubt the German bomber squadrons would have suffered even more serious losses if they had not received such dedicated support from their escort fighters. On the other hand, the Germans might well have won the battle for air supremacy if they had possessed an effective long-range escort fighter. As it was, the short-range Me 109 — the twin-engined Me 110 proved to be a failure in this role — constantly operated near to the limit of its fuel endurance, and could not provide the continuous support that was essential to the survival of the ill-armed bombers.

The American experience of strategic bombing was gained by the squadrons of the Eighth Air Force which operated from airfields in eastern England from 1942 until the end of the war. In spite of the clear evidence of failure of both the British and German daylight bombing operations, the American air staff were still convinced that the self-defending bomber formation was the key to success in this type of operation. They believed that if their heavy bombers, the Flying Fortresses and Liberators, could fly at greater altitudes and in larger and more heavily armed formations than had been attempted before, they would be able to fight their way to their targets. They were also confident that in the ensuing air battles the bombers would destroy the enemy fighter force and gain control of the skies over Germany. In the event, the role of the escort fighter again proved to be crucial. As soon as the American medium-range escort fighters were forced by their limited endurance to leave the bombers and return to base, the un-protected Fortresses and Liberators proved to be no match for the German fighters. They suffered such heavy losses that the bombing offensive was brought to the very brink of defeat, and it seemed as if the pattern of the daylight air war was about to be repeated. Then, unexpectedly, the Americans turned the tide of battle in their favour when they introduced into the force a long-range fighter, the Mustang, which proved to be one of the most outstanding aircraft of the war. Operating from bases in England, the Mustangs escorted the bomber formations to and from even the most distant targets and inflicted a crushing defeat on the German fighter force.

Finally, to seek an answer to the first question, as to whether in the prevailing circumstances the Air Staff should have been able to build up a more effective force. Again, a negative answer must be given; and the main reason for this is to be found in the serious decline which occurred in British aviation generally during the inter-war period. The decline began immediately after the First World War when, under Churchill's direction, the Air Force was reduced to a handful of squadrons and the newly formed airlines were left to fend for themselves in the unequal struggle to compete with the state-sponsored foreign airlines. Successive administrations followed the precedent set by Churchill and within a few years the lead in aviation which Britain had attained at the end of the war had been lost. Many of the major foreign airlines were subsidized by their governments, and soon it became common practice for governments to finance the construction of airports and the provision of essential facilities such as navigational aids and lighting devices for night flying;[3] the British Government, on the other hand, were not prepared to spend more than the absolute minimum on aviation. However, the near collapse of civil air transport in this country compelled them to face the fact that the civil airlines could not survive without state aid. In truth, the Government had no alternative but to intervene, and the solution to the problem was sought in the creation of a national airline, Imperial Airways. Government aid was provided, but the sum that was set aside, one million pounds to be spread over ten years, was wholly inadequate to enable the new airline to keep pace with the rapid developments in aviation which were to take place in the next decade.[4]

It will be remembered that Sir Edgar Ludlow-Hewitt had contrasted the poor operational performance of Bomber Command with the excellent all-weather capability of many foreign airlines. Without doubt, these airlines attained this degree of efficiency because governments in most major countries – Britain was a notable exception – encouraged the development of civil aviation in every way possible. The United States and Germany were particularly far-sighted in this respect. A few years after the war the American Post Office inaugurated an air mail service to a few major cities and during the course of the 1920s extended it to cover most of the country. Selected airlines were awarded subsidies for the carrying of mail, and the method used to determine the amount of subsidy to be paid worked in such a way as to encourage the airlines to operate with the most efficient types of aircraft. By the early 1930s the American government had covered most of the air routes of the country with a network of radio beams which enabled aircraft to navigate with safety in all weathers and had equipped many of the major routes with electric beacons and other night flying facilities.[5] In Germany, the national airline, Deutsche Lufthansa, was given direct state aid on a generous scale, but this did nothing to make it less efficient and competitive. It established an excellent reputation for all-weather flying, and like the American airlines flew regular night schedules. It developed into one of the most modern and efficient airlines in the world, and among its many notable achievements was the introduction into service of the first aircraft capable of flying non-stop from Europe to North America.[6]

In Britain the contrast could not have been more marked. Owing to the lack of adequate financial support Imperial Airways lagged far behind the major foreign airlines and was never able to offer the standard of service which was typical of, say, Lufthansa or Pan American Airways. It was equipped with slow, obsolete aircraft and operated only in daylight.[7] During these years it did not practise the modern flying techniques which had been pioneered in Europe and North America, and so could offer nothing in the way of experience which would help to solve the many operational problems which beset the bomber force.

When Sir Edgar Ludlow-Hewitt was appointed to Bomber Command he soon discovered to his dismay that he commanded a fair-weather force which was incapable of operating with any degree of safety in bad weather and at night. The many years of severe financial retrenchment had left in their wake deficiencies so serious that there remained too little time to make them good; and it was a matter of great concern to the Commander-in-Chief that his task of preparing the bomber force for war would be overtaken by events and that his aircrews would be forced to complete their training in the skies over Germany.

NOTES

This study is based mainly on the collection of official documents held at the Public Record Office in London (Kew). Material from these documents is identified by a two-part reference. In the reference AIR 2/4467, for example, AIR 2 indicates Class 2 in the Air records, and 4467 refers to the piece number, which is a collection of papers entitled 'Air Navigation – General Policy 1938 to 1942'.

The most detailed and scholarly study of this period is to be found in the first volume of the unpublished Air Historical Branch narrative *The RAF in the Bombing Offensive against Germany. Prewar Evolution of Bomber Command 1917–1939*. A copy is to be found in the Public Record Office under the reference AIR 41/39.

The most important published works which cast light on the development of military aviation during the inter-war years are *The War in the Air* by Sir Walter Raleigh and H. A. Jones – 6 volumes and a volume of appendices (1922–37) – and *The Strategic Air Offensive against Germany 1939–1945* by Sir Charles Webster and Noble Frankland, volumes I and IV (1961). References to these works are indicated by the letters WIA and SAO respectively.

In addition, the following abbreviations are used:

ACAS	Assistant Chief of the Air Staff
ADGB	Air Defence of Great Britain
AHB	Air Historical Branch (Air Ministry)
AM	Air Ministry
AS	Air Staff
BC	Bomber Command
CAS	Chief of the Air Staff
CID	Committee of Imperial Defence
COS	Chiefs of Staff
D	Director
DCAS	Deputy Chief of the Air Staff
DD	Deputy Director
HMSO	Her Majesty's Stationery Office
JWAC	Joint War Air Committee
ORB	Operations Record Book
RFC	Royal Flying Corps
RNAS	Royal Naval Air Service
RUSI	Royal United Service Institution (now Royal United Services Institute for Defence Studies)
WO	War Office

INTRODUCTION

1. This omission is still to be found in modern works. See, for example, *British Air Strategy Between the Wars* by Malcolm Smith, who scarcely mentions the Naval Air Service in his chapter dealing with the First World War.

2. See *Sailor in the Sky* by Vice Admiral R. B. Davies, 1967, p. 184.

3. WIA, Vol. II, pp. 451–3; Vol. VI, pp. 118–22.

4. For Lord Tiverton's Papers see AIR1/460. Many of Lord Tiverton's recommendations seem to fit more naturally into the period after 1941 rather than into the years 1917–18. For example, it is interesting to compare his suggestions on aircrew training in map-reading and target recognition (AIR 1/460, 15/312/97) with those made in the Bomber Command Bulletin – May 1942, AIR 14/511.

5. BC file 'Operational Research 1941–44', AIR 14/1218. For the importance of Operational Research in the Second World War see Part II of *Studies of War* by P. M. S. Blackett, 1962. See also *O.R. in World War 2* by C. H. Waddington, 1973, Ch. 1.
6. See RFC paper 'Future Policy in the Air', 22 Sept. 1916, WIA, Vol. II, pp. 472–5.
7. See undated AHB paper 'Design and Supply of Aircraft 1914–18', AIR 1/678.
8. WIA, Vol. VI, p. 552.
9. WIA, Vol. V, p. 471.
10. Bailhache Committee Interim Report, 3 Aug. 1916; Final Report, 17 Nov. 1916, AIR 1/2405.
11. W. J. Reader, *Architect of Air Power*, 1968, pp. 67–8.
12. Ibid., pp. 73–5.
13. Memo. Director of Flying Operations to CAS. Sept. 1918, AIR 1/460, 15/312/101. See also Brigadier-General P. R. C. Groves, *Behind the Smoke Screen*, 1934, pp. 137–8.
14. See HQ RFC paper 'Long Distance Bombing', 26 Nov. 1917, AIR 1/725, 97/7.
15. CAS meetings July and August 1923, AIR 2/1267.
16. Such a situation did in fact exist during the heavy German attacks on this country in the early part of 1941. While the German bombers were able to operate during periods of bad weather, our night fighters were grounded and our bombing effort was seriously curtailed. See undated AHB paper 'Flying Control in the RAF During the War', AIR 20/4018.
17. See undated AHB paper 'The History of Flying Control in Bomber Command', AIR 14/1417.
18. ORB No. 102(B) Sqdn, AIR 27/807.
19. See note 17.
20. Court of Enquiry into Accident Involving DH86B aircraft L7596 on 28 July 1939, AIR 2/3677.
21. See note 17.
22. Sir Maurice Dean, *The Royal Air Force and Two World Wars*, 1979, p. 67.
23. See note 17.

CHAPTER ONE

1. Esher Committee Report, 28 Jan. 1909, AIR 1/2100.
2. WIA, Vol. 1, pp. 158–9.
3. WIA, Vol. 1, p. 142.
4. CID paper, 29 Feb. 1912, AIR 1/21.
5. Ibid.
6. See Admiralty papers of 1913, AIR 1/626.
7. WIA, Vol. III, pp. 74–6.
8. See *The Aeroplane* (aeronautical magazine), 5 Jan. 1916, p. 1.
9. Henderson later admitted that this ruling had been mistaken. Memo to JWAC, 1 April 1916, AIR 1/2319.
10. See undated AHB paper (written between the wars), 'Design and Supply of Aircraft 1914–18' by J. C. Nerney, AIR 1/678.
11. HQ RFC Memo, July 1915, AIR 1/921.
12. See file dealing with cases of pilots being sent to France with inadequate training, AIR 1/997.
13. See file concerning RNAS training, AIR 1/660.
14. WIA, Vol. I, pp. 389–405.
15. Report, 'No. 3 Wing RNAS' by Capt. W. L. Elder R. N. (Elder Report), 24 May 1917, AIR 1/2266.
16. Report on Admiralty meeting, 17 Dec. 1915, AIR 1/625.
17. Elder Report. See note 15 above.
18. Ibid.
19. WIA, Vol. VI, p. 122.
20. See WIA, Vol. VI, p. 552 and WIA, Vol. V, p. 471.
21. Memo 'Duties of the RNAS and the RFC', 4 Feb. 1916, AIR 1/270.
22. Paper, 'Policy of Army Council with regard to RFC (Military Wing)', 2 March 1916, AIR 1/270.

23. 'Note by the Naval Representatives on the JWAC', 23 March 1916, AIR 1/2319.
24. Minutes of Air Board meeting, 1 Nov. 1916, AIR 1/515.
25. Letter Haig to WO, 1 Nov. 1916, AIR 2/123.
26. WIA, Vol. V, pp. 25–8.
27. WIA, Vol. V, p. 29.
28. WIA, Vol. V, pp. 36–8.
29. WIA, Vol. V, pp. 41–2.
30. For this report see WIA, Vol. of Appendices, Appendix II.
31. See memo by Henderson, 19 July 1917, WIA, Vol. of Appendices, Appendix I.
32. WIA, Vol. VI, p. 6.
33. WIA, Vol. VI, pp. 19–22.
34. WIA, Vol. VI, p. 26.
35. WIA, Vol. VI, pp. 26–7.
36. Report by Lord Tiverton, 3 Sept. 1917, AIR 1/462.
37. Report by Lord Tiverton, 2 Nov. 1917, Halsbury Papers.
38. Air Policy Committee memo, Jan. 1918, AIR 1/463.
39. Paper, 'Long Distance Bombing', 26 Nov. 1917, AIR 1/725.
40. Memo, Director of Flying Operations to CAS, Sept. 1918, AIR 1/460. A complete list of the industrial targets attacked by the 41st Wing and the Independent Force, from Oct. 1917 to Nov. 1918, is contained in WIA, Vol. of Appendices, Appendix XIII. A narrative of the operations is to be found in WIA, Vol. VI, Ch. IV.
41. See two staff reports on the Independent Force, 9 Sept. and 11 Oct. 1918, AIR 1/454.
42. See, for example, memo, Tiverton to Director of Flying Operations, 10 June 1918, AIR 1/460.
43. The Course Setting Bombsight Mk. I is described in an Admiralty pamphlet of Jan. 1918, AIR 1/2103.
44. See note 42 above.
45. Report of the British Commission, Jan. 1920, AIR 1/2104.
46. See translation of a paper by Major Grosskreutz in *Die Luftwacht* (Oct. 1928), AIR 1/711.
47. This information was given to the Air Staff by the Air Historical Branch in a letter dated 11 Dec. 1923, AIR 9/69.

CHAPTER TWO

1. Maj.-Gen. Sir Frederick Sykes, *From Many Angles* (1942), p. 262 seq.
2. Sykes, op. cit., p. 266.
3. Ibid.
4. Trenchard Memorandum, Cmd. 467, Dec. 1919.
5. Sykes, op. cit., p. 273.
6. BC Annual Report for 1937, 19 March 1938, AIR 2/2961.
7. Sykes, op. cit., p. 267.
8. Ibid., p. 294.
9. Ibid., p. 301.
10. Cadman Committee papers, 1937, AIR 2/2214. This file contains papers dealing with every aspect of civil aviation for the period 1918–37.
11. Sykes, op. cit., p. 302.
12. See note 10 above.
13. Brig.-Gen. P. R. C. Groves, *Our Future in the Air* (1935), Chs. I and II.
14. Minutes of Cabinet Meetings of 5 and 15 Aug. 1919, CAB 23/15.
15. See Basil Collier, *The Defence of the United Kingdom* (1957), pp. 14–15.
16. See AS paper, 'The Expansion of the RAF for Home Defence', 1 June 1923, AIR 2/1267.
17. CAS meetings July and August 1923, AIR 2/1267. Hereafter reference is made to the date of the meeting.
18. 'Future Policy for the Air', 22 Sept. 1916, WIA Vol. II, pp. 472–5.
19. 31 July 1923.
20. 10 July 1923.
21. Ibid.

22. The reasons for this decision are given in AS memo No. 11A, March 1924, AIR 9/8.
23. 19 July 1923.
24. Ibid.
25. Ibid.
26. 25 July 1923.
27. 10 July 1923.
28. Ibid.
29. 19 July 1923.
30. 8 Aug. 1923.
31. 'The Development of the RAF' by Sqdn. Ldr., J.C. Slessor, *RUSI Journal*, May 1931.
32. Viscount Templewood, *Empire of the Air* (1957), pp. 41–2.
33. WIA, Vol. V, p. 471.
34. For an account of air defence in the First World War see *Air Defence* (1929), by Maj.-Gen. E. B. Ashmore.
35. Statement in the House of Commons, 10 Nov. 1932.
36. Minute Churchill to Portal, 7 Oct. 1941, AIR 8/258. This minute is quoted in full in SAO, Vol. I, pp. 184–5.
37. AS note, 13 Oct. 1941, AIR 8/258.
38. Churchill was a leading member of a parliamentary deputation which met the Prime Minister on 28 and 29 July 1936 to express concern at Britain's inadequate air defences. The records of these meetings are on AIR 9/8.
39. AS memo, 24 May 1924, AIR 9/69. For even higher estimates of casualties see AS memo, 20 Oct. 1923, AIR 9/69.
40. See AS paper, 17 Nov. 1925, AIR 9/69.
41. Minutes of CID meeting, 29 Sept. 1930, CAB 2/5.
42. The Earl of Halsbury, *1944*, pp. 7–8.
43. Article in the *Daily Mail*, 8 July 1927.
44. Speech in the House of Lords, 11 July 1928.
45. Ibid.
46. Collier, op. cit., p. 69.
47. There were several references to Paris as an important target at the CAS meeting, 26 July 1923, AIR 2/1267.
48. Despatch of General Trenchard, 10th Supplement of the *London Gazette*, 31 Dec. 1918.
49. AS memo 11A, March 1924, AIR 9/8.
50. AS memo 11, Aug. 1923, AIR 9/8.
51. Speech by Trenchard, 2 Nov. 1926, AIR 9/7.
52. This memo, 2 May 1928 (CAB 53/14), and replies of Sir George Milne (16 May) and Sir Charles Madden (21 May) (CAB 53/16), are reproduced in full in SAO, Vol. IV, pp. 71–83.

CHAPTER THREE

1. See various AS papers in Plans Archives Vol. 7, AIR 9/69 and Plans Archives Vol. 9, AIR 9/36. *Prewar Evolution of Bomber Command 1917–1939*, pp. 30–2, AIR 41/39.
2. See undated AHB paper, 'Air Defence of Great Britain 1923–1940', AIR 2/4004.
3. Collier, op. cit., p. 18.
4. Collier, op. cit., p. 6.
5. Minutes of CID meeting, 5 July 1928, CAB 2/5.
6. SAO, Vol. I, pp. 58–9; The Marquess of Londonderry, *Wings of Destiny* (1943), Ch. IV.
7. Londonderry, op. cit., p. 65.
8. The bomber squadrons at the end of March 1933 were as detailed below.

Day Bombers (Regular): Nos. 12, 15, 18, 22, 33, 35, 40, 57, 101, 207. Nos. 15 and 22 were skeleton squadrons and two others would form the air element of the Expeditionary Force. Day Bombers (Special Reserve): Nos. 501, 504. Day Bombers (Auxiliary Air Force): Nos. 600, 601, 602, 603, 604, 607, 608.

Night Bombers (Regular): Nos. 7, 9, 10, 58, 99. Night Bombers (Special Reserve): Nos. 500, 502, 503.

9. Templewood, op. cit., Ch. XVII.
10. Minutes of CID meeting, 5 July 1928, CAB 2/5.
11. See note 38, Ch. 2.
12. C. R. Fairey, 'The Future of Aircraft Design for the Services', *RUSI Journal*, Aug. 1931.
13. Minutes of CAS meeting, 8 Aug. 1923, AIR 2/1267.
14. Minutes of CAS meeting, 25 July 1923, AIR 2/1267.
15. Marshal of the RAF Sir Arthur Harris, *Bomber Offensive* (1947), p. 23. See also *Prewar Evolution of Bomber Command 1917–1939*, pp. 45–6, AIR 41/39.
16. Quoted by Sykes, op. cit., p. 267.
17. Air Chief Marshal Sir Philip Joubert de la Ferté, *The Third Service* (1955), pp. 74–5.
18. *The History of 9 Squadron* (1965) by Flying Officer T. Mason, p. 32.
19. See Harris, op. cit., p. 110.
20. WIA, Vol. III, pp. 109–12.
21. WIA, Vol. III, p. 135 seq.
22. WIA, Vol. III, pp. 136–7.
23. See, for example, AS paper (undated, but circa 1926), AIR 9/7.
24. ORB No. 9 Sqdn., AIR 27/125.
25. There are many recorded cases of seriously inaccurate bearings being given to aircraft on war operations. For example, the bearings given by the bomber stations Linton and Leconfield on the night of 15/16 October 1939 were up to 100 degrees in error. BC file, 'Violations of Neutral Territory', AIR 14/158.
26. 'The Air Force' by Air Commodore H. R. M. Brooke-Popham, *RUSI Journal*, Feb. 1920.
27. CAS Air Liaison Letters to the Dominions, 1934–9: letter 31 Jan. 1939, AIR 20/6042.
28. Letter Harris to Sir John Steel, 2 Sept. 1937, AIR 14/54.
29. See, for example, the ORB No. 58 Sqdn. during the period 1924 to 1939, AIR 27/543.
30. ORB No. 12(B) Sqdn., entries Jan.–May 1932, AIR 27/164.
31. Report of sub-committee on Coastal Defence, 9 May 1932, AIR 8/139.
32. ORB No. 58 Sqdn., June 1933, AIR 27/543; ORB No. 9 Sqdn., May 1933, AIR 27/125.
33. Minutes of CAS meeting, 19 July 1923, AIR 2/1267.
34. See, for example, minute by CAS, 2 Aug. 1928, AIR 2/1267.
35. Minute DCAS to CAS, 13 Dec. 1930, AIR 2/1015.
36. Decision reached at AM conference, 14 Oct. 1932, AIR 2/1015.
37. Report on ADGB Exercises, July 1927, AIR 9/69.
38. AS paper, 'Air Exercises 1932', undated, contains figures of interceptions during the exercises of 1931, AIR 9/69.
39. 'British and Foreign Air Exercises' by Major C. C. Turner, *RUSI Journal*, Nov. 1931.
40. Meeting of sub-committee of ADGB, 17 Oct. 1934, AIR 2/1388. See also *Prewar Evolution of Bomber Command 1917–1939*, p. 50, AIR 41/39.
41. BC Annual Report for 1937, 19 March 1938, AIR 2/2961.
42. AS memo by Sqdn. Ldr. J. C. Slessor, 24 March 1930, AIR 9/8.
43. 'The Strategic Role of Air Forces' by Sqdn. Ldr. J. O. Andrews, *RUSI Journal*, Nov. 1931.

CHAPTER FOUR

1. See *The Rise and Fall of the German Air Force*, AM Pamphlet No. 248 (1948), pp. 1–11.
2. Ibid., p. 3; *The Rise of the Luftwaffe 1918–1940* by H. M. Mason (1973), pp. 151–64.
3. Groves, op. cit., pp. 46–7.
4. See note 2 above.
5. See note 1 above.
6. COS papers, CAB 53/23; Ian Colvin, *Vansittart in Office* (1965), pp. 23–4.
7. Minutes of COS meetings, CAB 53/4; COS Annual Report, 12 Oct. 1933, CAB 53/23.
8. Collier, op. cit., pp. 25–7.
9. See AS note to the Ministerial Committee on Disarmament concerning the integrity of the Low Countries, June 1934, AIR 9/69.
10. Minutes of conference on Defence Orientation attended by staff officers of the WO and the AM, 28 June 1934, AIR 2/697.
11. COS paper No. 341, 12 June 1934, CAB 53/24.

12. Minutes of COS meeting, 27 June 1934, CAB 53/4.
13. COS paper No. 344, 11 July 1934, CAB 53/24.
14. Details of Scheme A and subsequent expansion schemes are given in SAO, Vol. IV, pp. 103–4.
15. CAS memo, 2 Oct. 1934, contains a review of the policy which led to Scheme A, AIR 2/1616.
16. See AS memo, 'The Re-orientation of the Air Defence System', 30 July 1934, AIR 2/697 and minutes of ADGB committee, 17 Oct. 1934, AIR 2/1388.
17. Minute CAS to DCAS, 1 May 1934, AIR 2/697.
18. AM conference to consider the 1934 to 1939 expansion programme, 25 July 1934, AIR 2/1269.
19. Minute to CAS, 24 July 1934, setting out how the expansion was strictly limited by finance, AIR 2/1269.
20. AM file, 'Classes of Aircraft Required by the RAF', AIR 2/2715.
21. AM file on the Bombing Committee, AIR 2/1369.
22. Letter Brooke-Popham to AM, 31 Jan. 1935, AIR 2/1583.
23. The chairman of the Bombing Committee, the DCAS, was Air Vice-Marshal C. L. Courtney.
24. Letter AM to Brooke-Popham, 15 April 1935, AIR 2/1583.
25. Letter Brooke-Popham to AM, 16 May 1935, AIR 2/1583.
26. Minutes of the first meeting of the Bomb Sub-committee, 20 May 1935, AIR 2/1015.
27. AS memo, 'The Re-orientation of the Air Defence System', 30 July 1934, AIR 2/697.
28. Papers relating to the Committee for Scientific Survey of Air Defence are: AIR 20/145 (1934–6); AIR 20/80 (1935–8).
29. See *Design and Development of Weapons* (1964) by M. M. Postan, D. Hay, and J. D. Scott, p. 373 seq.
30. 6th meeting of the Air Defence Committee, 10 April 1935, AIR 20/80.
31. 1st meeting of the Air Defence Committee, 28 Jan. 1935, AIR 20/145.
32. See *Sir Edward Appleton* by Ronald Clark (1971), Ch. 3.
33. 'The Scientific Principles of Radiolocation', lecture given by Sir Edward Appleton at the Institution of Electrical Engineers, London, 26 April 1945. See also *Most Secret War* by R. V. Jones (1978), p. 16.
34. See note 29 above.
35. Memo, CAS to Secretary of State for Air, 23 May 1934, AIR 9/8; CAS minute, 1 Aug. 1934, AIR 2/697.
36. CAS minute, 1 Aug. 1934, AIR 2/697.
37. SAO, Vol. I, pp. 69–70.
38. Londonderry, op. cit., pp. 162–3.
39. SAO, Vol. I, p. 70.
40. See papers on AM file AIR 2/1269.
41. For the provisions of Scheme C see AS paper, 4 May 1935, AIR 2/1269.
42. Letter Churchill to Cunliffe-Lister, 8 Aug. 1935, AIR 2/2691.
43. 'Notes on the Air Situation' by W. S. Churchill, 25 Aug. 1935, AIR 2/2691.
44. AS note, 17 Sept. 1935, AIR 2/2691.
45. Minute CAS to DCAS, 19 June 1935, AIR 2/1269.
46. Minutes of the Committee of the ADGB, 17 July 1935, AIR 2/1388.
47. *The Rise and Fall of the German Air Force*, Air Ministry pamphlet, pp. 1–2.
48. *Luftwaffe* ed. H. Faber (1979), pp. 23–4.
49. Ibid., pp. 160–3.
50. Ibid., pp. 219–21.
51. AS papers forwarded to Lord Weir through the Secretary of State, 10 July 1935, AIR 2/2715.
52. Ibid.
53. AS note, 'The Possibility of Dispensing with the Armament in the Light Bomber Class', June 1935, AIR 2/2715.
54. Minute CAS to DCAS, 8 Dec. 1935, AIR 2/2718.
55. AS paper, 15 Jan. 1936, AIR 2/2718.
56. Minute DCAS to CAS, 18 Jan. 1936, AIR 2/2718.

57. Memo, DD Plans to DCAS, 16 Jan. 1936, AIR 2/2718.
58. Minute CAS to DCAS, 29 Jan. 1936, AIR 2/2718.
59. SAO, Vol. I, p. 89.

CHAPTER FIVE

1. AS paper outlining Scheme F, Feb. 1936, AIR 9/36.
2. Minutes of CID meeting, 3 March 1936, Appendix E, CAB 4/24. The fact that Chamberlain was the author of this memorandum should serve as a reminder that it was he who initiated the action to expand and re-arm the Air Force. It should be remembered, too, that he was the driving force behind all the rearmament schemes which were approved before the outbreak of war.
3. Letter Weir to Cunliffe-Lister, 22 Aug. 1935, AIR 2/2691.
4. See undated AHB paper, 'Air Defence of Great Britain 1923–40', AIR 20/4004.
5. Deputation to the Prime Minister, 28 and 29 July 1936, AIR 9/8.
6. AS paper, 11 Nov. 1936, AIR 2/2617.
7. It was estimated that the 1,022 bombers would comprise 402 Battles, 252 Blenheims, 32 torpedo bombers, 108 Hampdens, 108 Whitleys, 36 Harrows and 96 Wellingtons. AS paper, 12 Oct. 1936, AIR 2/2617.
8. See the biography of Lord Weir, *Architect of Air Power* by W. J. Reader (1968), p. 252 seq.
9. Statement of policy by Sir Thomas Inskip at COS meeting, 25 March 1936, AIR 9/8.
10. Minute CAS to Secretary of State, 18 Oct. 1936, AIR 2/2617.
11. SAO, Vol. I, p. 75.
12. An extract from this report is given in SAO, Vol. IV, pp. 88–95. See also SAO, Vol. I, pp. 89–90 and COS papers 1937–9, AIR 2/2731.
13. The report of the Mobilisable Committee, 14 April 1937, AIR 2/2584, gave an assessment of the readiness state of the bomber squadrons. The night bomber squadrons, for example, were considered to be no more than 25% operationally efficient.
14. BC Annual Report for 1937, 19 March 1938, AIR 2/2961.
15. Letter Steel to AM, 2 Sept. 1937, AIR 9/36.
16. Harris, op. cit. p. 35.
17. See note 14 above.
18. Letter Harris to Steel, 2 Sept. 1937, AIR 14/54.
19. CAS Air Liaison Letter to the Dominions, 18 Feb. 1938, AIR 20/6042.
20. See AS paper, 'Air Navigation Policy in the RAF', 9 June 1938, AIR 14/69.
21. Ibid. See also minutes of meeting of Group Navigation Officers at Headquarters BC, 14 Nov. 1939, AIR 14/65.
22. Minutes of Bombing Committee, 2 March 1938, AIR 2/4452.
23. Minute DD Plans to DCAS, 19 Oct. 1938, AIR 2/2604.
24. Manual of Air Tactics (1937), AIR 2/2024.
25. See note 19 above.
26. For the terms of reference see AS paper, 7 Jan. 1937, AIR 2/2730.
27. AS paper, Jan. 1937, AIR 2/2730.
28. Minutes of Air Offence Committee, 4 May 1937, AIR 20/17. See also *Prewar Evolution of Bomber Command 1917–1939*, p. 167, AIR 41/39.
29. P. M. S. Blackett, *Studies of War* (1962), p. 106.
30. SAO, Vol. I, p. 114.
31. *Guilty Men* was the work of three authors (Michael Foot, Frank Owen, and Peter Howard) using the pseudonym 'Cato'. Quotations from the chapters attacking both Inskip's appointment and his achievements as a minister have been used without discernment by writers ever since.
32. See AM file, AIR 2/2767.
33. Ibid., AS paper, Oct. 1937.
34. Letter Inskip to Swinton, 4 Nov. 1937, AIR 2/2767.
35. Letter Swinton to Inskip, 4 Nov. 1937, AIR 2/2767.
36. Letter Inskip to Swinton, 9 Dec. 1937, AIR 2/2767.
37. SAO, Vol. I, p. 77; Colvin, op. cit., pp. 135–8.

38. For Scheme K see AS paper, 13 Jan. 1938, AIR 2/2767.
39. For a review of the situation with regard to the rejection of Scheme J and the preparation of Scheme K see AS paper, 21 Jan. 1938, AIR 2/2767. An AS paper of 8 Feb. 1938 estimated that the German first-line strength at the beginning of 1939 would be 3,700 aircraft, of which 1,750 would be bombers. AIR 2/2731.
40. Minutes of CAS meeting, 18 Jan. 1938, AIR 2/2767.

CHAPTER SIX

1. Letter CID to AM, 13 May 1937, AIR 2/2731.
2. Note from DD Plans, 10 Aug. 1937, initiating work on the plans, AIR 2/2731.
3. Letter Steel to AM, 7 June 1937, AIR 2/2731.
4. AM conference, 1 Oct. 1937, AIR 2/2731. See SAO, Vol. IV, pp. 99–102 for details of the Western Air Plans.
5. Letter AM to BC, 13 Dec. 1937, AIR 2/2731.
6. SAO, Vol. I, pp. 92–3.
7. See, for example, letters from Group Captain Don to the AM, 4 and 31 Jan. 1938, AIR 2/2731.
8. Letter Ludlow-Hewitt to AM, 4 Feb. 1938, AIR 2/2731.
9. Letter AM to BC, 13 Dec. 1937, AIR 2/2731.
10. BC appreciation of WA 4, July 1938, AIR 2/2604.
11. Letter Don to AM, 3 May 1938, asking for authority to get the bombing trials started without delay. AIR 2/2604.
12. See, for example, AS memo No. 11, Aug. 1923, AIR 9/8.
13. Minutes of AM conference, 1 Oct. 1937, AIR 2/2731.
14. SAO, Vol. I, pp. 95–6. See *Prewar Evolution of Bomber Command 1917–1939*, p. 189, AIR 41/39.
15. Letter AM to BC, 13 Dec. 1937, AIR 2/2731.
16. Letter Ludlow-Hewitt to AM, 20 July 1938, AIR 2/2805.
17. Minute, D of Plans to CAS, 3 Feb. 1939, AIR 2/2805.
18. Air Targets Intelligence Report on Transportation, 9 Sept. 1938, AIR 2/2805.
19. AS note, 21 Jan. 1938, AIR 2/2767.
20. Letter Ludlow-Hewitt to AM, 19 March 1938, AIR 2/2731.
21. Manual of Air Tactics (1938), AIR 2/3295.
22. See AM file, AIR 2/4452.
23. See minutes of first meeting of Bombing Policy Sub-committee, 22 March 1938, AIR 2/4452.
24. Report on Sector and Combined Training Exercise 1937 by the Air Officer Commanding No. 3 (Bomber) Group, 1 Sept. 1937, AIR 9/64.
25. Letter Ludlow-Hewitt to AM, 25 Oct. 1937, AIR 9/64.
26. See note 23 above.
27. Memo by the Minister for the Co-ordination of Defence, 15 Oct. 1938, AIR 8/250.
28. See papers relating to the Bombing Committee 1936–9, AIR 20/4436.
29. CAS Air Liaison Letter to the Dominions, 20 Nov. 1937, AIR 20/6042.
30. CAS Air Liaison Letter to the Dominions, 20 June 1938, AIR 20/6042. See *Prewar Evolution of Bomber Command 1917–1939*, pp. 217–20, AIR 41/39.
31. See AS paper 'Considerations Affecting the Design of the Ideal Bomber for the Royal Air Force', March 1938, AIR 8/250. The officer who wrote this paper, later Marshal of the RAF Sir John Slessor, describes in detail the factors which influenced his findings in *The Central Blue* (1956), pp. 174–8.
32. Documents relating to the rules of air bombardment are contained in AM files AIR 2/3071 and AIR 2/3072.
33. Parliamentary Debates Commons Vol. 337, Cols. 937–8, 21 June 1938.
34. Letter Ludlow-Hewitt to AM, 14 Sept. 1938, AIR 2/4478.
35. SAO, Vol. I, p. 100; Letter Ludlow-Hewitt to AM, 25 Sept. 1938, AIR 14/323.
36. Letter Ludlow-Hewitt to AM, 25 Sept. 1938, AIR 14/323.
37. Committee on Defence Programmes and Accelerations, 28 Oct. 1938, AIR 8/250.

38. Report of the Mobilisable Committee, 15 Sept. 1938, AIR 2/2584.
39. For the provisions of Scheme M see AM file AIR 8/250.
40. Minutes of AM conference, 18 Oct. 1938, AIR 8/250.
41. See various papers in AM file AIR 8/250.
42. *Documents Concerning German–Polish Relations and the Outbreak of Hostilities between Great Britain and Germany on September 3 1939* (1939), HMSO, Cmd. 6106, p. 9.
43. Ibid., p. 36.
44. COS Memo 905, 3 June 1939, CAB 53/49.
45. For BC Order of Battle at 27 Sept. 1939 see SAO, Vol. IV, pp. 400–2.
46. BC Annual Report for 1938, 11 March 1939, AIR 14/298.
47. AM letter, 22 May 1939, AIR 2/3078.
48. Letter Ludlow-Hewitt to AM, 25 May 1939, AIR 2/3078.
49. BC Annual Report for 1938, 11 March 1939, AIR 14/298.
50. Ibid.
51. Ibid.
52. Ibid.
53. Ibid.
54. Minutes of AM conference, 6 April 1939, AIR 8/270.
55. Letter Ludlow-Hewitt to AM, 25 May 1939, AIR 2/3078.
56. Minute on AM file, 13 April 1938, AIR 2/2961.
57. CAS note, May 1939, AIR 2/3078.

CHAPTER SEVEN

1. Report of the Sub-committee on Coast Defence, 9 May 1932, AIR 8/139.
2. Minute DD Plans to ACAS, 4 Nov. 1938, AIR 2/2947.
3. Minutes of AM meeting, 30 Nov. 1938, AIR 2/2947.
4. See note 2 above.
5. Minute ACAS to DD Plans, 30 Nov. 1938, AIR 2/2947.
6. See note 3 above.
7. Letter Naval Staff to AM, 16 Sept. 1938, AIR 2/2770.
8. See various papers on AM file, Sept. 1938, AIR 2/2770.
9. See various papers on AM file, AIR 2/2772.
10. Letter AM to BC, 2 June 1939; BC report to AM, 10 Aug. 1939, AIR 2/2772.
11. Letter Ludlow-Hewitt to AM, 27 Sept. 1938, AIR 2/2770.
12. BC report, Sept. 1938, AIR 2/2770.
13. For the papers relating to the Propaganda Plan (WA 14) see AIR 2/4478.
14. Air Targets Intelligence Report, Oct. 1937, AIR 2/2805.
15. Letter Ludlow-Hewitt to AM, 28 July 1938, AIR 2/2805.
16. Paper prepared by D of Plans for CAS, 3 Feb. 1939, AIR 2/2805.
17. Letter Ludlow-Hewitt to AM, 20 Feb. 1939, AIR 2/2805.
18. Letter AM to Ludlow-Hewitt, 27 March 1939, AIR 2/2805.
19. Letter AM to BC, 1 July 1939, AIR 2/2805.
20. Minutes of the meeting, 5 April 1939, AIR 2/2884.
21. Letter AM to Ludlow-Hewitt, 17 April 1939, AIR 2/2884.
22. Letter Ludlow-Hewitt to AM, 21 April 1939, AIR 2/2884.
23. Note by Plans 2, 25 April 1939, AIR 2/2884.
24. French Army Staff note, 11 April 1939, AIR 2/2890.
25. Ruhr Plan (WA 5b), March 1939, AIR 2/2805.
26. AS note, 26 April 1939, AIR 2/2884.
27. French Air Staff note, 1 June 1939, AIR 2/2890.
28. AM note to French Air Staff, 16 Aug. 1939, AIR 2/2890.
29. Letter Ludlow-Hewitt to AM, 22 April 1939, AIR 2/2884.
30. French Staff paper, 22 May 1939, AIR 2/2884.
31. Letter Ludlow-Hewitt to AM, 7 July 1939, AIR 2/2884.
32. William L. Shirer, *The Rise and Fall of the Third Reich* (1959), p. 471 seq.
33. Keith Feiling, *The Life of Neville Chamberlain* (1946), p. 403.

34. Lord Strang, *Home and Abroad* (1956), Ch. V.
35. Shirer, op. cit., p. 427 and p. 476.
36. Ibid., pp. 490–3 and 513 seq.
37. Ibid., p. 541.
38. Ibid., pp. 525–6.
39. Ibid., p. 668.
40. Ibid., pp. 666–7; see also W. N. Medlicott, *The Economic Blockade*, Vol. I (revised ed. 1978), p. 312, pp. 321–3, 633–59, 667–71.
41. Shirer, op. cit., pp. 666–7.
42. Paper by D of Plans, 'The Question of Relaxing the Bombardment Instructions and Initiating Extended Air Action', 7 Sept. 1939, AIR 14/194. See also Ivan Lajos, *Germany's War Chances* (1939), pp. 122 seq. and 135 seq.; *The Von Hassell Diaries* (1948), pp. 31–2, 73; William L. Shirer, *Berlin Diary* (1941), p. 134.
43. The British War Cabinet discussed the implications of Soviet–German trade at a meeting held on 14 March 1940, CAB 65/6. The basis of their discussion was a memorandum prepared by the Minister of Economic Warfare, CAB 65/12.

CONCLUSIONS

1. An analysis of these operations is to be found in AM file AIR 20/6106; see also SAO, Vol. I, pp. 192–6.
2. SAO, Vol. I, p. 198.
3. Groves, op. cit., pp. 36–7.
4. Sykes, op. cit., pp. 300–2.
5. Groves, op. cit., Ch. 1; R. E. G. Davies, *A History of the World's Airlines* (1967), p. 39 seq. and p. 123 seq.
6. Davies, op. cit., pp. 56–9, 118–19; Groves, op. cit., pp. 19–25.
7. Sykes, op. cit., p. 302. See also the Cadman Committee Report 1937, AIR 2/2214.

BIBLIOGRAPHY

Air Ministry, Air Publication 1234, *Manual of Air Pilotage* (1930)
Air Ministry Pamphlet No. 248, *The Rise and Fall of the German Air Force* (1948)
Ashmore, Major-General E. B., *Air Defence* (1929)
Birkenhead, The Earl of, *The Prof in Two Worlds* (1961)
Blackett, P. M. S., *Studies of War* (1962)
Blunt, Flight Lieutenant V. E. R., *The Use of Air Power* (1942)
Boyle, Andrew, *Trenchard* (1962)
Clark, Ronald W., *Tizard* (1965)
——, *Sir Edward Appleton* (1971)
Collier, Basil, *The Defence of the United Kingdom* (1957)
——, *A History of Air Power* (1974)
Colvin, Ian, *Vansittart in Office* (1965)
Davies, R. E. G., *A History of the World's Airlines* (1967)
Davies, Vice Admiral Richard Bell, *Sailor in the Sky* (1967)
Dean, Sir Maurice, *The Royal Air Force and Two World Wars* (1979)
Dilkes, David (ed.), *The Diaries of Sir Alexander Cadogan 1938–1945* (1971)
Douglas, Marshal of the RAF Lord (Sholto Douglas), *Years of Combat* (1963)
——, *Years of Command* (1966)
Faber, Harold (ed.), *Luftwaffe* (1979)
Feiling, Keith, *The Life of Neville Chamberlain* (1946)
Galland, Adolf, *The First and the Last* (1955)
Grey, C. G., *A History of the Air Ministry* (1940)
Groves, Brigadier-General P. R. C., *Behind the Smoke Screen* (1934)
——, *Our Future in the Air* (1935)
Halsbury, The Earl of, *1944* (1926)
Harris, Marshal of the RAF Sir Arthur, *Bomber Offensive* (1947)
Higham, Robin, *Armed Forces in Peacetime* (1962)
Hinsley, F. H., *British Intelligence in the Second World War*, Vol. 1 (1979)
Hughes, Arthur J., *History of Air Navigation* (1946)
Hyde, H. Montgomery, *British Air Policy Between the Wars* (1976)
—— and Falkiner Nuttall, G. R., *Air Defence and the Civil Population* (1938)

Jones, Neville, *The Origins of Strategic Bombing* (1973)

Joubert de la Ferté, Air Chief Marshal Sir Philip, *The Third Service* (1955)

Lee, Asher, *Air Power* (1955)

Londonderry, The Marquess of, *Wings of Destiny* (1943)

Mason, Herbert Molloy, *The Rise of the Luftwaffe 1918–1940* (1975)

Medlicott, W.N., *The Economic Blockade*, Vol. I (Revised ed. 1978)

Morison, Frank, *War on Great Cities* (1937)

Munch, P. (ed.), *What Would Be the Character of a New War?* (1933)

Peden, G.C., *British Rearmament and the Treasury 1932–1939* (1979)

Postan, M.M., Hay, D., Scott, J.D., *Design and Development of Weapons* (1964)

Raleigh, Sir Walter and Jones, H.A., *The War in the Air*, 6 vols. and 1 vol. of appendices (1922–1937)

Reader, W.J., *Architect of Air Power* (1968)

Richards, Denis, *Royal Air Force 1939–1945*, Vol. I (1953)

Sassoon, Philip, *The Third Route* (1929)

Saundby, Air Marshal Sir Robert, *Air Bombardment* (1961)

Saunders, Hilary St. George, *Per Ardua. The Rise of British Air Power 1911–1939* (1944)

Shirer, William L., *Berlin Diary* (1941)

——, *The Rise and Fall of the Third Reich* (1959)

Slessor, Marshal of the RAF Sir John, *The Central Blue* (1956)

Smith, Malcolm, *British Air Strategy Between the Wars* (1984)

Snow, C.P., *Public Affairs* (1971)

Spaight, J.M., *The Beginnings of Organised Air Power* (1927)

——, *Air Power and the Cities* (1930)

Speer, Albert, *Inside The Third Reich* (1970)

'Squadron Leader', *Basic Principles of Air Warfare* (1927)

Strang, Lord, *Home and Abroad* (1956)

Swinton, Viscount, *I Remember* (1948)

Sykes, Major-General Sir Frederick, *From Many Angles* (1942)

Templewood, Viscount (Sir Samuel Hoare), *Nine Troubled Years* (1954)

——, *Empire of the Air* (1957)

Waddington, C.H., *O.R. in World War 2* (1973)

Watt, D.C., *Personalities and Policies* (1965)

——, *Too Serious a Business* (1975)

Webster, Sir Charles and Frankland, Noble, *The Strategic Air Offensive Against Germany 1939–1945* Vols. I and IV (1961)

Weems, P.V.H., *Air Navigation* (British Empire Edition, revised and edited by Arthur J. Hughes and P.F. Everitt 1942)

Zweng, Charles A., *Radio and Instrument Flying* (Pan American Navigation Service, North Hollywood, California, revised ed. 1942)

INDEX

Abyssinia, 98, 103
Aden, 54
Admiralty, 2, 3, 4, 6−7, 10−11, 14, 27, 152−3
Advisory Committee for Aeronautics, 2
Aeronautical Research Committee, 86
Air Battalion (Royal Engineers), 2
Air Board, 10, 13, 14, 15, 16
Air Council, 14, 16, 17, 101−2
Air Defence, xiii, xiv, 2−3, 11−12, 20, 21, 27−9, 32, 33, 34, 36, 44, 65, 66−7, 69, 76, 85−6, 90, 102−3, 131, 143−4
Air Defence of Great Britain Command, 48, 63, 66, 68, 84, 101−2
Air Ministry, xi, xvi, xviii, xix, xx, xxi, 14, 18, 22−3, 34, 62, 77, 84, 86, 88, 90, 95, 111, 114, 116, 118−19, 120−1, 124, 126−8, 129, 135, 146, 147, 149, 150−1, 153, 154−5, 157, 159, 160, 165
Air Parity Sub-Committee, 90
Air Policy Committee, 16
Air raid casualties, 11, 34−5, 108
Air Raid Precautions (ARP), 35−7, 41
Air raids, 8, 11−12, 34−5, 36−7
Air Tactics, Manual of, 118−19, 133
Air Targets Intelligence Committee, 127, 132, 157
Air Traffic Control, xx, xxii, xxiii, xxiv, 113
Air transport, 22, 23, 24−5, 26, 172
Aircraft Factory, 3, 4
Aircraft Industry American, xxii; British, xxii, 25−6, 52, 53, 77, 89, 106, 137; German, xxii, 71, 73, 90, 100, 107
Airships, xv, 2, 4, 6, 8, 56−9
Alcock, Sir John, xxi
Aldeburgh, 57
Aldergrove, xxii
All-weather flying, xx, xxi, xxiii, xxiv, 24, 26, 67−8, 72, 85, 98, 111, 112−13, 163, 172−3
Alsace, 20
America, 46
Anderson, Sir John, 35−7
Andrews, Squadron Leader J.O., 69−70
Anschluss, 145

Anti-Comintern Pact, 104
Appleton, Dr E.V. (later Sir Edward), 87
Armaments (air), 4, 31, 69, 95−6, 97, 98, 107, 119, 138, 147−8, 168−9, 170−1
Armaments Truce, 49, 50
Armour plating, 138
Assistant Chief of the Air Staff, 151
Astro-navigation, 59, 61−2, 116−17
Atlantic, xxi
Australia, xxi, 95
Austria, 137, 139, 140, 145
Automatic pilot, 66, 98, 111, 116
Auxiliary squadrons, 47, 50−1, 53
Axis, Rome−Berlin, 104

Bailhache, Mr Justice, xviii
Bailly, Commandant, 160−1
Baldwin, Stanley, 33, 35, 104, 126
Balloons, 156
Battle, 82, 91, 101, 114, 128, 130, 143, 144, 146, 147, 158−9, 164
Battle of Britain, 119, 171
BE 2, xvii, 3, 4
Beacons (electric), xxiii, 26, 113, 173
Beam approach, xxiii
Belfort, 7
Belgium, 11, 12, 48, 56−7, 103−4, 109, 128, 130, 160, 165
Berlin, 39, 72, 156
Birkenhead, 58
Birmingham, 58
Blackett, Prof. P.M.S., 86, 120−1
Blenheim, 101, 110, 128, 130, 142, 143, 144, 146, 147, 158−9, 164, 168
Blind landing systems, 26, 72, 113
Bomb aiming, 4, 6, 15, 16, 18, 19, 45, 64, 88, 111, 119−20, 135
Bomb dropping gear, 4, 5
Bomber Command, xiii, xxiv, 18, 26, 55, 101−2, 110−13, 116−17, 118−19, 120−1, 126−31, 135, 136, 142, 143, 144, 149, 150−1, 153−5, 157−8, 159, 160, 161, 168, 170, 172, 173
Bomber Groups, 102, 114, 116, 135
Bombing and Gunnery Camp, 63
Bombing Areas, 48

Bombing Committee, 83–5, 117–18, 120, 133–7, 138
Bombing Development Establishment, 118, 129, 137, 148
Bombing policy, xii, xv, xix–xx, 3, 6, 15–16, 18, 34, 41–4, 46, 65–6, 117–18, 121, 138, 146, 151, 152
Bombing results, xii, 5, 65, 119, 134–5
Bombing tactics, 5, 16, 17, 18, 20–1, 30, 65, 113–14, 118–19, 128–9, 130, 132–7, 151, 152
Bombs, types of, xiii, 19–20, 37–8, 65–6, 83–5, 105, 117–18, 138, 151, 154
Bombsights, 4, 5, 19, 64–5, 98, 111, 120
Breit, Dr Gregory, 87
Bremerhaven, 153
Brifaut, Captain, 38
British Airways, 26
British Expeditionary Force (BEF), 4, 8, 9, 10, 50, 100
Brittany, 54
Brooke-Popham, Air Commodore H.R.M. (later Air Marshal Sir Robert), 28, 31, 61, 68, 84–5
Brown, Sir Arthur Whitten, xxi
Browning gun, 139
Brunsbüttel, 153, 154
Brussels, 38
Bulldog, 68–9
Bulletproof glass, 138

Cadman, Lord, 25
Camera obscura, 136
Central Flying School, 2, 3
Chalk Farm, 40
Chamberlain, Neville, 100–1, 140–1, 145, 166
Chemical weapons, 36–41
Chief of Naval Staff, 44–6
Chief of the Air Staff, xiv, xv, xvi, xviii, xix, xx, 14, 17, 21, 22, 23–4, 29–31, 34, 41, 44, 55, 64, 65, 66, 77–80, 82, 91, 123, 125, 149, 158 (see also Trenchard, Sykes, Salmond, Ellington, Portal)
Chief of the Imperial General Staff, 44–5
Chiefs of Staff Committee, 41, 43–6, 74–5, 76–7, 80, 107, 110, 123, 140, 146
China, 164
Churchill, Winston, xxi–xxii, 23, 24–5, 26–7, 34–5, 48–9, 51–2, 55–6, 88–9, 90–1, 104–5, 172
Civil aviation, xxi–xxii, 22–3, 24–6, 71–2, 112–13, 172–3
Civil defence, 35–7, 41, 77–8, 105
Clapham, 40
Cloud flying, 64

Coast Defence, Committee on, 64
Coastal Command, 113
Cologne, 26, 68, 85
Committee of Imperial Defence, 2, 36, 42, 51, 80, 100, 126–7, 146, 155
Controller General of Civil Aviation, 23, 25
Counter offensive, doctrine of the, xvi, xx–xxi, 28, 29, 32, 35, 36, 42, 46, 53, 54, 67, 77, 79, 80, 81, 88, 101, 107, 109, 123, 142
Courtney, Air Vice-Marshal C.L., 97
Cowdray, Lord, 13
Cromer, 58
Cross-Channel Subsidies Committee, 24
Croydon, 68, 85
Cunliffe-Lister, Sir Philip (later Lord Swinton), 90
Cuxhaven, 153
Czech crisis, 140–3, 160
Czechoslovakia, 139–40, 144–5, 160, 165

Daily Telegraph, The, 67
Danzig, 72, 165
Dean, Sir Maurice, xxiv
Death ray, 86
Defence Committee, Air (Tizard Committee), 86, 87, 119, 120, 133
Defence Policy and Requirements, Ministerial Committee on, 100
Defence Requirements Committee, 75–6
Deputy Chief of the Air Staff, 83, 97, 156
Derby, 58
Deruluft, 72
Detling, 6–7
DH 9a, 53, DH 86, xxiii, DH 88 (Comet), 95–6
Dietrich, Kapitänleutnant, 58
Direction Finding (D/F) Wireless, 59, 60–1, 62, 63, 66, 111–12, 113, 114–16
Disarmament, Ministerial Committee on, 76, 80–1, 100
Disarmament Conference, 49–50, 74, 75
Don, Group Captain F.P., 128–9, 136
Doncaster, xxii
Dornier, Do 17, 50; Do 19, 92
Douglas, Air Vice-Marshal W.S., 151
Dowding, Air Marshal Sir Hugh, 102–3
Dunkirk, 56

Early warning system, 87–8, 119
East Anglia, 142
Eastchurch, 3
Economic blockade, 167
Eighth Air Force, United States, 171
Ellington, Sir Edward, 77–80, 90, 97–8
Engines, aero, 4, 70, 98, 138, 139

Esher, Lord, 2
Evacuation of bomber aerodromes, plans for, 142
Expansion Schemes, Air, A, 81, 89; B, 90; C, 90, 101, 106; D, 100; E, 100; F, 100–1, 105, 106, 110; G, 106; J, 122, 124; K, 124, 137; L, 137, 143–4; M, 143–4, 146

Fairey, C. R., 53
Fawn, 53
Felmy (German Air Force officer), 92
Fifty-two Squadron Programme, xvi, xx, 28, 47–8, 76
Fighter Command, 101–3, 113, 143–4, 171
Fighter defence, 29, 32, 66, 69–70, 81–2, 85–6, 90, 102–3, 131, 143–4, 170–1
Fighter escort, 29, 96–7, 131, 149, 170–2
Fighter groups, 102
Fighting area, 48, 102
Finningley, xxii
Flamborough Head, 58
Flares, 135
Flight planning, 62, 136
Flying Fortress, 171
Flying Training Manual, 55
Foch, General, 17, 42–3
Focke-Wulf FW 200 (Condor), 93
Foreign Office, 74–5, 124
Forster (Nazi Gauleiter of Danzig), 165
Fox, 68
France, xvi, 41–2, 48, 54, 67, 69, 74, 75, 79–80, 98, 102, 103, 104, 107, 109, 128, 140, 145–6, 160, 165–6, 171
Franco, General, 104
Frankland, Dr Noble, xiv
Freeman, Sir Wilfrid, 121
French Air Force, xii, 5, 28, 142, 160
Friedrichshafen, 6

Gainsborough, xxii
Gases, war, 36–41
Geneva, 49
German Army, 73, 94, 110, 160, 162
German Air Force, 9, 33, 50, 71, 73–4, 77, 78, 89–90, 91–4, 100, 104, 105, 106, 107, 109, 123, 127, 142
German Navy, 152–5, 168–9
Germany, xx, xxii, 2, 26, 27, 33, 38, 46, 48, 50, 52, 71, 74–5, 76–7, 79–80, 81–2, 83, 84, 85, 95, 97, 99, 101, 102–6, 107–10, 127, 128, 138, 139, 140, 145–6, 150, 152, 157, 159, 162, 170, 171, 172, 173
Giant type of aircraft, 53
Goering, Hermann, 73, 93, 94, 103

Goole, 58–9
Gotha G. IV, 11, 56
Guilty Men, 121
Gunners, air, 62, 147–8
Gunnery, air, 111, 147–8

Hage, 58
Haig, Sir Douglas, xii, 10–11
Haldane, J. B. S., 38
Halifax, 107, 144
Halsbury, The Earl of (see also Viscount Tiverton), 37–41
Hamburg, 38–9
Hampden, 70, 82, 91, 101, 114, 122, 130, 139, 144, 147, 164
Hankey, Sir Maurice, 75
Hanover, 26
Harris, Air Commodore A. T., 55, 62–3, 98, 112, 114
Harrow, 130, 143
Hart, 54, 68–9, 70, 82–3, 101
Hebden Bridge, xxii
Heinkel, He 46, 73; He 51, 73; He 111, 50, 73; He 177, 93
Heligoland, 168, 169
Henderson, General David, 2–3, 4, 8–10, 12–13
Henlein (Sudeten-German politician), 165
Heyford, xxii, 82
Higgins, Air Vice-Marshal J. F. A., 28, 30, 54
Higgins, Air Commodore T. C. R., 28, 29, 30
High altitude flying, 139
Hill, Professor A. V., 86
Hind, 83, 101
Hitler, Adolf, 49, 52, 73–5, 89, 92, 94, 103, 104, 139–40, 145–6, 165–7
Hoare, Sir Samuel (later Viscount Templewood), 32, 51
Holland, 61, 103, 128, 130, 160, 165
Homing aids, xxiii, 113
Hull, 58
Humber, 58, 79
Hurricane, 69, 88, 143, 171

Icing, aircraft, 113, 139
Immingham, 58
Imperial Airways, xxii, 25, 26, 172, 173
Independent Force, xiv, xv, xix, xx, 14, 17–18, 20–1, 56, 57, 66, 84
Industrial Intelligence Centre, 42
Inskip, Sir Thomas, 121, 122–4
Intelligence officers 136, 149
Iraq, 48, 54
Irish Sea, xxiii
Italy, 48, 75, 98–9, 103, 104

Japan, 75, 99, 103, 104
Joint Planning Committee, 99, 107–10,
    122, 129, 131
Joint War Air Committee, 10
Jones, H.A., xi, xiv
Joubert, Air Vice-Marshal P.B., 56, 86
Junkers Company, 72
Junkers, Ju 86, 73; Ju 88, 161; Ju 89, 92;
    Ju 90, 93

Kennelly, A.E., 87
Kesselring (German Air Force officer), 92
Kiel, 153, 154, 155
Kiel Canal, 153, 154
Knatchbull-Hugessen, Sir Hughe, 155–6
'Knock-out blow' (from the air), 77, 78,
    99, 107, 123–4, 131, 143
Königsberg, 72

Lancaster, 107
League of Nations, 49, 75, 98, 103
Leopold (King of the Belgians), 103–4
Leuchars, xxiii
Liberator, 171
Lighting, aerodrome and airway, xxiii, 26,
    72, 113
Lille, 54
Lipetsk, 72
Lithuania, 145
Liverpool, 58–9, 67
Lloyd George, David, 11, 27
Locarno, Treaties of, 48, 75, 103–4
Loewe, Kapitänleutnant, 58
London, xv, xviii, 1, 2, 11, 19, 36–8,
    40–1, 45, 52, 57–8, 66–7, 69, 76,
    78–9, 82, 86, 99, 105, 108–9, 142
Londonderry, The Marquess of, 50, 86,
    89–90
Longmoor (Royal Engineers Railway
    Training Centre), 129
Lorenz (Blind landing radio system), 113
Lorraine, xv, 20, 54
Low Countries, 76–7, 78, 79–80, 99, 100,
    108, 128, 140, 158–9, 160, 163
Ludlow-Hewitt, Air Chief Marshal Sir
    Edgar, 112, 128, 131–2, 135–6, 141–3,
    146–9, 154–9, 169–70, 172, 173
Ludwigshafen, 16
Lufthansa, Deutsche, 68, 72, 73, 85, 173
Luftwaffe, 50, 71, 103
Luxeuil, xii, 7, 11, 14

MacDonald, Ramsey, 49
MacRobertson Air Race, 95
Madden, Sir Charles, 44–6
Maginot Line, 160
Maidstone, 6

Mail carrying, 25, 172
Manchester (aircraft), 107, 144
Manchester (city), xxii, xxiii, 58, 67
Manston, 61
Map reading, xx, 15, 18, 59–60, 62–3,
    114, 116
Mediterranean, 54
Memel, 145
Mersey, 79
Messerschmitt Me 109, 159, 169, 171;
    Me 110, 169, 171
Meteorological facilities, xxiii, 15, 17
Michelin, Monsieur, 38
Middle East, 23, 55
Middlesbrough, 82, 102
Midlands, 82, 85
Milch, Erhard, 72–3, 93
Mildenhall, 156
Milne, Sir George, 44–5
Minister for the Co-ordination of
    Defence, 121 (see also Inskip)
Mobilisable Committee, 143
Möhne Dam, 132
Morale (as a factor in war), xix, xx, 4, 7,
    16, 17, 20–1, 24, 29–30, 31, 33, 34,
    42–4, 46, 78–9, 108–10, 141, 149
Moscow, 72, 166
Mosquito, 95–6
Munich crisis, 140, 150
Mussolini, 103, 104
Mustang, 171–2

Nancy, xiv, 14, 17, 20, 56, 57
National Physical Laboratory, 86
Navigation, xiii, xx, 4, 6, 15, 17–18,
    56–63, 67–8, 72, 88, 111–14, 116, 119,
    136, 147, 153
Navigators, 116–17
Nazi party, 50, 73
Netheravon trials, 161
Newall, Sir Cyril, 125
Night flying, xx, xxii, xxiii, xxiv, 26, 55,
    56–60, 63, 67–8, 85, 111, 112–13, 130,
    152, 153, 163, 172–3
1944, 37–8, 39
Nordholz, 58
North Sea, 131, 171
North West Frontier, 64
Northern Ireland, xxii
Nottingham, 59

Observer Corps, 63
Observers, air, 6, 62, 114, 147
Ochey, 14
Offence, Committee for the Scientific
    Survey of Air, 119–21, 133
Oldham, xxii

Oosterhout, 61
Operational Research, xiii, 15, 97
Ostend, 15
Overstrand, 82, 91, 95
Oxygen, 139

Pan American Airways, 173
Paris, 24, 38, 42, 54, 67
Paris Air Agreement, 71, 72
Pattern bombing, 135
Peirse, Air Vice-Marshal R. E. C., 155, 156
Phosgene gas, 38-9, 40
Photography, aerial, xii, 4, 136, 149
Pilots, xvii, xxiii, 5-6, 30, 61, 62, 77, 114, 144, 147
Poland, 145-6, 165-6
Police work, imperial, 23, 53, 54-5
Portal, Squadron Leader C. F. A. (later Sir Charles), 28, 29, 30, 34
Portsmouth, 82
Propaganda plan, 141, 155-6, 168

Radar, 87-8, 168-9
Radio navigation aids, xx, xxiii, 26, 60-1, 62, 111-12, 113, 114-16, 173
Raleigh, Sir Walter, xi, xiv
Reconnaissance, xii, 2-3, 127-8, 136, 149, 168
Reichtag, 165
Regional Control Centres, xxiii, xxiv
Reserve squadrons, 47, 50-1
Respirators, 41
Restricted bombing plans, 140-2, 150, 152, 155-7, 160, 168
Rhine, 15
Rhineland, 48, 75, 79, 84, 103-4, 128, 140, 145
'Roll up' (reduce first-line strength to create reserves), 142, 143, 146
Rothermere, Lord, xv, xviii-xix, 14
Royal Air Force, xi-xiii, xv-xvi, xviii, xxii, 1, 6, 14, 21, 22-3, 27, 101
Royal Flying Corps, xii, xiv-xv, xvi-xviii, 1-5, 7, 8-10, 13, 59, 114
Royal Naval Air Service, xii, xiii, xv, 1, 3-4, 5-8, 9-11, 13, 14-15, 56
Royal Scots Fusiliers, xiv
Ruhr, 27, 69, 79, 127, 128, 131-2, 142, 157-8, 159, 162
Rumbold, Sir Horace, 74
Russia, 72

St Eval, xxiii
Salisbury, Lord, 28
Salisbury Plain, 18, 102, 130, 164
Salmond, Air Marshal Sir John, 48, 66

Sashalite, 134
Schillig Roads, 169
Secretary of State for Air, xv, xviii, xix, xxi, xxiii, 14, 17, 22, 23, 32, 51, 90, 143 (see also Rothermere, Weir, Churchill, Hoare, Londonderry, Swinton, Wood)
Seely, Colonel J. E. B., 2
Self-defending bomber formations, 20, 95-6, 97, 138, 168, 170, 171
Sextants, air, 61-2, 116-17
Sheffield, 58
Sheppey, Isle of, 58
Shrewsbury, 59
Sidestrand, 70, 82
Simon, Sir John, 89
Slessor, Air Commodore J. C., 32, 68-9, 118, 151, 158, 160, 167
Smuts, General J. C., xviii, 12-14
Somme, 7, 9
Sopwith 1½ Strutter, xii, 6-7
Sorpe Dam, 132
South Africa, xxi
Soviet Union, 72, 92, 94, 103, 166-7
Spanish Civil War, 93, 104
Sperrle (German Air Force officer), 92
Spitalgate, 61
Spitfire, 88, 143, 171
Squadrons (Bomber), No. 9, 56, 61, 65; No. 12, 64, 68; No. 24, xxiii; No. 58, 55, 65; No. 102, xxii
Stalin, Joseph, 166-7
Steel, Air Marshal Sir John, 102, 111-12, 126
Stirling, 54, 107, 144
Strategic operations First World War
British, xi-xiii, xiv, xv-xvi, xviii, 6-7, 9-11, 14, 17-18, 20-1
German, 57-9
Second World War
American, 171-2
British, 168-70
German, 170-1
Strategic policy and planning
British, 1, 12, 14-17, 18-20, 21, 24, 32, 33-4, 54, 55, 56-7, 96, 122-4, 146
German, 92-4
Stumpff (German Air Force officer), 92
Sudeten Germans, 139-40
Sudetenland, 145, 165
Surplus Aircraft Fleet, 13
Swinton, Lord (formerly Sir Philip Cunliffe-Lister), 122
Sykes, Major-General Sir Frederick, xix, 14, 22-3, 25

Tanks, self-sealing fuel, 138
Target identification, 15, 18, 30, 46, 120,
    135, 136
Targets (general), xiii, xix, 133–5, 149,
    151; aerodromes/airfields, xix, 17, 123,
    130, 161; aircraft industry, 161; air-
    ships, 6; communications, xix, 17, 34,
    84, 129, 132, 138, 162–4; dams, 132;
    German air striking force, 109, 123,
    130, 161; German Army units, 164–5;
    German Navy, 84, 153–5; munitions,
    15; oil, 34, 60, 159; power, 34, 60,
    131–2, 157–8; submarine construction,
    xii, 6; war industries (general), xii, 6,
    16, 17, 30, 40, 43–6, 138, 162
Templewood, Viscount (formerly Sir
    Samuel Hoare), 32
Ten Year Rule, 26–7, 48–9
Thames, 58, 79
Thirty Years Rule, xxiv
Thrapston, 58
Times, The, 38–9, 56
Tiverton, Viscount (later the Earl of
    Halsbury), xiii, 14–16, 18–20, 37, 55
Tizard, H.T., 86, 87, 119–21, 133
Tondern, 58
Toul, 15
Training (aircrew), xiii, xvii, 5–6, 18–19,
    27, 34, 47, 51, 60, 62, 68, 89, 110–11,
    113, 135–6, 137, 144, 147–8
Transjordan, 54
Trenchard, Marshal of the RAF Sir Hugh
    (later Viscount Trenchard), xii, xiv–xxi,
    8–9, 10, 14, 16–18, 21, 23–4, 27,
    28–31, 32–4, 36, 37, 41–4, 48, 65, 81
Turner, Major C.C., 67
Turrets, power-operated gun, 95, 107, 111
Tuve, Dr Merle A., 87
Tyne, 82

Ulverston, xxiii
United States, xx, xxii, 26, 170, 172
Unrestricted bombing plans, 140, 150,
    157, 160
Uralbomber, 92, 94

V 1500, 53
Vansittart, Sir Robert, 74, 75
Verdun, 15, 20
Versailles, Treaty of, 71, 73, 103, 144, 145
Vimy, 53
Virginia, 53, 61, 82
Von Seeckt, General Hans, 71, 92

Wallace, 102
War Office, xv, 3, 4, 8, 9–10, 11, 27, 77
Wash, 102
Watson-Watt, R.A., 86–7
Webster, Sir Charles, xiv
Weir, Sir William (later Viscount Weir),
    xv, xix, 14, 22–3, 95–6, 101, 106
Wellesley, 114, 143
Wellington, 70, 82, 91, 122, 130, 139,
    144, 146, 164, 168–9, 171
Wenke, Oberleutnant, 57–8
Western Air Plans, 127, 132, 138; W.A.1,
    127, 129, 141, 161–2; W.A.4, 127,
    128, 141; W.A.5, 127, 131, 132, 141;
    W.A.5a, 162; W.A.5b, 162, 163;
    W.A.7a, 153
Western Front, xv, xviii, 4, 10, 12, 33, 39
Wever, General Walther, 92–3, 94
Whitley, 70, 82, 91, 110, 114, 122, 130,
    139, 143, 144, 153, 156
Wilhelmshaven, 153, 159, 169
Wilkins, A.F., 87
Wimperis, H.E., 19, 86
Wind finding, 18, 135
Wireless operators, 62, 147
Wireless telegraphy, xxiii, 4, 98, 115
Wolverhampton, 58
Wood, Sir Kingsley, xxiii, 143
Worthy Down, 55

Yarmouth, 58
York, xxii
Yorkshire, 142

Zeebrugge, 154
Zeppelins, 4, 56, 57